Published by Disciples of Mercy Foundation, Inc.,
P.O. Box 4074, Deerfield Beach, FL 33442
Toll Free: 1-888-722-7332 (1-888-Sacred2)
Web site: http://www.disciples-of-mercy.org
e-mail: peace@disciples-of-mercy.org

The Disciples of Mercy is an organization registered as a non-profit corporation in the state of Florida. Federal designation as 501(c)(3) tax-exempt organization has been granted by the IRS.

First printing, 1996   Third printing, 2004
Second printing, 1999   Fourth printing, 2011

In the spirit of obedience and accord with the *Code of Canon Law*, particularly canon 823 ("...writings published by the Christian faithful which touch upon faith or morals be submitted for judgement") and canon 824 ("...permission and approval by the local ordinary of the author be sought"), the Disciples of Mercy have submitted *Volumes I, II,* and *III* of *The Heart of God* for review to the ordinary of the Archdiocese of Miami where Lori G., the recipient of the messages, resided until her death. On June 6, 2000, the Great Jubilee Year, his Excellency, John C. Favalora, Archbishop of Miami, "officially declared that the three volume text *Heart of God: Messages from Jesus and the Blessed Mother* is free from doctrinal or moral error and may be published. No implication is contained therein that the one granting this imprimatur agrees with the contents, opinions or statements by the author of the texts."

Imprimatur: ✠ Most Reverend John C. Favalora, D.D.
                  Archbishop of Miami

Nihil Obstat: Very Reverend Tomás M. Marín, J.C.L.
                  Chancellor of the Archdiocese of Miami

The messages contained in this book follow the recommended formats of the *International Committee on English in the Liturgy, Inc.* and the *Chicago Manual of Style, 14th Edition*. No intent of irreverence or disrespect is implied by the use of lower case letters when referring to pronouns, articles, and nouns other than official titles associated with the Lord and his Blessed Mother.

ISBN: 0-9720991-1-5

The Heart of God:
Messages from Jesus and the Blessed Mother

Volume Two

Recorded

by

Lori G.

CONTENTS

Introduction to the Fourth Printing

Since the first printing of this work and the writing of these acknowledgments, preface, and foreword, many events have transpired. Lori G. was to pass to her heavenly reward on September 23, 1996, three weeks after her forty-first birthday. Sadly, Lori G. was to be joined at the eternal banquet by husband, John, on November 9, 2008. Preceding John's death two beloved priests who provided enormous spiritual assistance to her and the Disciples were to join Lori and John in heaven: Fr. Seamus O'Shaughnessy (April 7, 1999), and Fr. Joachim Tierney O.C.S.O., (May 25, 1999).

In addition, renowned Mariologist and author of *Dictionary of Apparitions of the Virgin Mary*, Fr. René Laurentin, had interviewed Lori approximately two months prior to her death and subsequently wrote three articles about her in the French Catholic periodical, *Stella Maris* (March, April, and May, 1997). We also witnessed the publication of three volumes encompassing over eight hundred messages and exactly 265,084 words. We have now arrived at the publication of our fourth printing of Volume II.

Special thanks is extended to Helen Marie Copley for her valuable editorial assistance.

We invoke your prayers for our continual perseverance in the work assigned to us by the Lord.

Disciples of Mercy Foundation
March 15, 2011
Feast of the Annunciation

Acknowledgments

The Disciples of Mercy Foundation has grown considerably since it began as a small band of people dedicated to fulfilling the commission from our Lord to spread the messages. The Lord had exhorted us "not to worry" for he would send the necessary people to facilitate our mission. He has been true to his word every step of the way. We have come to realize in our particular endeavors the words of the Archangel Gabriel to our Blessed Mother: "nothing is impossible with God." These words certainly ring true to us since our initial group was at a quandary of how we might proceed in realizing the publication of volume I. Now, we arrived at the publication of a second run of volumes I & II (Editor note: this is the fourth printing as of 2011), a true milestone and testament to the Lord's grace, the Holy Spirit's guidance, the Blessed Mother's intercession, and the vigilant protection of the entire heavenly court of angels and saints. This is not to infer that the assaults of the evil one did not occur. They certainly did, but through it all our refuge has been the merciful Lord, the Blessed Mother, Archangel Michael, Angel Stephen (an angel the Lord has assigned to the Disciples of Mercy as special protector and intercessor), and St. Maximilian Mary Kolbe, our patron saint. We are eternally grateful for their help and pray that we may continue to act in a manner that gives them honor and glory as we persevere in our apostolate which we recognize is only in its infancy.

It is fitting that the Disciples of Mercy express their heartfelt thanks to several individuals whom the Lord has sent to be our little Simons of Cyrene. First, our deep gratitude is extended to our spiritual advisor, Father Roman Schaefer. His strong faith in God and conviction in the teachings of the Catholic Church has helped us to follow a very exacting framework of spiritual direction. The Lord has always told us that we are to do nothing on our own initiative, even if the directive came from him, without Father Schaefer's knowledge and permission. Truly, his deep abiding faith, unwavering commitment to the Gospel, and discerning assessment of the messages contained in *The Heart of God* has helped us remain on the course we have been placed by the Lord. We are proud to follow this holy priest's example. In addition, we are indebted to all the priests and religious who have read *The Heart of God* and given us spiritual support and guidance, especially when circumstances and events were extremely difficult for us to grasp concerning the ways of the Lord. On this particular list, the name Father Seamus O' Shaughnessy, pastor of St. George's Catholic Church, Ft. Lauderdale, is at the top. He has always been receptive to hearing our spiritual needs and facilitating our prayer life. He has afforded the

Disciples of Mercy a beautiful home for our Rosary prayer group. To be included in this inspiring registry are Frs. Joachim Tierney O.C.S.O., and René Laurentin for their willingness to entertain the possibility that God does speak to his people, even ordinary and sinful people such as us, in miraculous ways. Their openness gave assurances of hope at a time when we, being completely in the dark about such occurrences in modern times, were bewildered as to how we might authoritatively determine the source of the "voices." The Lord's mercy and ways are truly unfathomable. We consider our encounter with both these astute discerners of the "Spirit" and holy, humble servants of God a tremendous blessing. May the Lord continue to shine the light of his Spirit upon them, for they are fine examples of the Apostle Paul's challenge "to encourage those who are in any difficulty with the encouragement which they themselves have received from God" (2 Cor 1:4).

Other individuals who truly merit our gratitude are Felicia Schipani and Ingrid DiMolfetta, the Lord's original disciples who were willing to listen at a time when things were very difficult to understand. Thanks to Mary Alonso, who particularly has donated a tremendous amount of time in assisting us in our family needs. Jim Urbanski, an early supporter and positive influence, warrants our appreciation as well. A dear friend who wishes to remain anonymous merits our indebtedness too. She has been our "Veronica" by supplying her strength and assistance in a manner that always lessened our anxieties. To our parents, John's for affording us some respite in parental duties when we were more actively engaged in the Lord's work, and Lori's for their aid when Lori was so ill, we are perennially grateful. We applaud our preteen and teenage children for their spirit of sacrifice and understanding. They have made us proud parents, especially on those occasions when the evil one would raise his ugly head attempting to foil our activities for the Lord by instilling disharmony. However, the children never succumbed to this strategy of subterfuge. Norm Dyko deserves much thanks for videotaping interviews of Lori and providing reproduction. His willingness to travel on behalf of the Disciples of Mercy has been a great asset.

Kudos to Ron Capardo and Sue Bermudez of the *Mailbox Store,* whose unrelenting support from the beginning in doing the work of God has enabled us to lay the foundation of the Disciples of Mercy. They provided the means to reproduce copies, send faxes, mail letters, and obtain a permanent mailing address. They also offer sound business advice.

A hearty thanks is extended to the administration and staff at *Food For the Poor, Inc.*, an organization that certainly mirrors our Lord's heart of compassion. Rarely does one find an organization whose entire membership is dedicated to being the Lord's hands and feet by ministering to the destitute of the world. Particular gratitude is accorded to Ferdinand G. Mahfood, founder and former president of *Food for the Poor*. The Disciples of Mercy are indeed blessed to have encountered a person of such trust, faith, and vision. He is selfless and indefatigable in his efforts to serve the poor of world. Despite his innumerable encounters with the despicable and inhumane living conditions that exist in third world countries, an experience that would dishearten even the most equanimous, his enthusiasm is never dampened. He is always focused on the transformative potential of every slum, ghetto, or shanty via the power of the Holy Spirit and the generosity of those on whom God has bestowed material blessings. Truly, Ferdinand is the embodiment of our Lord's exhortation "to have the faith the size of a mustard seed, for then you can say to the mountain: go from here to there, and it will go"(Mt 17:20). Ferdinand and the *Food for the Poor* organization have been instrumental in helping us establish our office and providing technical support, thereby making it possible to ready the Lord's messages for publication and distribution "to the four corners of the world."

Blessings to Sid and Claudia Schumann, whose arduous efforts have made our work so much easier in making the messages available to the world via the Internet. Thanks to Mark Hellstern of *Crosslists Company*, whose prayers, charity, and business acumen have helped us to publicize the messages on the national and international level. We will continue to rely on these generous people for their valuable assistance and cherished friendship. Robert Ray offered unstinting time and energy to promote continually the messages in a multitude of ways. He is truly our "Paul", whose evangelical activities are assuredly appreciated by us and by the Eternal Father who "so loves a cheerful giver"(2 Cor 9:7).

Finally, we want to honor our friend, advisor, and guiding light, John Sause. John is the person responsible for making *The Heart of God* happen. Yes, the messages were spoken by the Lord and our Blessed Mother, received through Lori, but it was John who transformed them into readable texts with clarifying footnotes ready for publication. John's assistance has been integral to the production of the present two volumes which Jesus has carefully reviewed, smiled upon, and blessed. As you read the messages, please say a prayer thanking the Lord for John. Many souls will benefit because of his efforts.

There are so many others who merit our appreciation for lending a hand and providing support in terms of prayer or financial means. We beg their forgiveness if we do not formally acknowledge them here. Their consolation comes from knowing that they are "the small hidden flowers in the belly of the bush." It is these "smallest hidden flowers in a vast garden that are given the most important tasks by the Eternal Father" (Message of December 4, 1995).

We realize that this expression of thanks fails to compensate fully all those who have generously given themselves in their efforts to bring the messages of Jesus and the Blessed Mother to the world. All we can say is that the Lord can never be outdone in generosity and they will be truly blessed. Nevertheless, we have much work ahead of us and we have only our Lord and his words (Message of February 8, 1996) both to challenge and comfort us:

> Children, I, Jesus, am weary, but I will *never* rest as long as souls are being lost to perdition. Work, children, work until your eyes burn, until your hands ache, until your throat is parched, and then work some more. If you were to see hell, you would understand the grief in my heart. I did not promise that your earthly life would be easy. I did not promise you would not suffer, but I did promise complete bliss in heaven.

> God's mercy is yours,

> Lori and John G.
> August 15, 1996
> Feast of the Assumption

Foreword

by

Rev. Roman Schaefer

My brothers and sisters, I'd like to take this opportunity to introduce the second volume of *The Heart of God* and to inform you of what has transpired for the Disciples of Mercy since we published the first volume. As I had stated in the forward to Volume I, I am a priest and parochial vicar at Our Lady Queen of Martyrs Church in Ft. Lauderdale, Florida (Editor's Note: Fr. Schaefer has retired to the Midwest). I have been a servant of God for 54 years and spent 25 years of my service as a chaplain in the United States Air Force. I have traveled the world, met many special people, and witnessed many marvelous events. Once again I have been blessed by Almighty God.

Two years ago I met a local woman who receives the messages you are about to read. It is extremely rare that Jesus and the Blessed Mother should choose to communicate to us in an extraordinary manner through the means of dictation to a human being. What makes Lori exceptional, even among those granted such supernatural gifts, is that she is able to converse with our Lord and the Blessed Mother at any time throughout the course of a day. Our Blessed Mother has explained to Lori that she has been granted a very special grace by God the Father, for which she is to thank him daily. Once a day, usually in the evening, she writes down an exact dictation, normally from Jesus but occasionally (averaging every eight to ten days) from our Blessed Mother.

Throughout this past year I have seen a tremendous development of the essential themes found in Volume I. Truly, the Lord loves all his children on earth in a way we will never fully understand. Even when the veil of earthly existence has fallen from our eyes with our entrance into heaven, we will never entirely grasp the infinite love the Lord has for each one of us. These communications of love and mercy are directly from heaven. There does not appear to be one word that contradicts the Catholic faith, teachings, traditions, the Bible, and our creed. They are a reflection of Sacred Scripture and a blessing to us all. Members of the clergy in the United States and several foreign countries who have read the messages are in total agreement with this assessment and have indicated the messages have been a catalyst to reevaluate their own personal relationship with God. This alone is powerful testimony.

The Lord has given those of us involved with the messages many tasks which we are striving to fulfill. The most important is the printing and subsequent distribution of his messages. This is no easy task since Jesus, our ultimate source of love and mercy, wishes these messages to be communicated to every person in the world. We must strive to cooperate fully with the Lord's desire to reach "all of his children on earth." In his wisdom the Lord has dictated these messages so that they may be considered as direct communications to the individual reader and not just to Lori. In essence, Lori is only the vessel that God has chosen, for we are all asked to drink of his love and mercy. Hence, it has come as no surprise that there seems to be a strong belief that these words emanate from God among my Protestant clergy colleagues in this country who have discerned the messages. The power of God can never be confined in any way.

This brings me to render a short update concerning our efforts to follow the Lord's directives. First, support for these messages has grown significantly over the past year. The Disciples of Mercy, (a title which the Lord himself bestowed upon those members directly involved in disseminating the messages), have come, through the grace of God, to understand better what the Lord expects of them in their spiritual life and to be of service in the distribution and evangelization of the messages. We have all come to realize deeply that the time we spend on earth is so very short compared to eternal life. Secondly, these messages that God is giving freely to each and every one of us have a specific purpose: *to attend to our souls and to heal us.* He is not a dispassionate God but one who entreats, yes, even "begs" us "to be reconciled to [him], thereby receiving grace for each situation." (Message of October 17, 1995).

Finally, there are four things God wants us to have as the focal points in our lives. First, love him with all our hearts, minds, and souls. Second, obey his commandments. Third, care for our souls. We need to work earnestly to make ourselves worthy of the setting at the heavenly banquet that he has prepared for us. With God's assistance we need to peel away tenderly the layers of resistance that hinder our spiritual growth and to establish a relationship with the very Essence within us. Finally, we need to love our neighbors as we love ourselves. We are responsible for the well-being of our neighbors. This includes caring about the condition of their souls as well. This may appear to be an unattainable goal to achieve, but in reality, with faith and grace, it can be accomplished to some degree, provided that we take this responsibility seriously. I believe it was Mother Teresa who said, "God doesn't call us to be successful, but he does call us to be faithful." We are all called to inform and model to our friends and acquaintances the message of the Gospel, the same message contained in *The Heart of God.* We should not be ashamed to speak openly of the Lord's love for all souls and how desperately he wishes for a greater closeness and devotion to him and his Mother. What a wonderful conversation it would be between two people, when in the course of their dialogue about Jesus and his Mother, they become aware of the "good news" which they either had never thought about in their lives or had chosen to forget because of a misunderstanding of what God's love for us is really all about. The book *The Heart of God* is one means given us to be the occasion for such a beautiful dialogue.

In closing, I wish to compliment the members of the Disciples of Mercy Foundation, established in the state of Florida as a non-profit foundation, for all their efforts in fulfilling what the Lord has specifically directed them to do. However, this small group of individuals needs your help in making the Lord's word available to others. Each day that souls are lost is a very sad day and as members of the Mystical Body we are exhorted to minimize this loss. I encourage the reader to assist them in any way he or she can. Please feel free to contact the Disciples of Mercy (P.O. Box 4074, Deerfield Beach, FL 33442). The phone number for the Disciples is 888-722-7332. One of the disciples would be happy to answer any question you might have in regards to the messages, such as how you may become a disciple or support us in our efforts to please the Lord.

God's mercy is yours,

Rev. Roman J. Schaefer
Our Lady Queen of Martyrs Church
Ft. Lauderdale, Fl 33312

Preface

by

John P. Sause, Ph.D.

The noted author, Trappist monk, and mystic, Thomas Merton, came to the conviction in his book, *The New Seeds of Contemplation,* that: "the secret of my identity is hidden in the love and mercy of God." [1] A few pages later Merton further states: "Love is my true identity. Selflessness is my true self. Love is my true character. Love is my name. If, therefore, I do anything or think anything or know anything that is not purely for the love of God, it cannot give me peace, or rest, or fulfillment, or joy." [2] Ironically, these statements of Merton, which encapsulate his own personal journey consisting of formal study, dialogical encounters with noted mystics of his time, and above all, his own unique experiential reflection, can be aptly applied in summarizing *Volume II* of *The Heart of God.* While the personal history and manner in which the principal subjects (Merton and Lori G) of these two books came to their convictions differ immensely, their conclusions are identical. Merton's modality is primarily founded upon an intuitive understanding of the contemplative experience that transcends ordinary cognition. Lori G's is solely derived from locutions, that is, statements actually dictated to the listener that come allegedly from a supernatural source. In the case with Lori G, the supernatural sources are our Lord and his Blessed Mother.[3] Despite their diverse paths, the end result of their respective journeys is the assertion that the meaning of our entire human existence and the joy that our hearts yearn to obtain can *only* be found in the love of God. The reader is invited to join the following excursus on the messages

---

[1] Thomas Merton, *The New Seeds of Contemplation*, New York: New Directions Books, 1961, p. 35.

[2] *Ibid.,* p. 60.

[3] For a developed background concerning Lori G, the reader is referred to the Preface of *The Heart of God, Volume I,* pp. ix-xvii.

contained in this book using Merton's statements as well as the typical questions we self-centered, cost/benefit-conscious humans would ask of the Divine prior to a commitment to his service.

The secret of my identity is hidden in the love and mercy of God.

Modern psychology attests to the indisputable fact that one's identity and self-esteem is inextricably wed to the measure of one's love relationships. Theodore Lidz, M.D., Professor and Chairman of Psychiatry at Yale University Medical School for many years, insightfully describes the search for identity:

> The answer to the query, "Who am I?" is largely founded upon knowing that one can love and be loved as an individual, and even more specifically, upon whom one loves and from whom one desires love. Ego identity involves the feelings of completion that come from feeling loved and needed, from being able to share the world with one another. [4]

The dictations given to Lori G by our Lord and the Blessed Mother profusely proclaim their love for each one of us for "as I [Jesus] speak to you [Lori], I am speaking to all my children." [5] Similarly, the Blessed Mother entreats us to "listen to the calls of your Heavenly Mother who loves you [us] to a degree that you [we] are incapable of understanding." (Message of July 22). Unfortunately, for many of us, our self-esteem has been largely shaped by the conditional love of others and a society that imposes goals and role models that are largely unattainable for the majority of the population. Hence, the message sent is that only these societal paragons of beauty, or intelligence, or success, are worthy of being loved. Sadly, such an environment ultimately contributes to a negative perception of self. Thus our self-image is severely damaged and subsequently the belief that we are worthy of loving and being loved for our

---

[4] Theodore Lidz, *The Person: His Development throughout the Life Cycle.* New York: Basic Books, 1968, p. 352.

[5] Message of June 17, 1995. Hereafter the day and month of the message shall be cited in body of the text since the year -1995 is the same.

true selves is cast into doubt. But such a status is not the case for those who have established a deep faith relationship with our Lord, his love for each of us is so deep and incomprehensible that " [he] would return to Calvary, he would die again for just one of us." (Messages of November 27 and July 27). In addition, this Lord of All Creation, Majesty of Majesties, has chosen to remain with us sacramentally in the form of ordinary bread imprisoned within the confines of only a few cubic feet : "I am a prisoner of love in the tabernacle, and I am the Prisoner of Love in the Holy Eucharist." (Message of August 10).

Despite these assertions of the Lord's love for us and his willingness to endure such an excruciating form of death and a humiliating sacramental presence, we think that he is speaking to only a small cadre of special individuals, souls that have never strayed, those who have always been within his flock. Such thinking is completely erroneous. His love is only matched by his mercy. "I have not come to call the righteous; on the contrary, I have come to call sinners, the ones who are weak and confused." (Message of August 4). His call of love is not that of a king demanding allegiance from his subjects but he "calls and begs for our love like a pauper on his knees." (Messages of February 19 and October 12). Nor is his love and mercy conditioned upon certain prerequisites: "Do I wait until you perform a certain way before I love you? No, children, I, the Lord, Jesus Christ, love you as you are. I accept you as you are. There is not one among you who has achieved perfection in my sight." (Message of January 31). Oh, we say to ourselves, these words of love and mercy are too incredible to believe, our past history with our loved ones who may have said comparable unconditional words were later betrayed by their actions. "Many of you cry to me, children, you have an earthly parent that is not trustworthy. I, Jesus, say to you, do not put faith in another person, it is not your [mankind's] nature to be faithful. It is only my nature to be faithful." (Messages of October 3 and July 29).

Another cause for our hesitation to approach the Lord is the number and kind of sins we may have committed. Surely, he could not love me. Look what I have done in my life, such offensive acts even repulse me when I reflect on them. How could the Lord possibly forgive me?

But the Lord lovingly assures us that "no matter what you have done, I, the Lord Jesus Christ, shall forgive you. Remember, children, my heart is infinite as is my mercy. Accept my invitation of love." (Message of February 23). Ah, here is where his mercy truly surpasses our understanding, for not only does he forgive the sins of a contrite and humble heart but he forgets them as well.   "Your sins are forgiven and forgotten. I remember them no longer."(Message of June 14). Truly, the Lord, "[casts our] offenses into the ocean of forgiveness, [he] remember[s] them no longer."(Message of November 5). His "mercy is greater than all the grains of sand in the universe." (Message of July 27). It is offered to us at this very moment for he comes "to meet us in the here and now, not in the past, nor in the future." (Message of March 21). Such love and mercy confidently enables us to start afresh, our slate of commissions and omissions of sin entirely wiped clean. A new beginning is entirely possible and the poison that has so afflicted our souls is completely flushed from our lives. "I, Jesus, have provided a way to loose yourselves from the weight of your sins. Go to Confession. Go frequently. Each time you go, I, Jesus, place a drop of my holy Precious Blood upon your hearts thereby healing you and discarding your burdens." (Message of November 12).   In addition, the Lord knows of our insecurities, and unlike others who tend to be judgmental regarding our failings, or even ourselves, who often prove to be our worst enemies due to the proclivity to be self-deprecating, he confides that "true love is always encouraging and never critical."(Message of August 31). He is "the only true and faithful friend of the soul."(Message of October 3).

But Lord, we say, we are afraid. If I surrender to you I will be deprived of what pleasures I now have. My friends may desert me, my perspective toward material possessions could change, my attitudes toward the poor and marginalized would need to be reassessed, and most of all, I may have to change my life orientation and the time allocations I now have for you. I could have no one but only you, Lord, and you are invisible. I'm fearful that your love is going to be too costly to me. It's not enough; I could lose everything! I'll be alone.

Ah, but this fear is based upon the refusal to acknowledge the perennial paradox of human existence: in order to find the true self, one must lose the self. Yes, it is precisely in the process of surrendering the self that one comes to the full realization of the true self. In short, our fears are unfounded. It is a deception of the evil one that the Lord will take the joy of life from us and replace it with pain, suffering, and only the cross. The Lord is a giver and not a taker. "I did not come upon the earth to bring illness and suffering; on the contrary, I despise sickness and it is my desire to heal the sick." (Message of November 2). Jesus is "not the source of our burdens [but rather] he hides us within his heart, he is the one who awaits an eternity for us to love him." (Message of November 25).   He "is not the reason for the numerous crises in [our] lives, it is [our] sins that bring about catastrophes." (Message of November

21).   His purpose for coming to this earth "is to bring hope to those who despair and life to those who are dead." (Message of November 6). Nor does the Lord "wish to remove the entertainment from our lives," (Message of October 20), but rather, he "assures us that our joy will be far greater now than when it was while we cherished our material possessions." (Message of September 8).

Foolishly, we contend that we want life on our own terms. We want to find ultimate fulfillment in another human being, in possessions, in fame, or in power. However, our hearts were made to find our ultimate joy and rest in the Lord, for as the Blessed Mother attests: "every soul was created by God to desire God." (Message of December 6) and that soul "trembles with loneliness for the soul was designed to rest in God." (Message of September 25). He is "the Treasure that the Heart is Always Seeking," (Message of September 8) the "only strength and consolation to the soul." (Message of November 25).   He is "the God of intimacy...[desiring] to share every aspect of our lives." (Message of March 27).   "With worldly things we shall always find misrepresentation and disappointment." (Message of February 22). The only source of lasting joy comes from the knowledge that "though we be dust, the Lord, Jesus Christ [is] infinitely in love with each of us." (Message of September 8). Yes, our identity and the need to be completed comes from the knowledge that "there is no greater love than the love of God and the love of your heavenly Mother, ... [and we need] not be afraid to trust [our] lives to [their] care." (Message of September 25). "Our only true and eternal home is in his heart." (Message of March 21).

Gratefully, though tentatively, we turn to the Lord and ask, what can I do, Lord?

First, he says, with tremendous gratitude, "throughout my suffering, I dreamt of the day that you would acknowledge me as Lord." (Message of October 9). Then, he asks that "you accept his invitation of love," (Message of February 23), for the Lord, "will not force your love." (Messages of January 30 and August 23).   He reassuringly states "do not be afraid for my will is sweet as honey to the bee, and all those who strive to live my will, receive courage and ability for all things are possible with me." (Message of January 9). He "desire[s] to teach [us] holiness and righteousness" (Message of February 3) and that we "show love and mercy to others." (Message of January 31). Nor is there any need to be jealous of his love for others for he "loves each of us equally and infinitely." (Messages of September 6 and August 25). He "think[s] of [us] constantly" (Message of September 1) and wishes that "we share everything with him." (Messages of May 19 and October 2). He breathes life into us each day and there is nothing we can do apart from him. (Message of August 6). He is truly the "God of intimacy" (Message of September 27) and "we are never out of his sight." (Message of July 21). Yes, the Lord "has a place and purpose for all of us." (Message of June 19). All he asks is that you place him first, (Message of September 29) and if you do so, "he assures you that you will reach each destination in your life with joy." (Message of June 8). Yes, offer your life to him and permit him to use you as he desires. (Message of November 26). He requests that you not be afraid to give him your life for all that you give him will be used for the glory of the Kingdom of God, and when the storms come, you will have the mighty branches of Love to protect you. (Message of December 23). He wants you to let your love for him be the basis of each relationship you have with others, (Message of July 10) for we "cannot love another unless [we] love him first." (Message of October 12). We are to live his commandments, for contrary to the contemporary purveyors of morality his "commandments are not old-fashioned, they are the foundation to our mortal and immortal lives." (Message of August 20). In essence, he "has given us [his] laws to keep us free of mortal shackles and humiliations,"(Message of July 12) and enable "the soul to soar freely in the world of the Spirit." (Message of September 30). He has given each of us many different gifts which are to be shared, and if we share our blessings with others who are less fortunate, then our blessings as well as the receiver's blessings will be multiplied. (Message of September 9).

To these requests and in the light of his overwhelming love, we say "yes, Lord," but with a proviso - please do not send me the cross.

Ah, foolish children, "If you desire to follow me, then you must embrace the crosses I send you." (Message of September 11). We need to understand "that when heaven sends a trial, it is a priceless gift from the Eternal Father... [for that] which is sent by heaven is ordained and sanctified in heaven, and is sent to increase virtue." (Message of October 17). But often the source of our tribulations is not heavenly in origin but due to the fact that much of our suffering is self-inflicted, for we distance ourselves from the Lord. (Message of October 17) Nevertheless, Jesus is calling his faithful ones to come to Calvary with him, for "all those who drink from the chalice of suffering, shall also drink from the chalice of consolation." (Message of December 23). Besides, we are never alone in shouldering this cross, as his beloved Mother accompanies every soul on [his/her] journey to Calvary, and Jesus provides

Simons to help us with the cross. (Message of November 14). Truly, he who "accepts the cross as a part of his life, is given a share in my [the Lord's] redemptive work ...for the cross brings countless graces to the one who carries it and countless graces to others as well." (Message of November 16). "[The Lord's] grief over lost souls is immeasurable," (Message of February 4) for we are all members of the Body and "all suffering that is offered to God is used as a salve to mend [the] Son's wounds." (Message of February 9). The Lord does not desire to impose reparation upon us, but our "sins are so grievous and ways so abominable that acts of reparation are accepted to tilt the scales from wrath to mercy " (Message of December 14). We also know that "the servant is not greater than the master," (Message of September 29) and "those who share in [his] suffering will share in [his] glory." (Message of October 2). We must trust the Lord's word "that the cross shall not harm us: in fact, it is the tool of our sanctification." (Message of October 9). Yes, "even if the cross were to kill the human body, surely, the cross will save your soul." (Message of October 11). But, "would the Shepherd hurt one of his flock? (Message of December 23). Of course not, we hold to the belief that the cross is the Lord's gift to us, (Message of February 14) and take consolation that"no matter what we are suffering, the Lord himself has suffered it. (Message of April 14). We cling to the solace of knowing that the heavier the cross, the closer the Lord is to us. (Message of January 18). And what does it matter that the cross may ultimately take our human life for "it is the spirit which is, in fact, the real and everlasting world"? (Message of September 30). Yes, "compared to eternity [our] life span is shorter than the blink of an eye." (Message of August 25). From this perspective, in spite of the cross, we can understand the Lord's definition of faith: "faith is the absence of fear in all situations."(Message of September 23). We have nothing to fear if we have faith. Truly, "blessed are those who believe...yet do not see." (Message of December 19).

What salient title would you say the Lord addresses himself that sets the tone of the messages?

When we follow the Lord's exhortation to"pray each day for an increase of faith" (Message of August 12), and "to have faith in all situations," (Message of August 15) we have entered the home of the Lord carrying our gift of "yes" to him, for "those who become saints are those who have always spent their time trying to please [him]." (Message of December 16). But ironically, it is the host who has the gifts. One of the most common titles the Lord attributes to himself in the messages is the Eternal Gift-Giver. Yes, "the gifts that I, the Lord, desire to bestow upon a soul are infinite." (Message of

November 5). Nor are the numerous gifts expected to be returned. "I solemnly assure you that I, Jesus, am neither a borrower or a lender. I am a Giver. I am a Nurturer. I am the Eternal Gift-Giver. When I give you a gift, it does not have to be repaid." (Message of December 15). These gifts are innumerable: "I am referring to the infinite amount of graces I have to bestow on each of you. Come with open arms and uncluttered hearts and take, take, take. It is my desire to give." (Message of October 26) and "never does a soul come into my presence or the presence of my beloved Mother and that soul does not leave with a gift." (Message of December 21).

Let us list some of the gifts the Eternal Gift-Giver bestows upon us.

Salvation:
"From the Cross, I purchased your salvation and power over diseases." (Message of May 22). Yes, even if physical disease were to eventually rob our body of physical life, his death and resurrection have conquered the power of evil. Eternal life is ours provided that we "repent and convert to obtain the kingdom of God." (Message of January 14). However, "when one rejects his mercy, then one is saying the final "yes" to satan," (Message of February 27) and "with deep sorrow [he] watches souls that are plunged into eternal darkness." (Message of September 3). Oh, if we but knew what awaits us in heaven, "a place created by Love and sustained by Love, the most magnificent places upon the earth are as barren wastelands compared to heaven." (Message of December 6). "The gift of salvation actually begins on earth [for] during Holy Communion [we] are closer to heaven than any other time." (Message of December 7)

The Mass:
"If you could visualize the events of the Mass, you would see me nailed to the Cross. You would see a priest holding a chalice under each one of my wounds to collect the blood. You would see my death and Resurrection. That is why you cannot comprehend the magnitude of graces at the holy Mass." (Message of November 28). The Mass is also a participation of the heavenly banquet; "it is at the Mass where heaven and earth actually become one time and one place. It is because of this union that you are given the power to share in my Resurrection." (Message of December 7). Besides the gift of being able to participate in the Mass, we have the benefit of the presence of his Mother, for the "Blessed Mother stands beside Jesus at every Mass." (Message of November 23). Incredibly, "Every grace is poured forth on those who come to Mass." (Message of July 24).

The Eucharist:
"The Eucharist is the Heart of God." (Message of July 24). The "[Lord] cannot emphasize enough the importance of receiving [him] in the Eucharist. It is then that [he] places a drop of [his] Blood upon [our] hearts... the same Blood [that he] shed at Calvary." (Message of December 20). The Majesty of Majesties has chosen to give us himself in the Eucharist but "concealed... for [he] wishes to hide [his] glory so that we may love him as an act of our will." (Message of July 6). The Lord "mourns day and night in every tabernacle, the eternal prisoner of [his] love for us." (Message of August 9). He "waits in every tabernacle throughout the world...as a parent eagerly awaits for his children to come home after being gone all day." (Message of October 26). "When [we] go to [him] in the Blessed Sacrament, [he] will grant all that [we] need so that [we] may continue on [our] journey." (Message of November 25). Yes, before "the Blessed Sacrament, [we] are given priceless gifts by the Eternal Father." (Message of December 21). If we were only to make use of this most generous of all gifts, so much of our anxieties in life would be dissolved, for "every answer that we seek shall be found in the tabernacle, the tabernacle is [the Lord's] footstep upon the earth." (Message of November 4).

The Blessed Mother:
"My beloved Mother was given to each of you at Calvary. This is one of the greatest gifts ever given to mankind by the Eternal Father." (Message of December 8). We are commissioned by Jesus to acknowledge and venerate his Mother, for "to honor [him], you must honor [his] Mother." (Message of November 4). She is the Queen of Heaven and Earth, the Refuge of Sinners, who is our true advocate, for "there is nothing that is denied [his] Mother by the Eternal Father. Just as [his] beloved Mother said the humble and selfless 'yes' to God, so it is that God always says 'yes' to his Mother." (Message of December 8). Her love for each of us surpasses our understanding for "[her] motherly love [for each of us] transcends all other love except the love of God," (Message of August 13), and she loves us despite our harsh and cruel torments to her Son. (Message of August 23). Sadly, her children's behavior on earth, their callousness and indifference to God, continues to inflict wounds upon her Son. (Message of February 9). "There is very little light upon the earth now and satan is trying to extinguish the existing light." (Message of January 1). It is because of this terrible state of affairs that the Blessed Mother "has been making her sorrows known throughout the world (Message of December 12). She is "the messenger from the Eternal City...given the task of bringing more children to full citizenship in heaven," (Message of October 18), and she speaks with the sanction and authority of Jesus because "her words come from her

Immaculate Heart and from the Sacred Heart of Jesus, hearts [that] are joined by his bitter passion. (Message of November 10). Our Mother is weeping because their messages [Jesus and the Blessed Mother] are ignored and ridiculed. She pleads for reparation, fasting, praying the Rosary and seeking reconciliation with God. (Message of January 29). She has "come to lead [us] all out of the darkness and back into the light of [her] Son's embrace." (Message of February 18). As the "messenger from the Most High, [she] delivers words of mercy" (Message of July 31) and her "visits have become more frequent because day and night, night and day, [she] pursues us relentlessly, seeking [our] love and return to God." (Message of September 25). But she "will not force us to love [her] Son and honor [her]" (Message of August 23), and tragically, "each day many, many are lost to the abyss of hell never to return." (Message of August 13). Subsequently, "all of heaven grieves when one dies and goes to the eternal pit." (Message of November 6).

The Church:
The Lord has ordained his Church to be an essential part of his Mystical Body, supplying the human means to sanctify and direct our lives on earth. The Church is the countervailing force to sin, for "sin not only affects the sinner, but affects his [Jesus'] entire Mystical Body, as a domino knocks another down...and the Sacrament of Reconciliation removes the poison that sin has brought upon his Mystical Body." (Message of December 26). In addition, just as "human beings are a part of his Mystical Body on earth, [so also is] his heavenly court part of his Body with heaven and earth becoming as one during the Holy Sacrifice of the Mass. (Message of December 16). The Church, the bride of Christ, and the present Pope, John Paul II, were so aptly described by Jesus in the following: "I, Jesus, desire all of you to listen to my high Bishop [the Pope], for truly he walks where I walk. I have set my high bishop to be the leader of my Church. I have given the Ten Commandments to be the walls of my Church. I have given the Scripture to be the life of my Church. I have given myself in the Holy Sacrifice of the Mass that my Church will neither hunger nor thirst. I have given my Spirit that my Spirit may breathe life into my Church, and I have given you my beloved Mother to be the Mother of my Church." (Message of November 4).

Jesus' Constant Presence and the Virtue of Prayer:
The Lord is present sacramentally in his Church, preeminently in the Eucharist, in the Mass as "high priest", (Message of August 10), in his Sacred Word, and also "when you are gathered together in [his] name." (Message of November 24). So generous is his love for us that where Jesus is present so also shall we find his beloved Mother. (Messages of November 24 and October 30). There is

another modality through which the Lord graciously bestows his presence, but sadly few resort to invoke or address him, that is, in prayer. In essence, we "cannot have a relationship with God if [we] do not pray." (Message of November 17). "Prayer is the way to communicate with [him]. The moment you utter [his] name, [he] hears you." (Message of October 16). Yes, "each time you call [his] name, [he] runs to you. [He is] forever at your side." (Message of January 3) "Prayer is the stairway to [Jesus] and all that is holy and righteous, it is the intellect giving permission to the soul to rest completely in his love and to receive abundant graces." (Message of January 24). The gifts the Eternal Father bestows by responding to our prayers cannot be underestimated for "Prayer can stop a hurricane. Prayer can stop a flood. Prayer can end a war." (Message of September 30). In essence, "there is nothing that cannot be accomplished by prayer." (Message of October 27). Oh, if "we but ask for the gift of prayer, it shall be granted us," (Message of October 27) and it is the prayer of a humble and contrite soul that shall be heard and answered." (Message of November 11). Though unworthy sinners we are, we "must ask [Jesus] to love [him] and praise [him] with [his] heart. And if we ask this, [he] will place [our] hearts within [his]." (Message of November 24). Then we are to pray "daily for an increase of faith," (Message of August 12), and "for our brothers and sisters" (Message of November 28) as well as unceasingly to the Holy Spirit for discernment "so that the veils over [our] eyes are lifted and [we] may see clearly." (Message of February 27).

What particular insights concerning our present state of affairs are to be derived from The Heart of God Volume II and the Holy Spirit, its ultimate author?

There are at least three that merit some explanation:

1) The false self built upon the illusion that the things of this world bring the ultimate security and love we all seek needs to be shredded. Our true self, the core of our being, is to be anchored in the inextinguishable reality of the Lord's incomprehensible love for each one of us. Hence, our own spiritual odyssey shall come to the conviction similar to that of Thomas Merton: "Love is my true identity. Selflessness is my true self. Love is my true character. Love is my name. If, therefore, I do anything or think anything or know anything that is not purely for the love of God, it cannot give me peace, or rest, or fulfillment, or

joy." [6] Yes, the barriers of fear causing us to hesitate in surrendering to the grandeur of God's plan for each of us need to dissolve and be replaced with daily confident acts of faith in his infinite love, mercy, and goodness. We are to spend our earthly life persevering in service to the Lord and others, always conscious that the Lord does not promise earthly riches, a life problem-free, freedom from prison or poverty, but he does promise eternal bliss and treasures beyond our imaginations. (Message of December 17). The innate desire of our being finds its complement only in Jesus, for he desires each of his children to have "perfect union with [him] in love." (Message of November 10) Truly, he is "the Treasure that the Heart is Always Seeking." (Message of September 8).

2) Sadly, our world is immersed in sin, "the earth has the virus of sin consuming it." (Message of July 25). Much of this "virus" is due to the machinations of the evil one whose reality and domicile we jocularly dismiss as pure myth but, in fact, it is he who mockingly laughs at our stupidity. The Blessed Mother cautions us not to have such a cavalier attitude toward satan, for he contributes toward "more and more souls being lost to the flaming pit, and [sadly] those of us who remain make a joke of it." (Message of July 26). It is "the ploy of the evil one to pretend he does not exist and come under the appearance of good." (Message of December 21).   "Aside from my youth, my priests are [satan's] largest target. (Message of November 30). Even chosen souls granted the gifts of visions and/or locutions are not free from such intrusions for, "the evil one is able to mimic Jesus and his beloved Mother." (Message of December 21). Fortunately, there are weapons that exist to fend off the onslaughts of satan; they consist in "becoming a consecrated soul, making the Immaculate Heart of his Mother your resting place, the Sacred Heart your pillow, the holy Scriptures your garments, the Rosary a sword of holiness, staying reconciled to Jesus, and frequenting the sacraments"... If [we] do these [the Lord] shall place a wall of holiness about [us] and the evil one shall not enter." (Message of December 29). Unfortunately, the Blessed Mother has stated that she and her Son "are grieving, for the society in which we live has no faith; materialism, pride, and greed have darkened the senses to God's call." (Message of January 8). We have constructed a world "more repulsive than Sodom and Gomorrah," (Message of January 17), the consequences of which are beyond our imagination - "many prison terms, as [we] know it, cannot begin to compare to

---

[6] Thomas Merton, p. 60.

the suffering inflicted upon those in hell." (Message of August 30). But dire consequences appear to await us in this life as well through usurping the authority of God concerning who decides life or death. (Message of January 12).

3) Abortion has become the scourge of our world, for "this generation has committed abominable sins, that of which killing the unborn is the most serious." (Message of August 13). "God grieves because every nation upon the face of the earth is sick," (Message of October 18), and "[he is] sickened by the atrocities and abominations upon this earth." (Message of November 19). We have made the greatest mockery of his creation by making the decision to murder his creation. We have murdered priests and prophets. (Message of January 12). This expression of our idolatrous self-indulgence has ironically brought its own nemesis, for the Lord has "provided cures for every disease upon the earth but we have aborted them." (Message of November 2). The blood of the unborn cries out for vengeance and sadly, "the time of mercy is almost over." (Message of November 17). We are entering into "an era of cleansing of humanity." (Message of June 29). "Reparation has been demanded, but it has not been made. A star shall fall from the heavens and so great will be its impact upon the earth that many will harken to [the Lord's] words." (Message of January 3). The Lord "will come as a tidal wave from a calm sea." (Message of March 5). Yes, "the chastisement of justice shall soon be upon us...we shall see ourselves as Jesus sees us...through the eyes of honesty and self-criticism." (Messages of November 12 and July 26). The time is approaching "when each person shall see the true state of his soul." (Message of August 31). "Every person on the face of the earth will hear this call." (Message of July 9). "There shall be plagues, and famines, and diseases, ... one catastrophe after another." (Message of October 10). "On this day of justice those of us who have not reconciled with the Lord will perish from fear alone. This is not the Lord's desire, his desire is to free us from sin, and that we frequent the sacraments and offer reparation for the lost brothers and sisters. (Message of November 12).

Despite the ominous tone of the upcoming events, one must follow the admonition of the Blessed Mother whose "role is to herald the coming of her Son" (Message of February 18). and "help prepare us to meet our Savior," (Message of March 23), that these "warnings are messages of mercy." (Message July 31). Hopefully, they will wake up this "foolish and prideful generation" to be open to the grace of repentance and conversion. (Message of December 1). And for those who have faith, our apprehension should be minimal for we have the words of Jesus, our Redeemer, to rely upon: "Those who consecrate themselves to my Sacred Heart and the Immaculate Heart of my Mother have nothing to fear." (Message of December 31). It is these consecrated souls, to use the words of Lidz, who have found their true "ego identity involving the sense of completion that comes from the feeling of being loved and 'needed' from Love itself and being able to share their world" with "the Divine Healer [Jesus] and the nurse of the soul [Blessed Mother]." (Message of June 13). As for our potentially lost brothers and sisters, we pray "may the ice of [their] hearts melt as the fire of the Lord's mercy dwells within [them]." (Message of January 20).

Before closing this excursus an acknowledgment is warranted. There is a small band of men and women who have come to the opinion that these messages are authentically originating from Jesus and his beloved Mother. This group is incorporated in the State of Florida as a non-profit organization entitled The Disciples of Mercy, a title Jesus himself bestowed upon them. (Message of August 16, 1994). Each disciple has a unique and grace-filled story as to how he or she came to the conviction that these messages are ultimately under the guidance of the Holy Spirit. If it had not been for their generous donation of time and energy in cooperating with God's graces, the messages could not have been produced. Their zealousness for the Lord is truly admirable and unceasing, for he has informed them "after each task you accomplish for me, I, Jesus, will assign you another task." (Message of November 1). However, following the admonition of the Apostle Paul, who said "those who have zeal for God,... let it always be discerning." (Rom 10:2), the Disciples of Mercy humbly submit their wills and intellects to the final authority of the Magisterium of the Catholic Church regarding the messages contained herein. They unanimously concur that this material is solely within the realm of private revelation and in no way does it take precedence over the canonically approved Scriptures or the preaching, teaching, sanctifying, and administrative authority of the Catholic Church.

Finally, this is not to imply that the Disciples of Mercy is an exclusive group. Quite the contrary, all of us are called to be disciples. "All those who know [Jesus] in their hearts and desire to follow [him] are [his] disciples." (Message of January 19). The disciples are those called to pray constantly and sacrifice daily (Message of February 18), and recognize that "each sacrifice of love removes a thorn from [the Lord's] brow and a rose is placed in [his] crown instead." (Message of September 6). To be a warrior in the Lord's army of souls we are commissioned to "touch every person you meet" (Message of November

21), with the message of the Gospel. How does one know he or she has begun to take the first step of discipleship? It occurs at the same time the Lord has attested to be his greatest consolation: "when he [the Lord] looks into one's eyes and sees them teary with love for [him]." (Message of November 21). There is no doubt that the reader of this volume will have many poignant moments when tears of love, gratitude, and sorrow will swell and fill the eyes. I exhort you not to motion immediately for a tissue or handkerchief to wipe away these tears, for they are truly beads of "blessed" water - water that springs directly from the soul awash in the knowledge, similar to Merton's own conclusion, that "the secret of one's identity is hidden in the mercy and love of God."

God's mercy is yours,

John P. Sause, Ph.D.
Professor
Dept of Philosophy and Theology
Barry University
Miami, FL 33161

I was instructed by the Lord that the following statements should be placed at the introduction of this volume. They set the tone of the volume and inform the reader of the unfathomable love the Lord and the Blessed Mother have for each one of us. God's mercy is yours. All one has to do is approach him with a contrite heart.

I have come to extinguish the darkness and light the candles of my love in every heart.

The Lord Jesus - May 12, 1995

Those that approach my mercy will be offered new garments of righteousness and new hearts of flesh. Those who seek my mercy will be hidden in the depths of my most Sacred Heart and in the Immaculate Heart of my beloved Mother. Together we will bring you to the heavenly banquet.

The Lord Jesus - May 20, 1995

I have come as a holy candle to light the way for you to return to God. The Savior is waiting for all of you with open arms.

The Blessed Mother - May 24, 1995

Children of my heart, be concerned for one another. You must not only concern yourselves with the physical well-being of someone. It is your responsibility to be concerned with their spiritual well-being.

The Blessed Mother - October 30, 1995

January 1, 1995

Lord Jesus, do you want to write?

My little one, I am here. Come let us begin.

Daughter, I am teaching you the way of the cross, which is the way to me. Take courage in me, my little lamb, for I AM has called you, and you, my servant, have been purchased by me, the Lord God. I have purchased you all, my children, by my death on the cross.

Yes, my children, you are all mine, but I will not force you into my service. For only those who truly love me desire to serve me. Remember, I AM WHO AM serves and nurtures his flock with love and mercy.

My shepherd's staff is the rod of compassion and my garments are made of love and mercy. Come to my flock, all of you, and leave the den of satan. Leave behind your garments of wickedness and be baptized, thus receiving garments of holiness and righteousness.

Be as a light upon the dark earth and despise the darkness of sin. Children, there is very little light upon the earth now and satan is still trying to extinguish the existing light. Unite, my children, unite. Remember the power of prayer and acts of charity.

Daughter, thank you for writing. Go in peace, little mercy of my heart. I bless you and I love you.

I bless you and love you, too, Jesus. Amen.

January 2, 1995

Lord Jesus, do you want to write?

Child, I have taken your concerns and have placed them in my heart.[1] I AM is

---

[1] I was very concerned about all the notoriety that may come my way as the messages began to spread. I was afraid that my ego would get in the way of giving all glory to God.

speaking. Let Wisdom instruct you.

My child, satan's power ravages the soul as a cancer, as the good cells are devoured by the bad. Remember what I have taught you, little one. The sins of pride and greed are poisonous to the soul for they are not easily recognized. How then, child, shall you recognize and be on guard of these great pitfalls into the abyss?

I tell you solemnly, put on the armor of God. Accept no honor and glory for yourself. Remain little and realize that it is I AM who dwells within you. Do not seek recognition from another, for you, my child, are only a vessel. If the vessel is sturdy before setting sail, it will not destruct in the midst of the storm.

Child, do not be afraid to proceed. I have set your concerns before my face and I, the Lord, shall not let you falter. Remain obedient to the tasks I have set before you, my little sparrow.

Never, my little one, shall you have to leave the nest of my love. I have given you many tools to help you in the face of temptation. Call upon St. Michael to protect you. The Rosary is a most powerful sword of holiness. Frequent the sacraments and stay reconciled to me. Satan shall not prevail, my little lamb.

Thank you, Lord. I love you.

I love you, too, little one of my heart. I bless you.

January 3, 1995

Lord Jesus, do you want to write?

My little one, I am here. Let us begin. My child, each time you call my name, I run to you. I am forever by your side, my child.

Oh, how my heart aches from loneliness. My beloved sons and daughters, why do you turn from me? You must realize that I am the only source of love and comfort. You are being deceived by satan's trickery, as he laughs at your ignorance.

Write all that you hear, my little disciple.

A star shall fall from the heavens. So great shall its impact upon the earth be, mankind, that many will hearken to my words. Ah, but for those who do not, their stubbornness and foolishness are as arsenic. By their own choice shall be their eternal destiny. Do not be afraid to write what I tell you, child.[2]

Reparation has been demanded but has not been made. Wake up, you foolish and prideful Generation, for the Lord God of Israel is calling you. I shall permit the trumpets to sound to mark the beginning of the chastisement. Fast, offer sacrifices, and do penance. Do not be afraid, my child. You are my prophet. You are to speak all that I, the Lord, tell you.

Be in peace, little one of my heart. I bless you.

I bless you, too, Lord God. Have mercy. Amen.

January 4, 1995

Lord Jesus, do you want to write?

My little one, how patiently I have been waiting for you. Come, let us begin.

Mercy shall fall from heaven as rain after a drought. You, children, shall be given the final choice. Saturate yourselves with my mercy and live, or hide from it and perish!

Be still in my presence, child. Listen carefully to my words.

My mercy shall heal all you sinners, and grant you the grace of conversion and repentance. Children, know that without a repentant heart, one cannot accept the graces I am freely offering. Without a repentant heart, one will linger in the shadow of satan until he eventually finds himself at perdition's gates.

But those who accept my mercy with humility shall be set free. They shall be unshackled and loosed from their condemnation. I AM shall raise them that they will soar above their earthly humanity. Children, again I am instructing you. Implore my mercy and you shall receive my mercy.

---

[2] I become uneasy when the Lord starts talking in terms of prophesy about upcoming events.

Child, thank you for writing my words. Go in peace, my little heartbeat. I bless you.

I bless you, too, my precious Jesus. Amen.

January 5, 1995

Lord Jesus, do you want to write?

My little one, listen to the voice of the Almighty and Sovereign God of Israel. Child, what does it mean for one to offer sacrifices? Remember, I am the Lamb. I am the Sacrificed Victim of Reconciliation. My blood has purchased salvation and the defeat of death.

Children, I am asking you to sacrifice so that you may become purified by the fire of holiness. I am asking you to offer small acts of reparation to show your humility and willingness to cast aside sin. I am asking you to make reparation on behalf of your many brothers and sisters who continue to mock me.

Remember, children, do not be discouraged. Those who persevere in faith shall be lifted by me to my Heavenly Father. The principle of offering reparation for others as well, brings the soul into the virtue of charity and generosity.

Remember how I, the Lord Jesus Christ, have instructed you that these virtues deliver a strong fragrance to the Throne Room of Heaven. Be not discouraged, my little lambs. Call upon me and I, the Lord, shall always help you.

I bless you, child. Thank you for writing.

I bless you and love you, too, Lord Jesus and Blessed Mother.[3] Amen

January 6, 1995

Lord Jesus, do you want to write?

My precious child, I am the Lord, the Holy Spirit.

---

[3] Although the Blessed Mother did not speak, I often address her, too, because the Lord has told me she is always present where he is.

Know that as soon as you utter my name, I am by your side. I am the All Powerful and Everlasting God of Abraham, Isaac, and Jacob. I have in my hand the Book of Truth and Life. Those of mine who have inscribed my name upon their hearts have I, the Lord, written in the Book of Truth and Life. But those who have erased me from their lives, I, the Lord, Jesus Christ, have cast from my eternal Book of Life.

Children, you do not realize the seriousness of these days. How is it, children, you arise and go to sleep each day in the shadow of my love and do not recognize me? Yes, children, I watch you sleep. I call your names in the night, yet by daybreak, children, you have forgotten. Yet who is it that makes the sun to rise and set each day? Who is it that breathes life into your sleeping bodies each day? "I am," says the Lord God of All Creation, "of the just and of the unjust." Does the sun rise over just the few? No children, my heart has infinite love for each of you.

Daughter, thank you for writing, my little one. Go in peace with my blessing.

Lord, I love you. You make my heart smile. I bless you, too. Amen.

January 7, 1995

Lord Jesus, do you want to write?

I do, my little child. Come into my heart and receive my message of love.

Children, sin is the plague of the soul. It multiplies and renders its victim incapable of healing himself without assistance. Children, I am the *only* assistance of the soul. I am the Divine Healer who comes to refresh the soul and purify it with love and mercy. Without me, children, the soul will wither and perish.

The sin shall multiply and so shall its effects. Oh, children, do you not see that the soul is as a clear river of water which was created to flow towards me? But the river of the soul has been polluted by the trash of sin and must be made clean and new. Children, by my death on the Cross, I, the Lord, Jesus Christ, have made each soul new. But to sustain yourselves, my little ones, you must rest in me. Children, be reconciled to me and rest in my heart of love.

I bless you, child. Thank you for writing.

I bless you, too, O Lord. I love you. Amen.

January 8, 1995

Daughter, I am here. I am Blessed Virgin Mary and the Mother of God. Daughter, I come to you wearing a crown of twelve stars and carrying my beloved Son, Jesus, in my arms. I come to you this way to show my unity to the Twelve Apostles and the Twelve Tribes of Israel. I am guarding the Twelve Tribes of Israel under my mantle of love.

Children, my mantle of love which was given to me by Almighty God is holy, and, therefore, all those who live under my motherly mantle shall obtain graces of holiness. Children, if you were to see the coming events, your desire to be reconciled with God would be immediate. You would find yourself on your knees begging for mercy.

Children, we are grieving, for the society in which you live has no faith. Materialism has replaced the heart, and pride and greed have darkened the senses to God's call. Wake up, my sleeping children. It is time to make your homes in order. The time for reconciliation and conversion is now. Children, you shall not have many tomorrows left. I am sad, my children. Please, return to God and amend your lives.

Daughter, I bless you. I love you, my little child.

I love you and bless you, too, Mama Mary.

Lord Jesus, do you want to write?

No, my little one. We will continue tomorrow. Be blessed, my little mercy. Stay in my love.

I love you and bless you, too, Lord Jesus and Holy Spirit. Amen.

January 9, 1995

Lord Jesus, do you want to write?

My little child, I have seen you in your despair.[4] Let us begin.

Child, understand that when I, the Lord, asked you to abandon your life to my care, I am asking you first to relinquish your attachment to your will. Tell me, my child, when did your self reliance ever benefit you? Which direction are you traveling when you are not carrying out my will? Yes, my child, the road to perdition is wide. It is wide from man's rationalizations and inability to recognize sin.

Child, I am asking you to give your will to me that I may dwell in you and be your God. Have an open mind, my little child. Do not be afraid for my will is sweet as honey to the bee, and all those who strive to live my will, receive courage and ability from me, the Lord God. Of your own, what ability and courage do you possess?

Nothing, Lord.

Remember, child, all things are possible with me. Never put a limit on my power, for I am the Omnipotent and Sovereign God of Abraham, Isaac, and Jacob. Come, children, rest in the sanctuary of my heart.

I bless you, child. Go in peace.

I bless you and love you, too, Lord Jesus, forever and ever. Amen.

January 10, 1995

Lord Jesus, do you want to write?

My little one, thank you for your sacrifice of love.

Hearken all of you who have ears to hear, for the Lord God of Israel is calling

---

[4] I wasn't feeling very well during my pregnancy and other personal events were causing me great stress. The term "despair" does not mean the theological concept of " a total loss of hope in salvation." Rather the more appropriate meaning employed here and in future mention of the term in this volume, is "disheartened and frustrated with one's physical, social, or economic circumstances."

you. Children, you turn your heads from me and pretend you do not hear. In your arrogance you say that my words must be for others, and, therefore, why should you listen. I tell you solemnly, children, that the day has come upon you to choose your eternal destiny.

I am watching all of you, children, and I, the Lord, am deeply saddened by those who continue to mock and scourge me. Children, remove the blinders from your eyes and you will see how your soul is standing at the entrance of hell. Children, accept my mercy which is offered to you in love. The King of Mercy has come to you, children, that you would not perish in hellfire, but live forever with me in splendor. Again, the choice is yours.

Daughter, thank you for writing. Rest, my beloved disciple. I bless you.

I bless you, too, Lord Jesus and Mother Mary. I love you. Amen.

January 11, 1995

Lord Jesus, do you want to write?

My little disciple, come and receive my message of love. I AM is speaking. Let Wisdom instruct you.

Through the ages I, the Lord, have watched as mankind has suffocated his heart with worldly possessions. I have seen the affliction of wealth and the absolute treasure of poverty. In poverty, my children, is where you shall find me, your Savior, who is your greatest treasure. Those who are bloated with earthly wealth have no room in their hearts for me. They are puffed up with ego and pride and feel no need for my help.

Oh, how you are deceived, my foolish children. You, my little lambs, are being led to the slaughter by satan because you have not hearkened to my calls. Children, why do you prepare for your earthly future and not your eternal future?

Children, my love is light to those blinded by arrogance. My love is food and drink for the hungry, and my arms are the everlasting shelter to those who return to me.

I bless you, child. Thank you for writing my words. Go in peace.

I bless you and love you, too, Lord Jesus. Amen.

January 12, 1995

Lord Jesus, do you want to write?

My little disciple of mercy, receive my message of love.

The earth is mine, children, and everything of the earth was created to bring glory to my holy name. Yet you, my children, have made a mockery of my creation and therefore, a mockery of my name. The greatest mockery is your decision to murder my creation. Oh, children, how you have grieved me. You have murdered so many that I, the Lord, have sent to help you. Priests and prophets have you murdered, children, by your
arrogance and hardness of heart.

I, the Lord, am the *only* author of life. Only I, the Lord, can grant life or take life. You, my children, have no authority from me to decide life or death. Your sins are atrocities and are poisoning you, creation. My children, open your eyes. Can you not see the poison of your sins upon your world?

O Wicked Generation, be prepared to account for your lives before me, the Lord God.

We shall continue tomorrow, child. I love you and I bless you.

I love you and bless you, too, my Jesus and Mama Mary. Amen.

January 13, 1995

Lord Jesus, do you want to write?

I do, my little disciple of mercy. Let us begin.

My children, why do you despair? You are under the protection of my angels at all times. Should I rescue you from the gates of perdition only to see you cast again as prey to satan? No, my children. You are mine. I have purchased you by my death on the cross. I, the Lord have won the victory by my blood.

We are present in the hearts of all those who call to us, but beware, my precious children, of satan's facade.[5] He is as the clown at the circus, masking his destructiveness under a joyful appearance. Beware, my little disciples. Use caution as you proceed, but remember, I shall always be with you. You must pray unceasingly to the Holy Spirit for the gift of discernment. Remember children, my adversary shall never win. His efforts shall all be thwarted by me, the Lord God. Be diligent, my special ones, and persevere. I have told you before, children, to always seek my confirmation.[6] I will not permit interference [from satan] during the confirmation. Be ever on guard, for satan wears masks of every sort. Be unblemished, my little lambs, and great will be your reward. Strive always to be obedient to my will. We will continue tomorrow, my child. Go in peace. I bless you.

I bless you and love you, too, Lord God and Mother Mary. Amen.

January 14, 1995

Lord Jesus, do you want to write?

My little child, receive my message of love and mercy.

Each drop of rain upon the earth cleanses it. It washes away the old and makes a path for the new. So it is, children, with grace. Grace, my children, is my gift to you. You cannot earn this gift for it is freely given to you in love. I have instituted my sacraments as avenues for you to obtain grace.

So many of you abuse my gifts of love. Children, I, the Lord, have witnessed

---

[5] I was asking Jesus whether he and our Blessed Mother were at an alleged apparition site.

[6] When I receive a specific directive from the Lord or a message that I consider to have serious consequences, I will often ask the Lord to send me a "confirmation" or sign that would verify it is coming from him and not the evil one.

your favoritism to earthly possessions. These have become your greatest treasures and you, children, have said "no" to my gift of love. Oh, what foolishness dwells in your hearts, children. You are living in the kingdom of satan, who is waiting to hurl you into the abyss.

I solemnly assure you, you must repent and convert to obtain the Kingdom of Heaven. You must return to my heart of love and mercy and I, the Lord, will invite you into my kingdom to dwell with me. Do not discard my invitation of love.

Thank you for writing, child of my heart. I bless you.

I bless you, too, Lord of my heart and Blessed Mother. Amen.

January 15, 1995

Lord Jesus, do you want to write?

My little child, come into my arms and receive my message of love. Concentrate, my little disciple of mercy.[7] I AM is speaking.

My child, the earth revolves around the sun depending on the light and energy of the sun for its very existence. I assure you, children, that I, the Lord, uphold the sun in my palm as all creation rests in my palm. I am teaching you, children, to recognize my kingship and authority over all creation. Children, I am the power and sustaining force behind all creation, which was created to serve me, the Lord God.

Children, by a breath of my nostrils the oceans can swallow the continents. Yet, children, in your arrogance you have labeled yourselves the gods over all the earth. The only contributions you have made to creation, children, are those which I, the Lord, have given you. By your very nature, children, you are a destructive force to all that is good and your sin has devoured my creation as a cancer.

---

[7] The Lord often corrects me when my mind drifts from what I am supposed to be doing. I was being distracted by my children in the next room.

Children, what path are you traveling when you have not reconciled and offered reparation to me, the Judge of the Living? Remember, my children, the Lord, thy God, has come to you from the throne room of heaven so that you might live in my mercy.

My child, thank you for writing my words. Go in peace, little disciple of mercy. I bless you.

I bless you, too, Lord Jesus and Blessed Mother. Amen.

January 16, 1995

Lord Jesus, do you want to write?

My little one, receive my words of love.

I am suffering, my child. I am the Suffering Redeemer. Yet who knows my name? Have all my efforts been in vain?

Lord, I'm sorry. I don't know what to say. Have mercy, O Lord.

My daughter, Jerusalem, you were once the delight of my heart. I, the Lord, have granted you gifts more valuable than gold and silver, for I delighted in you. But now, my Jerusalem, you are as ashes for I, the Lord, have quenched the fire of my love for you. You, my children, are my grief and my heartache. Oh, how I am grieving, for your sins have pierced my heart.

You have forgotten me, my Jerusalem. The god of idolatry is your god, yet I, the Lord, will absolve you by my mercy if you repent before me. Thus, says the Lord God of Abraham, Isaac and Jacob: "rebuke and dismiss your evil ways. Cast your eyes from sin. Humble yourselves before me and repent, and I, the Lord, shall forgive you."

My beloved servant, thank you for writing. Go in peace.

I love you and bless you, Lord. Have mercy, O Lord. Amen.

January 17, 1995

Lord Jesus, do you want to write?

My children, listen to the words of the Lord God of Abraham, Isaac and Jacob.

From the mountain of the God of his people, Israel, shall come the justice of the Lord. Oh, how the heavens and earth shall tremble at his majesty. Who among you by his deeds can say, "Lord, judge me not for I am upright in thy sight?" Is there even one among you? No, children, but I, the Lord, am offering you my mercy which will envelop you and carry you across the threshold of the abyss of hell.

Listen carefully, little child, to the Holy Spirit of Truth and Right Judgement. I shall teach you a prayer, my precious ones. Open your hearts to the Fire of Truth and Life.

> Redeemer of Israel, Sanctifier and Purifier of Souls, we long to dwell in the land of the righteous. We desire to build a new house which we may call the Temple of the God of Israel, who is Holy, who is One. Let the fire of your love purify us. Make us pliable and useful to you, that we may become upright in thy sight. Close not your eyes. Make not your ears deaf to our pleadings. O Lord, drown us in your mercy and hear our lamentation, for the Lord is our God and holy is his name. Blessed be the name of the Lord forever. Amen.

My children, you are more repulsive than Sodom and Gomorrah, and who shall you send as a representative to me to implore my mercy? No, there is not one among you. Remember my patience and kindness to you, children. You must call upon the Spirit of Truth to heal you and unshackle you. Return to me and I, the Lord, will help you.

Thank you, child. Go in peace. I bless you.

I bless you, too, Lord Jesus. Amen.

January 18, 1995

Lord Jesus, do you want to write?

My little child, unburden yourself. Come to the foot of the Cross. Tell me, child, what do you see? [8]

I see that you are crucified, Lord. Your head is bowed down. I see the blood from your wounds.

Child, who have I, the Lord, given my life for?

For me?

Yes, child, for you - for all. Tell me, child, do you believe I, the Lord, will forsake you?

No, Lord. It's just that so many difficult things happen and it feels like you are far away from me sometimes.

Child, I am faithful as the sunrise. I never leave your side. My child, each time the weight of the cross is increased for you, you doubt in my loving care of you. Child, know that the heavier the cross is for you, the closer I, the Lord, am to you.

Little one of my heart, I will not abandon you. I will help you with everything. Go in peace, little child. Do not despair.

I love you, Lord. I bless you. Amen.

---

[8] I closed my eyes and the Lord placed a vision in my head. He appeared in his crucified form with his head sloped down so I did not see his face but I did see blood oozing from his wounds. I would say he appeared about five feet away from me in this momentary vision.

January 19, 1995

Lord Jesus, do you want to write?

Daughter of my heart, record my words of love.

Listen carefully, my little child. My disciples are honored in heaven by my heavenly court of angels and saints. For each of you is a place setting at the banquet of my Heavenly Father. For each one of you has a special place been reserved. Remember, great is the reward and consolation for all those who persevere. Let me assure you that all those who come home to heaven are without possessions, for they have learned to relinquish their earthly possessions and be only attached to me.

Remember, children, place your desire for the Kingdom of God first, and everything you need shall be granted you. When the time comes for each of you to put aside his cross you shall find yourselves in my loving embrace.

Do not be discouraged, my disciples. I, the Lord, shall always help you. All those who know me in their hearts and desire to follow me are my disciples.

Child, we shall continue tomorrow. I bless you.

I bless you, too, Jesus and Mama Mary. Amen.

January 20, 1995

Lord Jesus, do you want to write?

Come, my devoted servant, and receive my message of mercy.

Child, my mercy shall blanket the earth as the first snow of winter. So pure is my mercy that those who are lost shall find their way back to my heart of love. My mercy will brand my love upon their hearts. Upon their hearts and minds will I, the Lord, brand my words of love and life.

Imagine, my children, the entire earth covered by pure white snow, untouched by human hands. So it shall be that my mercy will consume mankind.

Continue to write all that I tell you, child.

Yes, the ice in your hearts shall melt as the fire of my mercy dwells within you. Do not turn from my divine mercy, children. There is not one among you who is not in need of my mercy and forgiveness. These words which I, the Lord, have spoken to you will engulf many in the flames of my mercy. Come to me, my children. I am Jesus, beloved Son of God and Eternal Fire of Mercy.

I bless you, little child of my heart. Go in peace.

I bless you, too, Lord of my heart and soul. Amen.

January 21, 1995

Child, I am here. I am Blessed Virgin Mary and the Mother of the Church. I am the Mother of the Church because my beloved Son, Jesus, is the head of the church as is his role of high priest.

Children, you all are members of the Body of Christ and as such, you must recognize my Son's guardianship and authority over his Church. Many of you have disregarded my Son's instructions to his Church and you desire to abolish the old ways to institute the new.

My children, my children, by whose authority do you act? You were not given authority from heaven to make these changes. No, on the contrary, the apostasy that exists within the Church is led by satan and his demons. They have declared war on heaven and all that would strive to follow Jesus. Beware, all of you, my little children.

You are only safe in my Immaculate Heart and the Sacred Heart of Jesus. My children, you must pray for the Church and for all those priests and laity who have been snared and pursued by satan. Persevere, my beloved children.

That is all we shall write, my child. I love you and I bless you.

I love you and bless you, too, Mama Mary.

Lord?

I am here, little one. We shall continue tomorrow. Go in peace.

I bless you and love you, Lord Jesus. Amen.

January 22, 1995

Lord Jesus, do you want to write?

Yes, my child. Receive my message of love.

Daughter, understand that the entire world is sitting under the umbrella of my mercy. For so strong is my love that I, the Lord, shall not rest until my mercy reaches every heart. Yes, daughter, despite my love, many will still reject me, for they have completely given their hearts to satan and shall suffer always for their grievous error.

Remember, children, your decisions are based on your heart and are not temporary. You need my help to restore your lives. You are drowning in satan's ocean of deception and I, the Lord, am offering you a life jacket. Children, the life jacket I am offering you is my mercy. If you do not accept my mercy, you shall perish.

Listen carefully, my child. I AM is speaking. I shall send my disciples forth into satan's ocean of deception and they will rescue those who desire conversion. But so many of my little ones shall drown because of their pride and hardness of heart. So many will let go of my life-giving mercy only to be devoured by satan's rage. Be on guard. Be on guard. Be on guard.

Child, thank you for writing my words. Do not be afraid, little mercy of my heart. I bless you.

I bless you and love you, too, Lord Jesus. Amen.

January 23, 1995

Lord Jesus, do you want to write?

My child of mercy, I desire to teach you what it means to dwell in the mercy of the Lord God.

Child, you were stricken by the cancer of sin and you, my daughter, lived as an outcast from my sight. But I, the Lord Jesus Christ, took pity upon you. I have lifted you from the stench of iniquity and have cleansed you by my holy Precious Blood. Now, my child, you dwell completely in my mercy.

Yet, Generation, understand this: I, the Lord, listen as you judge the sins of another. It is best for all of you, children, to be sealed in silence for you are all guilty in my sight. Judge no one, children. The only hiding place for you, children, is in the shelter of my divine mercy. Do not make the fatal error to consider yourselves above the need for my mercy.

My child, tell others of my mercy and how I, the Lord, have rescued you from your pitiable state. Continue to dwell in my mercy for therein lies your only freedom.

I love you and bless you, child. Be at peace.

I love you and bless you, too, Lord Jesus. Amen.

January 24, 1995

Lord Jesus, do you want to write?

My little disciple, listen carefully to the words of the One Who Is.

I, the Lord, shall teach you the significance of prayer. Prayer is the soul's fortification and lifeline to me, the Creator. Prayer from the heart strengthens the heart and encompasses the heart in a fortress of my love and guidance. Prayer, my children, is the stairway to me and to all that is holy and righteous. Prayer acts as a filter to impurities of the soul and fragrances the soul with the perfume of righteousness. Prayer, my little ones, is the intellect giving permission to the soul to rest completely in my love and to receive abundant graces.

Continue, my little mercy.

My children, you cannot live without oxygen nor can the soul survive without prayer. Be mindful of this, children. Accept my teachings. Children, when you pray for others, their blessings are multiplied and so are yours. Be considerate when you pray, children, and remember all prayers, whether spoken or unspoken, are answered by my Heavenly Father. Remember always to seek the will of my Heavenly Father and to persevere in your efforts. Daughter, I bless you. Go in peace.

I bless you, too, Lord Jesus. Amen.

January 25, 1995

Lord Jesus, do you want to write?

My little disciples of mercy, can you see how my heart has guided you to this point?

You, my children, are reflections of my love to shine upon the earth. Today, my beloved, I am rejoicing. Yes, the fruits of my labor have begun to multiply.[9] I am preparing you, children, to harvest the crop I, the Lord Jesus Christ, have planted and nurtured in the fountain of my tender mercy.

Continue to write, my child.[10]

Understand the different roles there are in my army. For my army is not created to maim and destroy. My army was handpicked by me to rebuild the foundation of my people, Israel.

My beloved disciples of mercy, you are the torches of light that reach to the heavens and bring joy to our grieving hearts. Yes, children, my heart has brought all of you to this point and I shall continue to nurture and sustain you. Continue in your efforts, children, to please me. I bless you all.

---

[9] Several members of the prayer group were present for this message. We had gathered together to run off the messages, assemble them in stapled packets, and to distribute them to those persons who would possibly be receptive. The Lord is acknowledging our efforts.

[10] I suddenly became very self-conscious and momentarily immobilized during the message, but the Lord dispelled this debilitating fear.

Thank you, Lord. We bless you, too. Amen.

January 26, 1995

Lord Jesus, do you want to write?

Daughter of my Sacred Heart, receive my message of love.

Children, I, the Lord, am offering you a share in the victory of my Sacred Heart. Yes, children, my disciples shall be called to the banquet of victory by my Heavenly Father. Oh, joyous day, the day that all of heaven rejoices as satan and his army are hurled into the abyss forever. The victorious shall dine with me, the Lord God, and shall drink from the cup of salvation.

Children, you must persevere and do not sit still, for those who cast aside their faith in lieu of earthly riches shall be swallowed by satan. No, my children, those who do not walk with me, walk away from me and shall not prevail against satan.

What must one do to dine at the banquet of the Lord God? Repent, children, and follow my commandments. Follow me and accept my holy will with humility and resignation, and you, my children, shall share my victory eternally.

I bless you, child. Go in peace.

I bless you, too, Lord God. Amen.

January 27, 1995

Lord Jesus, do you want to write?

My little child, rest in the sanctuary of my heart. My daughter, my daughter, where is your focus?[11]

Do you see when your eyes stray from me that your heart is next to follow?

---

[11] I was not feeling very well and thus drifted into a lazy state for the last few days and occupying my mind with merely passing impressions.

Lord, I'm sorry. For two days I've been sick and lying on the couch watching TV.

My child, I, the Lord, do not wish to remove the recreation from your life. But understand how television is satan's largest source of infiltration. When you focus on television, you do not focus on me, and your heart cannot hear the call of the Holy Spirit.

Beware, all of you, my little children. You do not realize how I, the Lord, wish you to discard your attachment to television. Remember, I am a jealous God. I desire that you spend more time with me.

Ah, my children, my children, why do you spend so much of your time in darkness and corruption? Come into the light, little ones. Come back to me.

Be blessed, little one of my heart. Do not lose your focus, child. Keep your eyes on me.

I love you, Jesus. I thank and bless you and Mother Mary. Amen.

January 28, 1995

Lord Jesus, do you want to write?

My little one, I have been waiting for you. Listen carefully to the words of the Spirit of Light and Truth.

Why is it, my children, that when you see a red light, you stop, and proceed at a green light? These, children, are the commandments of the road and you follow them to remain unharmed and within the law. But I tell you this, children, how much more valuable are the commandments I, the Lord, have given you. My laws are directions to keep you on the path to me and to keep your immortal soul on the path to heaven.

Yet, children, you are quick to ignore my direction as you feel it is insignificant. Truly, I tell you that when you stand at the intersection of judgement I will ask you if you followed my commandments, or did you disregard them? Did you place the emphasis of your life on worldly possessions and laws and ignore mine? Those who strive first for the kingdom of heaven shall obtain all that they ask for. I am Jesus, beloved Son of God, and I am calling you to walk eternally with me.

Thank you for writing, child. Go in peace.

I bless you and love you, Jesus, and Mother Mary. Amen.

January 29, 1995

My child, I am here. I am Blessed Virgin Mary and the Mother of God. Again I have come to deliver the message of my Son's love to others.

Daughter, we are weeping. Our messages are ignored and ridiculed. My Son is scourged by mankind's cruelty and rejection of him. I cannot still the hand of God's wrath much longer.

My child, I have come to warn you of another catastrophe. A great storm with severe intensity is approaching and many shall perish. Daughter, do not be frightened. Write all that I tell you.[12]

Children, I need your prayers. Where is the reparation we have asked for? Fast, children. Offer reparation on behalf of those who continue to scourge my Son. Do all that we ask of you, children. Pray the rosary daily and seek

---

[12] I always get anxious and fearful when the Blessed Mother and the Lord begin telling me of upcoming events. Nevertheless, a huge snowstorm occurred in the mid-Atlantic and Northeast states six days later. I quote directly from the Sunday, February 5 issue of the *New York Times*: "After six weeks of languorous winter, the first big snowstorm of the season roared across the New York metropolitan area and the Northeast with a vengeance yesterday, obliterating the region under accumulations 6 to 16 inches deep and turning the day into a hardship for some and a magical adventure for others. As if making up for lost time, the storm -- a comma-shaped Northeaster, 300 miles across -- barreled up the Atlantic Seaboard and transformed landscapes from Virginia to Massachusetts. It disrupted air, rail and highway travel, knocked out power to thousands, closed businesses, flooded low-lying coastal areas and shut down all but emergency government services."

reconciliation with God.

I shall not dictate any more words tonight. Go with my blessing.

Thank you, Blessed Mother. I love you.

Lord, are we going to write?

No, my precious one. We shall continue tomorrow. I bless you.

I bless you, too, Lord Jesus.

January 30, 1995

Dear Jesus, happy ninth month anniversary of messages. I love you, my precious God. Do you want to write?

My little one, come. Record the words I, the Lord, dictate.

My child, do not despair, for you are held high in the light of my mercy. I have lifted you in my palm above the earth and have given you the choice.[13] Understand, children, I, the Lord, will not force your love. You, children, have the choice whether to love me or not, and whether to follow me or follow satan. My children, you must see the confusion and misery in your lives and bring yourselves, though completely wretched, to the foot of the Cross. It is there, children, where I shall receive each and every one of you.

There is not one among you that has ever called to me and not been lifted into my compassionate heart. But in the hardness of your own hearts, you do not see the truth because you do not see me, and I am the Truth.

Remember, children, if you seek the truth, then you must seek me.

---

[13] I was sick at the time due to my pregnancy, but I became momentarily engrossed in a vision where I found myself in the palm of the large hand of the Lord. Suddenly, I fell off the hand and started falling toward the earth, but I cried out to the Lord who indicated that I had the choice to stay in his palm or fall to earth.

My child, go in peace. Thank you for writing my words.

I love you, Jesus and Blessed Mother Mary. I bless you forever. Amen.

January 31, 1995

Lord Jesus, do you want to write?

My little child, do not despair. Receive my words of love.

My child, what conditions do I, the Lord, place on love? Do I wait until you perform a certain way before I love you? No, children, I, the Lord, Jesus Christ, love you as you are. I accept you as you are. There is not one among you that has achieved perfection in my sight.

My children, you must show love and mercy to others. Why are you so quick to judge another's situation and so slow to recognize your own?

All of you see through false eyes and false values, for you do not follow my values. I, the Lord, say: "Honor and respect one another. Do not condemn another, children, as you shall find yourselves condemned. Be cautious and persevere in your journey to holiness. Do not let pride and arrogance rob you of my love and the love of another."

We shall continue tomorrow, child. Go in peace. I bless you.

I love you, Lord. I bless you, too. Amen.

February 1, 1995

Lord Jesus, do you want to write?

Child of my heart, let us begin. There are many paths to me, my little one. But remember what I, the Lord, have told you. All paths converge into one, which leads the soul to my heart of love.

So many of you have not yet placed a foot on the path to me, and I tell you, children, you must hurry. Time is running out. Call to me to help you and I, the Lord, Jesus Christ shall help you.

My children, think of climbing a ladder. Often you ask someone who is trustworthy to steady the ladder so you would not fall. Children, open your hearts to my teaching. Ask me to help you stay on my path. Call upon my beloved Mother to assist you. Children, we are waiting for your calls of love.

Children, the ladder to heaven is the cross which I, the Lord, have given you. The wise man is the one who accepts the cross as his way of life. The wise man is the one who calls upon me to help him carry the cross.

My child, I bless you and I love you.

I bless you and I love you too, Lord Jesus. Amen.

February 2, 1995

Lord Jesus, do you want to write?

My child, come into my heart and rest. Allow my love to strengthen and refresh you.

I know you are weary, my little lamb. Continue on your journey to Calvary and I, the Lord, will help you.[14] Persevere in your walk with me. Persevere to your eternal destination as I, the Lord, have done. Allow me to lead and be your example.

My child, each time you fall, you must stand again, and I will help you. You must continue always. Do not give up, for satan is stalking you as a vulture eagerly awaiting to devour you.

Place your hope and trust in me, my children, and believe that I will provide for all your earthly as well as spiritual needs. Would you possess courage and fortitude if I, the Lord, did not provide it? Tell me, child, what would you possess if I, the Lord, had not granted it?

---

[14] I was having many complications with my pregnancy and becoming extremely fatigued. The Lord kept assuring me all would be fine and that I was to trust him.

Nothing, my Jesus.

Rest your fears, little one of my heart. Take courage in my goodness. Children of mine, hearken to my calls of love. I bless you all.

I bless you, too, Jesus. I love you.

February 3, 1995

Lord Jesus, do you want to write?

My little disciple of mercy, record my words of love. My child do not despair, for I AM shall help you. My child, remember how I, the Lord, explained I was the welder. Everything that returns to me must first endure the fire I, the Lord, submit them to. Yes, I take you, precious child, and place you through the fire of my love which is a purification. This enables you, children, to come to me, the Almighty.

For those I chastise and purify are loved infinitely by me, the Creator. Oh, children, I am a Loving and Compassionate Father. I desire to teach you holiness and righteousness, and you, my children, shall be made new in my sight. Only through the Holy Spirit can man acknowledge me as Lord and Creator. Children, open your hearts to receive my spirit of love and reconciliation.

Children, do not turn your backs on my call of love. We shall continue tomorrow. Be blessed, my little student.

Be blessed, too, my God of Mercy. I love you and Mother Mary. Amen.

February 4, 1995

Lord Jesus, do you want to write?

My little one, rest in my Sacred Heart of Love and Hope. Listen carefully to my words.

My heart has begun to beat upon the earth. My spirit of love is igniting the flame of love in cold hearts. Some of you are starting to return love to Love.

Child, I, the Lord, shall breathe love into every wretched soul. Those who pursue my mercy shall blossom in virtue which I, the Lord, shall teach them. Woe to those who reject my mercy. My love shall depart from them and I shall cast them from my sight.

My grief over these lost souls is immeasurable. Who amongst you shall console your Savior? Child, I am Jesus. I am the Origin and Continuation of Mercy and Goodness. All virtue is given you by me and all life is sustained by my hand.

My children, see me with the eyes of your soul. Understand that I, the Lord, am faithful and generous. I am patient and slow to anger. I am a just Judge. Can any of you imitate me in virtue? Come to me, all of you, and allow me to be your holy teacher.

I love you and I bless you. Go in peace.

I love you and bless you, too, Lord, and Blessed Mother. Amen.

February 5, 1995

Lord Jesus, do you want to write?

My little child of mercy, step under the umbrella of my love. Record my words.

Many of you, children, are as those who are lost at sea. My mercy is your life-preserver, children, but if you refuse to accept my mercy, you shall drown. I, the Lord, am preparing many of you, children, to assist your brothers and sisters on their journey back to me. My little disciples, you must stay in my light and love.

Do not stray from the path to me for powerful is my adversary who shall confuse and distort your perceptions. Always, children, keep your eyes on me in any situation and you shall not falter. Trust in my guidance and my goodness, and you, children, shall shine as torches upon the earth.

Today I'm so tired, Holy Spirit. Please give me energy.

My child, perseverance is a gift and a grace given by me. Oh, children, I, the Lord, am waiting to grant you gifts that are priceless. Will you accept my love? Will you accept my gifts?

Rest, my little one. We shall continue tomorrow. Be blessed.

Thank you for your patience and understanding, Lord. I bless you, too. Amen.

February 6, 1995[15]

February 7, 1995

Lord Jesus, do you want to write?

Come, little one. Receive my words of love. Listen carefully, little one of my heart.

My heart is mankind's sanctuary. For as my heart continues to beat with love and mercy, so the earth and all its inhabitants which I, the Lord, created, are sustained. Children, realize that I AM wears the crown of kingship and authority, and you, my children, do not. This crown of glory is Eternal to Eternal as I AM and will never change.

Oh, foolish children, why do you grant yourselves authority over human life? You have not received my permission to act in this manner. No, my children, and you shall be held accountable by me, the Lord God.

So many of you are blinded by your arrogance and pride that you actually perceive my crown upon your very head. I tell you solemnly that the day will come when you shall see me in my glory, and you shall know, mankind, of your foolishness. Remove the crown of pride from your head and humble yourselves before me. I am Yahweh, the Everlasting to Everlasting, Lord God of Hosts. Hear my words.

Thank you, child, for your sacrifice of love. I bless you, little mercy of my heart.

I bless you and love you, Jesus Mercy. Amen.

---

[15] I was feeling the ill-effects of my pregnancy and the Lord dispensed me from taking a message today.

February 8, 1995

Lord Jesus, do you want to write?

My little disciple of mercy, record my words of love.

My child, what does it mean to follow in my footsteps? The cross is both sorrowful and joyful. The cross breeds humility of spirit, perseverance, and fortitude. Child, those who follow in my footsteps progress in virtue and perfection. They progress in holiness because the cross is the fire of purification.

Each time you stumble and then continue, breeds courage as well as compassion. Child, realize that only the truly humble of heart are strong. Only those who persevere in my footsteps achieve the Kingdom of God.

Listen carefully, my little one. I AM is molding you into a precious rose. My child, learn from me. I am Jesus, the Resurrection and the Life. My little rose, allow me to remove the thorns from your life. Accept the cross willingly for my sake, as I have for yours.

We shall continue tomorrow, my precious one. I bless you. Go in peace.

I bless you, too, Lord Jesus. I love you and Mother Mary. Amen.

February 9, 1995

Lord Jesus, do you want to write?

My little one, my beloved Mother shall dictate my words of love.

I am here, my daughter. I am Blessed Virgin Mary and the Mother of God. Listen carefully, my little daughter.

All suffering that is offered to God as reparation is used as a salve to mend my Son's wounds. Children, the wounds Jesus continues to receive are inflicted by your callousness and indifference to God. My Son is bleeding and his blood shall cover and cleanse humanity. Remember, my children, that Jesus accepts Crucifixion again and again for your transgressions. Even your small acts of charity bring joy to our sorrow.

My children are all members of my Son's body. Remember, little ones, though you are all different, you are equally precious and important to God.

My Mother, I'm sorry. This is really difficult.[16]

Remember, child, perseverance is the bridge to salvation. I am always by your side helping you. Be secure in my love, child. Go in peace.

Thank you, Mama Mary. I love you.

Lord, do you wish to write?

My little one, rest in my merciful heart. Be blessed. I love you.

I love you and bless you, too, Lord Jesus, my merciful God and Friend. Amen.

February 10, 1995[17]

February 11, 1995

Lord Jesus, do you want to write?

My little children, I am here. I have come to dictate my message of love.

At each sunrise the earth is freed temporarily from its prison of darkness. At each sunset the earth is once again made a prisoner of darkness. I am giving you this example, children, to show you how the soul can be both in light and

---

[16] I am pausing in this message because I am almost nine months pregnant and very uncomfortable. I'm trying to find a comfortable position. The Blessed Mother told me to be comfortable and to take my time.

[17] I was near term and not feeling very well today so the Lord dispensed me from receiving a message. The next few messages were very difficult to record since my hands had become extremely swollen. The Lord indicated that he would dictate the message to me, and I, in turn, would dictate it to another disciple who would do the actual recording.

in darkness within the same day. My children, I wish you to understand that if you are focused on me, and me alone, though it be dark around you, you shall walk in the light of my love.

My children, I desire that you visit others in prison. My child, I shall clarify how I, the Lord, view prison. Being in prison does not necessarily require metal bars. Many of my children are prisoners of hunger, loneliness, despair, addiction, and wealth. Yes, I say wealth because this in itself is the prison of satan's facade. My children, there are many forms of prison and when I ask you to visit your brother in prison I am asking you for your generosity. Generosity softens the heart of both the giver and the receiver, and again brings those souls into closer union with me, the Creator.

My beloved children, thank you for your sacrifice of love. Persevere, my little ones. I am Jesus, the Eternal to Eternal Light. Stay in my heart, little children. We shall continue tomorrow. Receive my blessing. Receive my love.

We love you, too, Jesus, and we bless and thank you. Amen.

February 12, 1995

Lord Jesus, do you want to write?

My precious children, record my message of love. Child, a false peace exists in the hearts and minds of many. For so corrupt and clouded is man's vision that he is easily deceived into a false sense of security. Children, unless your foundation is of the Holy Spirit, there shall not be peace. Unless you repent and return to me, the mirror you perceive yourself by, will continue to lie to you.

I am the Lord, the God of Abraham, Isaac, and Jacob. It is I AM who has come to remove the blinders upon your eyes. Remember, children, that satan is also a fisherman of souls and most of you, children, have become his prey. But my mercy, children, shall lift you from his net into new waters which I, the Lord, shall provide.

From the everlasting fountain of my mercy shall come an ocean of mercy upon the earth. Those who refuse my mercy shall remain satan's prey. For by their arrogance and hardness of heart, they have chosen this path. Children, understand that I, the Lord, shall not force my love upon you. I desire your love freely.

We shall continue tomorrow. I bless you, my little disciples of mercy. Go in peace.

We bless you too, Lord. Thank you. Amen.

February 13, 1995

Lord Jesus, do you want to write?

My precious children, I am pleased by your unity. Receive my message of love.

My children, unity of one's heart must begin with me. Unless your heart is joined to mine, you shall be as one who is isolated from all. A member of the body cannot exist outside of and apart from the body, for it shall wither and die. Unless you are a part of my Mystical Body you shall perish, for what strength shall you have?

Each one of you, children, is precious to me. I welcome each of you to become a part of my Mystical Body, and as such, love and mercy will nourish and sustain you. Children, in my mercy I, the Lord, sustain and care for each of you. Those who know me, know of my goodness and compassion. But many of my poor children are fools and are blinded by their own arrogance, and even still I, the Lord, sustain and care for them.

What grief have I because so many of my little ones do not know me. Again, in my humility I am making this appeal for conversion and reconciliation with me. Oh, children, that you may find even a shred of compassion for me who loves you infinitely.

My beloved children, thank you for your sacrifice of love. Remain in my heart. Remain in my light. I bless you.

We love you and bless you, too, Lord. Thank you.

February 14, 1995

Lord Jesus, do you want to write?

My little children, I am here. I am your Consolation and your God. My children, each small step you take to Calvary with me grants you innumerable graces. Each time you pick up your cross and persevere on your journey another gem is added to the crown you will be given in heaven.

My children, you must not look at suffering as a curse. No, but view it as you would a landmark to mark a familiar setting. For you see, my children, suffering is marked by the nails in my hands and feet. The crown of thorns upon my brow is another landmark to mark your salvation.

Children, when you open a tool box you expect to find some very basic tools such as a hammer. I use this example in simplicity. Some tools are used frequently and some are not, but they comprise the entire set.

Listen carefully to what I, the Lord, am trying to teach you. Without suffering there should be no joy. Without humiliation there should be no compassion. Without nails there should be no need for a hammer. Yet I, the Lord, solemnly assure you that all these things are necessary in each one of you so that virtue may develop and be enhanced. I know you are weary, my little children, but do not be afraid of the cross. The cross is my gift to you.

Be blessed, little children of my heart. Thank you, for recording my words of love.

Thank you, Father. Please help us. We love you. Amen.

February 15 and 16, 1995[18]

February 17, 1995

Lord Jesus, do you want to write?

---

[18] On February 15, 1995, the Lord blessed my family with a baby girl. Consequently, I did not record today and tomorrow.

My little disciple, come and record my message of love.

Child, in all situations you must strive to learn what I, the Lord Jesus, have desired to teach you. Remember, child, my plan is perfect and my way is perfect. I, the Lord, open my heart to sinners, that all may know and receive my gift of eternal life. I desire to give you all this gift, children, but so many of you have rejected my offer because you have rejected me.

My child, perseverance requires patience and courage. Perseverance is learned when you humbly accept the cross I have given you. Listen carefully to my words, daughter. If you choose a goal for yourself, consider that you must persevere and be patient in order to achieve this goal. Children, these virtues are gifts from me, the Eternal Gift-Giver. I am waiting to give you all these gifts.

Child, rest in my heart of love. We shall continue tomorrow. Go in peace.

Thank you for your patience, kind Jesus. I love you. Amen.

February 18, 1995

My little one, I am here. I am Blessed Virgin Mary and the Mother of God.

My children, I, the Mother of Jesus Christ, shall make another appeal to your cold hearts on behalf of my beloved Son and the entire heavenly court. Children, do you see the catastrophes falling upon mankind? We have warned you to convert and repent, yet you have scorned us.

My children, my role is to herald the coming of my Son and to bring his messages of love. By the graces granted by Jesus, I have come to lead you all out of the darkness and back into the light of my Son's embrace. Children, you must live in the embrace and heart of God. Nowhere else shall you be safe from the evil one.

He has devoured many of our poor children and he continues with his evil hunt of souls. Pray, children. Pray constantly. Offer sacrifices daily. Your reparation has been asked for many times, children.

I bless all those who shall read my words. Please extend my love to others. Go in peace, child of my heart.

Thank you, Mama Mary. I bless you, too.

Lord?

My little one, rest. We shall continue tomorrow. Be blessed, little mercy of my heart.

Be blessed, Lord of my heart. Amen.

February 19, 1995

Lord Jesus, do you want to write?

Little mercy of my heart, record my words of love.

Child, my army of disciples is growing for I, the Lord, Jesus Christ, have called you by name. I am gathering my sheep and I, the Good Shepherd, shall lead all of you to new pastures. Where I, the Lord, shall take you shall be unblemished. Water shall flow from the everlasting fountain of my mercy and the food I shall feed my people shall be holy.

Oh joyous day, my little children, for all those who persevere in faith through these dark and terrible hours, shall go from famine to the great banquet feast of the Lord God.[19]

Children, I am Jesus. I am the Eternal to Eternal Light and Love of Every Heart, Mind, and Soul. I am the Alpha and the Omega, from Everlasting to Everlasting. All of you, children, who are feasting now shall find the famine of your hearts at the end. For the day will come when hearts shall hunger for me, but I shall not hear them. For I have called and begged for your love as a pauper on my knees, yet you have rejected me.

---

[19] At this moment I had an internal vision of our Lord standing in the sky with his arms outstretched overlooking a large banquet table in a green valley. People were coming from all directions and sitting down to eat. There was much rejoicing.

Remember my children, loyalty begets loyalty. Thank you for writing, my little one. Go in peace. I bless you.

I bless you and love you, too, Lord. Amen.

February 20, 1995[20]

February 21, 1995

Lord Jesus, do you want to write?

My little child of mercy, I am pleased by your perseverance. My little one, I, the Lord, have blessed you and have instilled the fire of my love within your heart. Child, I have shared my grieving heart with you. Can you, little one, comprehend my grief over my lost children?

My child, I am permitting you to experience this grief so you will understand the importance of reaching out to others.[21] My daughter, I have called you and placed you on a mission of love. Bring souls to me, little mercy of my heart. Tell others how I grieve for my lost children. My grief is infinite for my love is infinite.

My daughter, sorrow comes from the pain of separation and rejection. I, the Lord, receive this treatment from the hands of my children. Each soul that returns to me offers me consolation.

Oh, children, do you see my humility? I come on my knees pleading for just one precious soul to return to my heart of love. Come home to my heart of love, my precious children. My heart of love is your only refuge.

---

[20] I was not feeling very well this day so the Lord dispensed me from recording a message.

[21] I was placed back in the hospital after my baby was born. I cried out to the Lord in anguish over missing my new baby. The Lord responded by explaining how he wished me to understand the grief he carries concerning his lost children.

Thank you for your sacrifice of love. I bless you.

I bless you, too, Lord. I love you, Jesus. Amen.

February 22, 1995

Lord Jesus, do you want to write?

Child of my heart, receive my words of love. Open your heart, child, to embrace the Spirit of Love and Truth.

Children, when you purchase an item from the store, you expect the item to be exactly what has been represented on the package. Many times it is not so. Open your heart, child, to my instruction. Wisdom is speaking.

The "only" truth is me, the Lord God. All that the prophets have spoken is true, for I am the Lord God of Abraham, Isaac, and Jacob, and I am the Truth. My children, with worldly things you shall always find misrepresentation and disappointment. If you place your hope and trust in me, you shall never be disappointed. My little ones, remember my faithfulness is eternal and from generation to generation to those who follow me.

Children, you are repeatedly being deceived by satan who has distorted your minds. No longer do you listen to my Spirit of Right Judgment who in love corrects and counsels each of you. Children, call upon me and I, the Lord Jesus Christ, shall hear you. My love shall embrace you and nurture you back into my light of holiness. Persevere, little ones, persevere.

Thank you, child, for recording my words. I bless you and love you.

I bless you and love you, too, my Jesus and Mother Mary. Amen.

February 23, 1995

Lord Jesus, do you want to write?

My little one, come into your Father's embrace and allow Love to nourish you.

My child, just as food is necessary to nourish the cells of the body, my love is necessary to nourish the soul. For without my love, the soul shall descend into darkness and away from virtue. My love, children, is the life and water of the soul to bring the soul into union with me.

Write all that I tell you, little mercy of my heart.

Children, my heart is the entrance to heaven. Just as certain monuments mark the entrance into a city, no one can enter heaven without first entering my Sacred Heart. Children, my heart reigns in heaven as on earth. How does one come into my heart?

Oh. precious ones, how simple my love is. Accept my invitation to repent of your sins and I, the Lord, shall carry you into my heart. This, children, is my merciful way. No matter what you have done, I, the Lord Jesus Christ, shall forgive you. Remember, children, my heart is infinite as is my mercy. Accept my invitation of love, children.

Thank you for writing my words, little one of my heart. Be in peace. I bless you.

I bless you and love you, too, Lord Jesus. Amen.

February 24, 1995

Lord Jesus, do you want to write?

My little disciple of mercy, I AM WHO AM is speaking. Record my words of love.

In every situation, child, you must strive to do my will. In doing so, you will progress in holiness, and I, the Lord, will grace you abundantly. Those of you, children, who desire to follow your own egotistical ways are sitting in a dark room. Without my love your soul shall remain in darkness. You are as the tree that needs to be watered, yet eventually perishes from thirst. Children, I have repeatedly told you that only I, the Lord, am the Sustaining Force of All Creation. I uphold all of you in my palm by grace which waters the soul and causes the soul to blossom in virtue.

Approach me, children. I, the Lord God, am waiting to tenderly receive you. Come to me in humility and with repentant hearts. You, my lost children, are thirsty and hungry. Come to me, children, so that I may give you life. The water I shall give you is the eternal water of faith and love. This, children, is my gift of love to you. There is nothing you can do to merit this gift.

Children, have compassion for me and do not deny me. I am Jesus, Almighty and Sovereign King of Peace. Thank you, child of my heart. I bless you and love you.

I bless you and love you, too, Jesus and Holy Spirit. Amen.

February 25, 1995

Lord Jesus, do you want to write?

My little one, come into your Father's arms and record my words of love. My child, do you see how your newborn infant depends on you? She places all her hope and trust in your care, and her love and loyalty is simple and pure.

Children, you see yourselves as adults, but I, the Lord, see you as infants. You are my precious little ones and I am your Holy Father. My children, come to me in simplicity. Place all your hope and trust in me. Did I not provide food for the newborn as well as for every creature of the land and of the sea? Children, allow me to nurture and care for you. My heart is the eternal flame of love which is never extinguished. Every drop of my Precious Blood has been shed for all of you, children. Children, I, the Lord Jesus Christ, have given my life for all of you. Why then will you not trust me to care for you?

The soul that trusts me is granted innumerable graces by my Heavenly Father. Children, open your hearts to receive the gifts offered by God. These gifts are priceless treasures of love.

Thank you, child, for writing my words. I love you and I bless you.

I love you and bless you, too, Jesus and Mama Mary. Amen.

February 26, 1995

Lord Jesus, do you want to write?

My beloved child, come into my arms and record my words of love.

Why do you despair, little mercy of my heart? You dwell in my heart and I, the Lord, uphold you. My little one, although you may struggle at times, know that I, the Lord, am with you always to encourage you. I watch you, child, as a tender newborn. As soon as you turn your face to me, I lift you into my heart of love.

Child, do not be intimidated by the things of the earth. Am I not stronger and wiser? Can I not help you in any situation you face? You must trust completely in my guidance and loving care of you. Remember always to call upon me, for my love is the salve to mend your wounds. My compassion shall give you dignity. My mercy shall enable you to stand up and begin again in any situation. Put on your helmet of faith and be completely covered in my mercy and love. Let my love shine upon you and renew your spirit. Allow me to dwell in your heart that our hearts shall be as one.

Daughter, I bless you and I love you. Go in the peace of my love.

I love you and bless you, Jesus. Amen.

February 27, 1995

Lord Jesus, do you want to write?

My precious one, listen to the words of the One, True, Living God.

When one rejects my mercy, then one is saying the final "yes" to satan. Children, all of you will ultimately be given the choice of your eternal destiny. Remember I, the Lord, desire your love and loyalty but I will not force your love. My heart is a sanctuary of love. It is not a prison.

Children, satan has cast his net over all creation and he uses many different types of bait to capture you. Children, you must persevere and pray to the Holy Spirit for discernment. Pray that the veils over your eyes are lifted and that you may see clearly.

Children, satan pollutes all that he touches and you must remember how he distorts your vision. Ask to see the truth and you shall be granted your request by me. I am the Truth. I am the only way to the Eternal Father. Children, many of you doubt in my teachings and the gifts I have given to those who speak my words. Ask, children. Ask that your soul be enlightened by the Holy Spirit so you may walk the path to me and with me.

Be blessed, little mercy of my heart. Go in the peace of my love.

I love you, Lord Jesus and Mother Mary. Help me with everything, Holy Spirit, please. I love you. Amen.

February 28, 1995

Lord Jesus, do you want to write?

My beloved child, receive my words of love.

Listen to my words, my little daughter. I AM has planted the seed of my love in many of my children. Little ones, many of you have been called, yet few have responded. Oh, children, I am grieving. Can I, the Lord God, close my eyes and my heart so that your cruelty will not affect me? No, my precious ones, for you are mine. From the dust I created you and I breathed life into your sleeping bodies.

Children, open your hearts to my call. I am inviting you to my dinner table to break bread with me, yet you continue to cast me aside. I am tormented, my children. Pay attention, O Israel. Your homes shall be shaken and your land will be devoured. For those who continue to dwell in the shadow of iniquity, the worms that never die shall be waiting for you.

Continue to write, child.[22]

My child, I am faithful. I extend my arms to all my children. Let those who hear come to me.

---

[22] Generally, when the Lord or the Blessed Mother interject this phrase in the message, it is because I am interrupted by one of my children. They are both very compassionate and understanding in permitting me to address the particular child's need and then return to recording the message.

I love you, Jesus. I pray the whole world will love you.

I love you, too, my little one. Be blessed, child of my heart.

Be blessed, Lord of my heart. Amen.

March 1, 1995

Lord Jesus, do you want to write?

Children of my heart, my devoted ones. You, my little lambs, have heard my call and have come. You, my children, are as the torches on an airplane runway in the darkness of night.[23]   In simplicity I give this example. So many of my children are coming home and they shall see your lights of love and hope.

These signals that you show others are reflections of my love for mankind. Without my love, children, one could not come into the light. My disciples, I, the Lord, have gathered you from the dust of the earth and by my blood have provided a place at the heavenly banquet.

My devoted servants, heavy is the cross upon your shoulders, but I AM is helping you and sustaining you. Children who believe they are free are really prisoners, and those who recognize they are prisoners of their sins are on the road to freedom. Pay attention, my sleeping children. Disciples of mine, I, the Lord, Jesus Christ, shall teach you a prayer about humility, for humility is a priceless gem to the soul seeking forgiveness and reconciliation. Listen to the words of the Holy Spirit of Truth and Right Judgment:

> Father, Eternal Master, grant us the garments of humility that we may come before you desiring reconciliation. For in that hour, Father, surely you shall not chastise the truly humble and repentant of heart. Though we be naked before you, take away our layers of pride and greed of heart, and gently cover us in the sweet fragrance of humility. Dear Father, turn not your face nor your ears from our cries, but in your mercy hear

---

[23] Our Lord was speaking to the small band of disciples who compose our prayer group.

and answer us Amen.

Lord, thank you.

Children of my heart, remember there are many parts to my Mystical Body. I, the Lord, have granted each of you innumerable graces to persevere. Go forth, my beloved disciples, and show others how you dwell in the mercy of the God of Abraham, Isaac, and Jacob.

Be blessed, my children. Continue on your journey in faith and I the Lord will help you. Extend my blessings to others.

We love you, too, Jesus. Amen.

March 2, 1995

Lord Jesus, do you want to write?

My child, I am here. I am Blessed Virgin Mary and the Queen of Peace.

My Mother, thank you for coming to me.

My daughter, there is a spirit of confusion lurking in your midst. I have come to help you. Children, you must pray unceasingly to the Holy Spirit for wisdom and discernment. You must request the aid of the Holy Spirit and the entire heavenly court. Do this at your prayer group and each step you take regarding my Son's messages.

My little children, many children will read these words of Jesus and their hearts of stone and discontent shall melt. Oh, children, satan is now closer to you than ever before. Increase your prayers. Increase your unity. My little ones, invoke the powers of heaven first in all that you do.

Take courage for you are all my Son's lambs, but we are here to help you. This, children, is the time of great power and grace from the Eternal Father. Remember, little ones, you are never alone.

Thank you, daughter, for writing my words. I bless you. Go in peace.

I bless you and love you, too, Mama Mary.

Shall we write, Lord?

No, precious one. We will continue tomorrow. Rest, my little child.

March 3, 1995

Lord Jesus, do you want to write?

My little child, come into my heart and receive my words of love. Child, allow the Truth of Humanity to speak to your soul. I AM has chosen you because of your sinfulness. I have chosen you from the pit of darkness and have covered you in my holy Sacred Blood. I, the Lord, Jesus Christ have placed the Heavenly Court of my angels and saints at your disposal. Little one, make use of the gifts I have given you.

Lord, are you mad at me?

Ah, my little child, remember I reprimand those I love. Do you not discipline your children? Do you not watch over them cautiously, prodding them to remain on the right path? I, the Lord, help you to accomplish this as well as guide your steps. For all those who have ears, listen.

Children, call upon me and I, the Lord, will guide your steps so that you may grow in virtue and holiness. You shall conquer and defeat satan as I, the Lord, shall walk beside you. You, my child, shall dwell in the shadow of the Holy One of Israel, and who then can harm you?

My child, follow my guidance and always strive to be obedient to my will. I will always help you. Be blessed, child of my heart. Go in peace. I love you.

I love you and bless you, too, Lord Jesus. Amen.

March 4, 1995

Lord Jesus, do you want to write?

My little child, I have been waiting for you. Allow my mercy to cover and sustain you. My child, how does one come to trust me? It is accomplished only through grace which I, the Lord, give to every precious soul. Many of my children choose to disregard the gifts I, the Lord, bestow, but for those who honor my gifts my life grows in them. Understand, child, that for a precious soul to trust me I must possess the heart. If one's heart is possessed by greed and selfishness, then it is to these two sins that the person's trust shall go. However, if one's heart is given to me, then how shall they trust another?

Listen carefully, children. Give your heart to me and I will bless you. I will touch your heart with my blood, and I shall grow in you and you in me. The graces which I bestow are as flowers that need sunlight to flourish. I am the Sunlight of the Soul and the Master of Graces. Allow me to nourish you, children.

My precious one, rest. We shall continue tomorrow. Be blessed, little mercy of my heart.

I love you, Lord. I bless your holy name. Amen.

March 5, 1995

Lord Jesus, do you want to write?

My beloved child, I know you are weary. Persevere, my little lamb. Walk to Calvary and drink from the cup of salvation. My child, when the seas are calm, many do not believe that a wave can rise up out of the still waters and consume the land. Child, just as in the past, man does not believe in my power and authority, and my ability to rise up in any situation. Yes, man is arrogant and gives himself credit if the outcome of a situation is good. If the outcome is not good, man denies his responsibility and blames me, the Lord God.

Oh, foolish Generation, I solemnly assure you I shall come as a tidal wave from a calm sea. I shall come with my heavenly host and all those who mock me shall drown. All those who curse me shall be cursed by me.

Let us continue.

My children, I am waiting to cover you in my mercy. Listen to my call of love.

My child, rest. We shall continue tomorrow. Do not despair, little one.

I love you, Lord. Thank you. Amen.

March 6, 1995

Lord Jesus, do you want to write?

My little child, let us begin. I, the Lord, am in your midst. Do you recognize my presence? Love is in your room and in your home for I am Love. I AM has come among you and has made a home in your heart. Child, you could not love apart from me.

My children, lift your voices in prayer to my Heavenly Father with faith in all that you ask. Lift the love in your hearts to him, Who Is. Remember those who are obedient shall be blessed and given the grace to remain obedient. Persevere, my children, persevere.

I love you and bless you, my Jesus.

I love you and bless you, too, child. Go in peace.

Thank you, Father. Amen.

March 7, 1995

Lord Jesus, do you want to write?

My little one, record my words of love. My child, each word that I, the Lord, speak is holy. My words, children, pierce the heart with the fragrance of purity. My words are purified by the fire of my love and they nurture the soul's longing for me.

Children, I have come to fulfill you. I have come to remove the emptiness in your lives and to grant you a new life. Children, you can only have fulfillment if you walk with me. I am Jesus, the Resurrection and the Life.

Stand up, my little ones, and begin your journey home. You were created, children, to dwell with me forever, but I, the Lord, shall not force your love. "If you wish me to be loyal and devoted to you, then be loyal and devoted to me," says the Lord God. Place no one before me. Learn to recognize the false idols in your lives and abolish them. Abolish sin and darkness, and live in the light of my love. Allow my love to heal and refresh you.

My child, thank you for writing. Go in peace, little one of my heart.

Thank you, Lord. I love you and bless you. Amen.

March 8, 1995

Lord Jesus, do you want to write?

My little one, how I love you. Ah, my little child, rest in my Sacred Heart of Love. Do not despair, little one of my heart.[24] Do not despair, any of my beloved children. I have heard all of you, my precious ones.

Prayer fills the great heart of heaven with its loveliness. Like a melody, prayer softens my heart, if it comes from a repentant heart. Oh, children, so many of you believe I cannot hear you. I tell you solemnly, I am by your side as soon as you utter my name.

Children, when you pray, you must persevere. All the answers you are seeking shall come according the Holy Perfect Will of my Heavenly Father. But remember, little ones, every prayer is heard and answered. Although you cannot see me, believe that I am present when you pray. Believe that my beloved Mother goes to all those who call upon her. We are listening and responding to you, children. But, children, are you listening and responding? Remember, children, without me you shall perish.

Thank you, child, for writing. Go in peace.

I love you and I bless you, Jesus. Amen.

---

[24] I was still sick and not returning to what I considered my normal health status prior to the pregnancy.

March 9, 1995

Lord Jesus, do you want to write?

My little one, you must persevere in your journey. Yes, child, record my words of love. Let Wisdom instruct you. I AM is speaking.

My child, you must open your heart and receive the gifts I desire to give you. Rise up, little one, and lean on me, your Savior. Place all your hope and trust in me. I shall not forsake you, child of my heart. My daughter, I am your Holy Teacher. I teach each one of my children according to their individual needs. Each one of you is infinitely precious to me.

Each one of you is a piece of coal that I, the Lord, shall make into a diamond. Children, of yourselves you do not possess ability to reach your potential. For only I, the Lord, know your potential. Children, the more you love, the more capable you are. The more compassionate you are, the more wisdom you shall be granted. Remember, child, I am the Giver of All Gifts. There is nothing you could do on your own apart from me.

Thank you for writing, child. Go in peace with my blessing.

I love you and bless you, too, Lord. Amen.

March 10, 1995

Lord Jesus, do you want to write?

My little one, I have been waiting. Come record my words of love.

My child, a great tree has many branches. The larger branches contain the most leaves, whereas the smaller branches are still a significant part of the tree, though they remain unseen. Listen to my teaching, child. The larger branches represent my Church and the leaves are the many souls they are responsible for. Yes, I, the Lord, place great responsibility on those I have called to shepherd others. The smaller branches are those children who have fallen away from the church, yet make up a large part of my Mystical Body. There are many members of my Body who are not aware of their role in my Mystical Body. Remember, child, though the members be individual, the Body is one. The Body has strength from those members who frequent the sacraments and stay reconciled to me. The Body has strength from those members who walk with me in righteousness and holiness.

Children, examine your place in my Body. Are you a small hidden branch still walking in sin? Are you still in darkness? Come into the light of my love, children. I am waiting to heal you.

Thank you, child, for writing. Be secure in my love. I bless you.

I bless you, too, Lord. I love you. Amen.

March 11, 1995

Lord Jesus, do you want to write?

My loving child, come into my heart and record my message of love. The soul, my child, is so precious to me that I, the Lord, spend eternity caring for and nurturing souls. Children, I created all of you from the dust of the earth, and then I breathed life into you. By my breath you became alive. By my love you were given a heart which was created to serve me.

My little one, you are distracted.[25] Come into my heart and renew your strength. Stay focused. My child, those who place me first work diligently to stay on my path. Yes, though my path is narrow, those who truly wish to follow me shall be granted the grace to do so. They shall be granted my Spirit who shall dwell with them and guide them in my ways.

Oh, children, call to me and I, the Lord, shall send my Holy Spirit upon you. He shall come to you and cover you in my love and mercy. Open your hearts, children, to my Holy Spirit of Love.

I love you, Lord.

---

[25] I was preoccupied with other events that were occurring in my life and it was becoming difficult to find some quiet time just to take the message. In short, I was thinking of worldly things and not the spiritual realm at all.

I love you, too, precious one. Go in peace.

I love you, my precious God. Amen.

March 12, 1995

Lord Jesus, do you want to write?

My little disciple of mercy, let us begin. Listen carefully to my words. My adversary comes upon unsuspecting souls. He preys upon their inability to fathom themselves within his powerful grip.

Daughter, all of Jerusalem has fallen prey to the devil. My city of glory is now a city of sin and demonic infiltration. My daughter, darkness surrounds this earth and satan's tentacles are squeezing all life from the earth. Be on guard, all of you, who would follow in my footsteps. Beware, children, for satan assumes the role of candy to a child. He appears innocent, yet make no mistake, he does not appear holy! For I, the Lord, Jesus Christ, am the "only" fountain of holiness and holiness comes only from me.

Children, you must do all of the many things I have told you. Be diligent in your prayers to the Holy Spirit. Read my Word and frequent the sacraments. Allow my life to grow in you for who then, children, could harm you?

Rest, my beloved daughter. Be secure in my love. I shall not forsake you. Go with my blessing.

I bless you and love you, too, Lord. Please make us strong. Amen.

March 13, 1995

Lord Jesus, do you want to write?

My daughter, come into my loving arms and receive my words of love. Child of my heart, I AM is speaking.

So many of you take great pain and effort to preserve your mortal bodies. Yet who among you places this type of effort on the care of your immortal soul? Children, you must begin now to prepare your soul for your future. Remember, the soul never dies.

Children, you spend too much time preparing the flesh when, in fact, the flesh will perish. Your mortal bodies shall return unto the dust from whence they came. But lo, your soul shall begin its eternal journey. Children, where does your final destination lie? You, my children, will ultimately be responsible for that decision. Many of you exercise your earthly bodies, but I tell you, children, you must exercise your spiritual ones. You must make the effort to pray and reconcile with me. If you do, a great weight shall be removed from your spiritual shoulders and great will be your reward.

Thank you, child of my heart. Go in peace, my little one. I bless you.

I bless you, too, Lord Jesus. I love you, Holy Spirit and Blessed Mother. Amen.

March 14, 1995

Lord Jesus, do you want to write?

My devoted one, come and record my words. My little child, you are one of my soldiers. I, the Lord, have placed you in my army to guard and protect my church. Child, I use these words in a special way. For all my devoted servants have I, the Lord, granted this important mission. My children, the time is at hand when you have been asked by me to defend my altar against the blasphemer. You are asked to defend my laws against the unrighteous.

Child, again the earth shall open up and swallow the unclean of heart, for they have the weights of sin about their ankles. You, children, have been called by me to defend my Holy Name to those who defy me and speak my name in vain. You, children, have been called by me to help those I have chosen to announce my words. Go with zeal in your hearts, children, and carry the banner of my love at all times. I love you all, my little children.

Go in peace, my daughter. Thank you for your sacrifice of love.

I bless you and love you, Jesus. Amen.

March 15, 1995

Lord Jesus, do you want to write?

My beloved and faithful children, I am Blessed Virgin Mary and the Queen of Heaven.[26]

Oh, my children, today I am weeping. I have tried to cover all my children with my mantle of love. But my children discard my mantle and put on the mantle of satan. Remember what my Son, Jesus, has told you. Children, satan weaves his covering over precious souls. He is also a fisher of men's souls. He is the great liar. He is alone the prince of darkness. I am grieving for all those who are living under the mantle of evil for they cannot see the light of my Son's eternal love.

My mother, what should we do?

My children, you must be reflections of my Son. Always persevere and be patient. If you mimic my Son, then the light of my Son's holiness will shine through you. You shall be mirrors of heaven. Children, I know you are discouraged but every step backwards shall be turned into a great leap forwards by my Son. I leave my motherly blessing upon you, little ones. Tell others of our love.

My child, thank you for writing.

My beloved Mother Mary, thank you. I love you.

Lord, shall we write?

No, precious one. Meditate on the words of my Mother. I bless you all, children of my heart.

We bless you, too, Lord. Amen.

---

[26] The Blessed Mother is referring to our prayer group who was present for this message.

March 16, 1995

Lord Jesus, do you want to write?

My child, come and record my words of love. Children, the Holy Spirit is planting the seeds of righteousness throughout the earth. The seeds of my love are being carried by my angels to the four corners of the earth. Soon the day shall come when there will not be one left among you who has not heard my call of love.

So many of you have discarded my seeds of love and have cast me from your sight. All those who shall forget me on the last day shall not be remembered by me. I am the Lord God of All Nations and of All People. Come to Calvary and witness my Crucifixion. My blood has been shed for all mankind so that whosoever believes in me may return to grace by my Eternal Father. That which was lost by disobedience can now be reclaimed by my death on Calvary. Remember, children, that it is my heart which reigns in heaven and upon the earth. Listen to my calls of love.

Thank you, child, for writing. I bless you.

I bless you, too, Lord Jesus. I love you and Mother Mary. Amen.

March 17, 1995

Lord Jesus, do you want to write?

Child of my heart, I shall give my message of love. Little one, I know you are weary.[27] Ah yes, the cross is heavy for those who follow me with patience and perseverance. Each one of my devoted children is being called by me to sustain other members of my Mystical Body.

Children of mine, you are wounded and scarred. My entire Body is wounded

---

[27] I was not feeling physically well and was having difficulty in meeting the demands of the routine daily activities of being a mother to my newborn, three other children, and a housewife.

and scarred. I have come to heal your wounds and erase your scars. Give your sins to me, children, and become a new creation. Begin again, all my little children.

Children, I, the Lord, Jesus Christ, am the High Priest of my Church. Though my Church be divided on earth, there is only one Church of which I am the head. Make no mistake of my authority, children.

Children, there are many types of flowers in a garden and so it is with my Church now. But all of you are part of my Body and the actions of one member affects the rest of the Body. Children, examine your lives and learn to place others' needs before your own. I will help you.

Child, we shall continue tomorrow. Go in peace, little one.

Thank you, Lord. I love you and bless you. Amen.

March 18, 1995

Lord Jesus, do you want to write?

Oh, little child of mercy, how it grieves me to see one of mine in despair. Listen to my words, my daughter.

All things of the earth are temporary and shall pass from sight quickly. My children, I, the Lord, have made provisions for all those who call on my name. For each one that calls upon the name of the Lord is heard and answered.

Give glory to the Lord of Hosts who travels the skies in chariots of fire. By his very breath he shall refresh the poor and make low the proud. By his breath and his word shall satan be defeated and cast from his sight forever.

My child, do not doubt in the incomprehensible power of the Lord, your God. Remember your vision is limited but I, the Lord, am not limited. Who then shall rise up against me and win? There is no one. Humble yourselves before me, Generation. Repent of your wicked ways and I, the Lord, shall place a crown of righteousness upon your brow. "Turn back to me," says the Lord of Hosts, the Lord God of Israel.

Child, thank you for writing.

I love you, Jesus. I bless you. Amen.

I bless you, too. Go in peace.

March 19, 1995

Lord Jesus, do you want to write?

My little one, gain strength in my heart of love.

Children, many of you are wandering aimlessly seeking comfort and fulfillment. You are like those in a valley surrounded by mountains on all sides, and you have no means to climb the mountain. Children, you shall never be able to rise above any valleys in your life without my help. Every mountain will be impossible to climb and every goal beyond your grasp. Only I, the Lord Jesus, can help you reach your true potential.

Let us proceed.

Children, you are all a part of my Body but not all of you dwell in my heart. Those whose hearts are of the world do significant damage to my Body. Children, I am Jesus. I am the Resurrection and the Life. Let all those who desire life come to me. Children, all the decisions you make are for eternity.

Remember to sow the seeds of your eternal future, and the harvest will be salvation and the abundant and glorious treasure of heaven.

Go in peace, child of my heart. I bless you.

I bless you, too, O Lord. I love you. Amen.

March 20, 1995

Lord Jesus, do you want to write?

My beloved disciple, record my message of love. Child, my flock has many sheep. Though many have strayed from the flock, they are still branded with my name. No matter where they have gone, they are still branded by my love, and eventually they shall return to me. Child, a soul is branded to me, the Creator, through Baptism.

Through this sacrament the heart is set apart from all other hearts. The heart is covered in my blood and my life begins to grow within that soul. O children, be baptized all of you. Come once again to the river of healing and reconciliation with me and be cleansed. I am Jesus, the Eternal Fountain of Grace. I have come with the entire heavenly host to reunite my flock and to bring others to my flock.

Children, if you do not follow me, then it is satan and the world whom you follow. Child, these words that I, the Lord, dictate are for my entire flock. Remember, child, you must persevere and I, the Lord, shall guide you.

Go in peace, little one of my heart. I bless you.

I bless you, too, Lord. I love you, Jesus and Mother Mary. Amen.

March 21, 1995

Lord Jesus, do you want to write?

My little one, come into my heart of love. How many of you, children, have moved from one house to another? Many times you must cut the ties at one home only to begin again. You must make arrangements to have the utilities shut off at the old location and turned on at the new.

My little children, I AM is instructing you. Children, your only true and eternal home is in my heart. If you dwell in my heart, then the old is washed away and the new is not yet known. Only if you dwell in my heart, shall you recognize the present. That is where you shall find me. I, the Lord, come to meet you in the here and now, not in the past, nor in the future. Children who make their home in my heart shall have a constant source of power for I AM shall dwell in those who dwell in me.

My Spirit of Love shall ignite the candle of your heart and know, children, I, the Lord, shall not extinguish that candle of love. That is your choice, my precious ones. As long as you accept my love and my commandments, that candle of love shall burn in your heart. Remember, children, I am the Eternal Light of Love. Come back to me, children.

I love you, Lord.

I love you, too, child. Go in peace. I bless you.

I bless you too, my God. Amen.

March 22, 1995

Lord Jesus, do you want to write?

My little child of mercy, allow me to use your hand as an instrument of my grace.

My children, you cannot know me if you know not my Word. My Word is the sword of life. My Word is nourishment for the soul and the caress and strength of the heart. My children, you must spend some time each day reading my Word. My Word clothes the naked and feeds the hungry. Prisoners shall find freedom in my Word and those who are scarred shall find comfort.

Children, do you see how much I, the Lord, love you? I have given you my Word. I have given you my heart. I have given you my life. What more could I have done to win your love?

Precious children are lost from me each day. Their opportunities to reconcile with me have passed and the gates of hell have closed them in. Now they cannot return to me. Do not procrastinate, my children. I have come among you offering salvation to you. Those who refuse my gift will burn in hellfire forever.

Thank you, child, for writing. Be secure in my love. I bless you.

I bless you, too, Lord. I love you and Blessed Mother. Amen.

March 23, 1995

My child, my beloved Mother shall dictate my words of love. Open your heart, little child.

My daughter, I am Blessed Virgin Mary and the Mother of God. My child, you must seek refuge in the heart of God. For the heart of God is infinite and has a special place for each one of his children.

Children, I am heaven's messenger. I have come as a servant of the Most High to announce the return of my beloved Son, Jesus. I have come, children, to help you prepare to meet your Savior. Most of you are not ready. Children, you must pray for God's mercy and forgiveness. If you do not heed my warnings and the warnings of Jesus, grace shall be lifted from your lives and from your land. God's protection will not be upon you and what suffering you shall endure.

I am pleading for you, children, my heart always in prayer for you. Will you respond to my calls of love? My invitation to return to God is for each one of you.

That is all, my daughter. I love you and bless you.

Thank you, my beloved Mother Mary. I love you and bless you, too. My Jesus?

We shall continue tomorrow, little one. Go in peace.

I love you and praise you, Lord. Amen.

March 24, 1995

Lord Jesus, do you want to write?

Come, child, and receive my words of love and hope. The time is approaching, my child, when the Cross shall be once again offered to my Eternal Father. Yes, the day of my Crucifixion is drawing closer and I have called you, children, to stand by my side. How many of you shall deny me? How many of you shall flee when questioned about me?

My beloved children, take courage in me. Allow me to be your strength. Do not fear the remarks of others, but fear my voice and my voice alone. Children, those who persevere in faith until the end shall be rewarded greatly by my

Heavenly Father. Yes, children, all those who would follow me shall come to Calvary with me.

Come to the foot of the Cross and there you shall receive forgiveness and abundant graces. My blood shall scorch you and my Spirit shall set you on fire with my love. It is at the foot of the Cross you shall find me patiently waiting for all of you. Come, children, come.

My child, thank you for writing. Go in peace with my blessing.

I love you, Jesus. I bless you, too. Amen.

March 25, 1995

Lord Jesus, do you want to write?

My little one, I am by your side. As soon as you utter my name, I come to you, child. Let us begin.

Lord, you are precious. I pray the whole world will love you.

Ah, my little sparrow, I am the keeper of the nest. Yes, that is where you shall find me. I am referring to your heart, the nest of my love.

Jerusalem is holy because I have sealed her in my heart of love. She is the great nest that will rise above all others, and my little sparrows shall come home. Yes, my Jerusalem, city of glory, shall shine like a diamond in the midst of pebbles. She shall be as a star in a blackened sky. "Holy Jerusalem is mine," says the Lord God of Israel. If you do not repent before me, you shall not enter my holy city. No, the gates of glory shall be sealed against you. Reconcile with me and become holy. Put on the garments of righteousness, and you shall receive virtue and dignity. Follow my commandments, and I, the Lord, shall carry you on my wings to my holy city. Please, children, return to my nest of love.

I bless you, child. Go in peace.

I bless you, too, my Jesus. Amen.

March 26, 1995

Lord Jesus, do you want to write?

My little disciple, I AM has come to offer my message of hope and love. My little one, you must follow my instructions . You must surround yourself and your home by prayer. Pray constantly, child, to the angels and saints. My child, the war has begun. Do not stand alone on the battlefield. I have provided heavenly soldiers to remain by your side. Utilize the gifts I have provided you. Listen carefully, my daughter of mercy. You will take my words as a bee goes from flower to flower. My words shall be as the pollen to travel from one heart to the next. I, the Lord, shall prepare the way for you, and always shall I go before you.

Child, understand that my mercy is flowing through this world as lava. My mercy is the red hot fire to burn through men's arrogance and to reduce the heart of stone to ashes.

Do not be afraid, my children, to go out and preach the gospel, and share these messages, for this is true life. This is for the salvation of many.

My little one, be blessed. Thank you for writing. Go in peace.

I bless you and love you, too, Lord Jesus and Blessed Mother. Amen.

March 27, 1995

Lord Jesus, do you want to write?

My little child, come into my sustaining arms and record my words of love. You must continue on your journey to Calvary and to the foot of the Cross. The climb is uphill now, my child, and each step you take shall be made more difficult by the weight of the Cross. The Cross was from the beginning as I AM. The Cross is eternal and from everlasting to everlasting.

My children, each word that I, the Lord, speak is for each of you. I desire you to realize that I am a God of Intimacy. I am a God of Nurturing and Creativity and I desire to share every aspect of your lives. Why do you only run to me when you are in despair? Why do you not share your joy with me?

My children, do you see the way in which I captivate the heart? I pursue you relentlessly, my children. My love is the fire of the heart. Each one of you is so precious to me that I have come to you holding my heart and begging for your love. When will you accept my invitation of love?

I bless you, my little servant. Go in peace.

I bless you, too, my God. I love you. Amen.

March 28, 1995

Lord Jesus, do you want to write?

My child, abandon yourself to my loving embrace. Record my words of love and hope.

Children, open your hearts to my call. I am knocking at the heart of creation and I, the Lord, am being ignored. I am ignored by the rulers and judges. I am cast aside by those in authority. I am shunned by my youth. You are all my children, but I solemnly assure you that by my breath the arrogant temples of your hearts shall be destroyed.

Remember, I am building my city of glory. The stones of my city are humility. The roads shall be paved by the repentant of heart. The gates of my city shall open for the meek and humble of heart. The arrogant shall be cast aside. They shall not enter my city of glory. My holy ones shall be as roses in my garden of delights. Those in my city of glory shall be as a new garden which receives water and sunlight from me, the Lord God of Hosts.

My daughter, lift up your eyes toward heaven. Soon, my beloved, you shall see the Son of Man descending in glory and splendor with mighty angels. Stay awake, my beloved children.

Thank you, child, for writing. Rest in my heart of love.

I love you, Lord, I bless you, too. Amen.

March 29, 1995

Lord Jesus, do you want to write?

My little lamb, I AM is speaking. Let Wisdom instruct you.

Faith, my beloved children, is a gift and a grace. Without faith one cannot know me, for without faith one would not enter into prayer. My precious, precious children, you possess priceless gifts from me, yet how easily you discard my gifts to seek earthly comforts.

Children, I, the Lord, have given you the gift of prayer. I am by your side each time you utter my name.

Be not distracted, my little one.

My child, prayer is as incense in the Throne Room of Heaven. For so powerful is its essence that the heart of heaven is shaken by its beauty and sincerity. Every prayer of the heart is mingled with my blood before it is answered.

Oh, children, do you see how my heart aches for your love? Have I died on the Cross in vain? Does my blood run upon the earth for nothing? I am offering you life and my eternal gift of salvation. I am holding my heart in my hands for all of you. You must increase your prayers, child. Yes, the strong shall carry the weak and I, the Lord, shall uphold you all. Persevere, my beloved children, persevere.

I bless you all, my consecrated souls. Go in peace.

We bless you, too, O Lord. Amen.

March 30, 1995

Lord Jesus, do you want to write?

My beloved disciple, come and record my words of love. Listen carefully, my little one. All of heaven is preparing for that joyous day. Yes, the return of the Lamb is at hand. I am the Lamb by whose blood mankind has been redeemed. "You have been purchased, Generation, and ownership is mine," says the Lord

God of Hosts. I have loosed the shackles of your slavery to death by my blood. You were born by the Cross, which is your key to heaven. Mankind, I, the Lord have defeated death.

My children, you were doomed. I came so that you may live. Children, even now I come to you so that you may live. Allow me to be first in your lives, and the Holy Spirit shall make your heart his sanctuary. My blood shall purify your heart so that I may dwell within a holy foundation. All those who invite me into their lives become a new creation in my sight. By my blood you shall be clothed by me, the Lord God. I shall dress you in holy garments. I shall place a crown of love upon your head and the spirit of my love shall rest in your heart.

Children, where is your love? I am the Lamb that was slain for your iniquities. Am I not worthy of your love?

Thank you for writing, child. Go in peace. I bless you.

I bless you, too, my Jesus. Amen.

March 31, 1995

Lord Jesus, do you want to write?

My beloved one, do not weary of writing my words. I AM shall sustain you.

Daughter, the Lord of Hosts has visited his people. For so mighty is the Lord in compassion that he has walked in every home. He has stood in every doorway. He has listened to every conversation. I AM is speaking, child. Listen carefully to my words.

Children, do not be so arrogant as to think I do not hear your conversations or thoughts. I AM has visited you and I know every dark and hidden secret. For what man can hide from me, the Lord God? You shall flee to the mountains and to the hills and they shall hide from the sight of the unrepentant on the day of judgement.

There is no place to hide, children, no place to flee. The Lord of Hosts has called for your return to my Sacred Heart of Love. My heart is your only resting place. Only in the sanctuary of my heart shall you find peace. Ah, my children, you say

I am harsh and cruel. I assure you, children, that not one of you has given another as many choices as I, the Lord, give you. Return to me, my little lost souls. You do not comprehend the tragic consequences if you do not.

Child, thank you for writing. I bless you. Go in peace.

I bless you, too, O Lord. I love you, Holy Spirit and Blessed Mother. Amen.

April 1, 1995

Lord Jesus, do you want to write?

My precious child, come into my embrace and record the words I speak to you.

Fear not, my little one. I AM has chosen you from my holy mountain and has placed the pen of my love within your hand. Ah, my child, I behold the earth, and all that is within the earth within a beat of my heart. Each time my Sacred Heart beats, rays of mercy pour forth and cover the earth.

The majestic fragrance of love descends upon the earth with each beat of my heart. No, my little sparrow, you must not try to comprehend me. I am Jesus, the Resurrection and the Life. I am the Heart of All Creation and the Judge who beckons you to eternal salvation. Though I am a Just Judge, my children, do not take advantage of my goodness. Approach me in humility. Approach me in honesty and I, the Lord, shall hear you. To those who lament before me shall I, the Lord, cradle and nurture.

I strengthen all those who call upon me. All those who love me shall be granted all that is asked in faith. Ask, children, and you shall receive. Look for me, children, and I shall manifest myself to you.

Child, thank you for writing. Go in peace, little mercy of my heart. I bless you.

I bless you and love you, too, Jesus and Mother Mary. Amen.

April 2, 1995

Lord Jesus, do you want to write?

My child of mercy, let us begin. The sword of truth is about to strike the earth. I AM has watched the abominations and the abandonment of morality upon the earth. Creation once sparkled as a light guiding a ship in a darkened sea. But now, oh, how I, the Lord, grieve. The heavens are shaken by my grief and so shall the earth be shaken. Yes, children, the sword of truth points to you. You do not see yourselves the way you really are, Mankind. Satan has covered you all with a blanket of illusion. But only I, the Lord, can reveal the truth to you.

Call upon me, children, and I will wash you in my holy Precious Blood. Each time a nail was hammered into me, your sins were driven into the ocean, deeper, and deeper. As my blood began to spill upon the earth your sins were devoured by the waves of the sea and carried to the deepest places. I have restored you to grace, my precious ones, but you refuse to accept my gifts. You claim that earthly gifts are finer than mine. "Children, if you wish to know the truth you must come to me," says the Lord God of Hosts.

Thank you for writing, child. Go in peace. I bless you.

I bless you, too, my God and my Savior. Amen.

April 3, 1995

Lord Jesus, do you want to write?

My little one, come and receive my words of love and hope. There is a great bridge that spans heaven with the earth. That bridge is me, children. I am Jesus. I am the Way to Eternal Bliss, the Truth of All Creation, and the Sustainer of All Life.

Children, I, the Lord, love you all so much that you have been given the choice by me to accept me or not. I have given you free will. Yes, I grant you many opportunities to repent and convert, but you must make the choice. Children, I give my love freely, and freely I desire its return. Children, I watch over your foolish ways. You are as the man who stores up his treasure in a safe deposit box; what you have placed in the box does not increase, it does not yield fruit. For surely I tell you that you cannot store up earthly treasures and merit the Kingdom of Heaven. For your hearts are as the safety deposit box, constant and unable to produce fruit. Children, realize that it is in mercy that I come to you this way. It is because I love you, precious, precious children.

Remember, do not store up earthly treasure, but store up acts of charity and love for my sake. Then shall your reward be great.

Child, thank you for writing. Go in peace, little disciple of mercy. I bless you.

I bless you, too, Lord Jesus. I love you. Amen.

April 4, 1995

Lord Jesus, do you want to write?

My little one, come and record my words of love. Child, do not despair. Place your hope and faith in me and me alone. You shall be crushed by humanity if you do not. I am Jesus, the only Source of Consolation and Love. Remember, my precious one, I am the Light of Love upon the Earth.

Little mercy of my heart, allow your faith to soar above your human bondage. In this I mean do not shackle your faith with intellect and pride, but allow it to grow and develop in my love. One can never have enough faith. Child, you must have faith to pray, and in turn, prayer shall increase your faith. Humility shall increase your prayer life which, in turn, shall increase your faith.

Remember how all paths shall converge into one for the soul who seeks me. I am the Giver of Faith and the Helper of the Humble. Come to me all of you who are weak and confused and I, the Lord, shall strengthen you.

We shall continue tomorrow, my little soul. Be blessed. Go in the peace of my love.

I love you and bless you, sweet Jesus. Amen.

April 5, 1995

Lord Jesus, do you want to write?

My precious one, I am here. I am Blessed Virgin Mary and the Mother of God. My child, I have come to you with the entire Heavenly Court. Today, child, my heart is filled with joy.

I am rejoicing, child, for today some of my lost children have returned to Jesus and to my motherly embrace. You are welcome, all my little children, no matter how far you have strayed. My Son's mercy shall cover you and you shall be healed. My child, today is a day of celebration in heaven for so priceless is the soul to us that we celebrate his return.

Remember that my Son, Jesus, explained about the return of the prodigal son and how his father rejoiced. So it is when a soul returns to God. Oh, children, I continue to need your prayers and acts of reparation. This is a time of great grace from the Eternal Father but I need my children's assistance. Pray the Rosary, children. Do not make excuses. The Rosary continues to secure great graces from God each time it is prayed. Children, do not doubt in the power of prayer. Remember, my children, I am here to help you. I love you, my daughter.

Go in peace. I bless you.

I love you, too, my Mother Mary, and I bless you, too.

My Jesus, I love you.

I love you, too, my child. We shall continue tomorrow. Rest, child. I bless you.

I bless you, too, Lord. Amen.

April 6, 1995

Lord Jesus, do you want to write?

My little child, your perseverance is pleasing to me. Come to my holy mountain and receive my words of love.

Listen carefully, my child. One by one, I, the Lord, am changing the stones of men's hearts into pearls. I am changing hearts into treasure chests, for the heart knows I am the treasure of humanity.

Children, the day is coming when all your gold and silver shall not purchase safety for you. For what power does gold and silver possess in the face of divine judgment? Your wealth is only temporary, my dear ones, and shall quickly abandon you that final hour.

But know then that your treasure in heaven is forever. Store up your treasure in heaven now, children. Begin by conversion and reconciliation. Offer acts of reparation and be charitable. Surely your treasure in heaven will begin to grow. Who shall guard your earthly treasure. my children?

Surely, the wise man will flee from you when he sees the millstone about your neck. Yes, you must eventually pay a very high price for your treasures. I AM is speaking. Receive my words of truth.

Thank you for writing. Rest, my beloved child. I bless you.

I bless you, too, Jesus, my God. Amen.

April 7, 1995

Lord Jesus, do you want to write?

My little one, come and receive my words of love and truth. Open your heart to receive the words of the Holy Spirit of Truth and Right Judgment.

Child, notice that I, the Lord, did not say, "Open your ears to receive my words." On the contrary, you must have an open heart to hear with. You must have a repentant heart that you may see and that you may hear.

Allow me to dwell in your heart and I, the Lord, shall give you a new heart. I shall fill your heart with virtues and give you a heart of flesh. The stone heart you have now, Creation, shall be crushed by me, the cornerstone.

My child, you must build walls about you to shield you from satan. These walls are made up of prayer and grace. My child, your prayers shall serve as a soft cushion to protect you against the temptations and assaults of my adversary. Be on guard. Be on guard. Be on guard. My daughter, my daughter, do not despair. I, the Lord, shall always help you. Be blessed, little one of my heart. Go in peace.

I bless you and love you, Lord. Amen.

April 8, 1995

Lord Jesus, do you want to write?

My child of mercy, come dwell in my heart. Listen to the voice of the One Who Is.

I have come to you, Humanity, to separate the pearls from the stones, and the seeds from the crops. Not all seed yields fruit, children, and I, the Lord, have come for the fruit. Yes, I am hungry for my children's love and I have come to gather the fruit of the Spirit.

Those who follow me and yield to my guardianship produce fruit, and the seed I, the Lord, planted and reproduced begins to flourish. The seed that I have planted bears witness to my Holy Name.

Hear, O Israel. I AM is calling you to repentance again and again. "Gather up the fruits of your spiritual harvest and bring them to me," says the Lord of Hosts. Which of you shall come with spiritual fruits and pure hearts? I tell you solemnly, you'd be best to spend some time evaluating your lives before the final judgment. Look at yourselves with honesty and humility and I, the Lord, shall help you to see. Then, and only then, will you begin to see the truth about your pitiable condition.

There are many of you who try to cultivate the seed in others yet disregard your own souls. Wake up, you foolish Generation. The time is at hand. The Kingdom of Heaven is upon you. Prepare your hearts. Thank you, child, for writing my words. Go with my blessing. I love you.

I love you and bless you, too, sweet Jesus. Amen.

April 9, 1995 Palm Sunday

Lord Jesus, do you want to write?

My precious, precious child, I have waited so long for you to love me. Thank you for responding to my call of love.

I am coming into Jerusalem, my children, for I, the Lord, have claimed her as my

Holy City before creation. She is the gem of all gems, my children, yet when I come, many shall be left outside the city gates. Once the gates of my Holy City close, those who are left outside shall never enter.

Oh, my children, so many of you did not honor me today. Do you know the heaviness of my heart? I came so that you might be reconciled to the Eternal Father, yet you do not honor me. You do not come to me. I tell you all, that I, Jesus, am the only way to my Father. I am the Gateway to Heaven and the Heart of All Creation. Yet just one word from you, children, and I would forgive you and cover you in my everlasting mercy.

My children, I have reserved a place for each of you at the heavenly dinner table, but I weep for I know there shall be many empty places. Children, do you see my humility? How I the Lord come begging for your love? If you wish my loyalty, then be loyal to me.

Thank you, my little disciple of mercy, for writing my words. I bless you and your family.

I bless you and love you forever, Lord. Amen.

April 10, 1995

Lord Jesus, do you want to write?

My devoted child, come into my arms of love. My child, listen to the words of your Savior, the Holy One of Israel. Allow the Spirit of Love to speak to your heart.

Children, so many of you ignore my Spirit of Love. Children, we are three, yet one. The Holy Spirit is Lord and is one with the Father who is one with the Son. Do not ignore the Spirit of the Lord nor grieve him with your idolatrous ways. Children, have compassion for your God. Is there not one among you to take pity on your Savior? How many of you would have me crucified again?

Oh, children, the truth is hidden from the arrogant. But the simple and humble of heart recognize their Savior; those, beloved of my heart, who think of me and offer me prayers of consolation.

Child, have faith. My little child of mercy, you must persevere in all avenues leading to me and I, the Lord, shall reward you for your efforts.
My little disciple of mercy, rest. I know you are weary. Thank you, child of my heart.

Lord, I love you and praise your mighty name forever and ever. Amen.

April 11, 1995

Lord Jesus, do you want to write?

My beloved daughter, allow me to use you as my vessel of grace. Listen carefully, little child of my heart.

Child, the Rosary is a powerful weapon against the evil one. It is the sword of praise and the lantern to guide those who are lost in the sea of sin. Yes, though the Rosary be simple it is clearly perfected by me, the Lord God. Those who persevere in praying the Rosary receive additional graces and assistance from my Beloved Mother.

Each time you bring yourself into the mystery of my life, death and resurrection, I water the many seeds of virtue I have planted at Baptism. Yes, my life grows and flourishes in you and you, my children, are transformed by Love. I am Love. I am the One who sees into men's hearts and despises the iniquity that rules them. By a wave of my arm sin shall be crushed and the flames of righteousness shall spread as the breath of my Spirit carries them to the four corners.

Yes, my children, the wind of the Spirit blows and you will not know the direction. Righteousness is coming, children. Holy, Holy, Holy, the Lord God of Israel, is coming for his people. With a crown of glory upon his brow he shall come with his mighty army of angels. Who then shall welcome Him Who Is?

Allow my blood to wash you and cleanse you that you may have in your heart a dwelling place for my Holy Spirit. Come, children, come.

I love you, child. Thank you for writing. Go in peace with my blessing.

I love you, too, Jesus, my Savior. Amen.

April 12, 1995

Daughter, I am here. I am Blessed Virgin Mary and the Mother of God. My child, I am covering the earth with my mantle of love. My crown is giving heavenly graces to all those who call upon me. Listen carefully to my words.

Children of my heart, I am again calling you to the sanctuary of the Most Blessed Lord in the Holy Mass. I am the Queen of Heaven and of Earth and I am present in the Mass praising my beloved Son, Jesus. Oh, my children, my Son is your King and High Priest who comes to you to offer life and love. At the altar of the Lord does my Son stand looking into the hearts of his children. The repentant bring him such joy.

Children, you do not realize the magnitude of graces you receive at the Mass. Continue, daughter, continue to write. When you come to Mass, children, your soul is presented to the Eternal Father who purifies it with the fire of his love thereby sanctifying you and making you righteous. These are gifts given you freely by God. There is nothing you could do, children, to merit these gifts.

Children, as my mantle covers you then shall you lift up the banner of David and proudly go forth proclaiming the gospel of my Son. I shall always go with you. Thank you for writing my words, child. I bless you all.[28]

We bless you, too, Mother Mary.

Lord, do you want to write?

Yes, child, but tonight my words shall be few. My devoted children, thank you for your sacrifice of love. Dear ones, you must be courageous in the face of temptation. My adversary should like to crush you and devour your hearts. Children, the blasphemy against me is increasing. Remember to all those who defend me, shall I, the Lord Jesus Christ, defend to my Heavenly Father.

Ah, children, I have called you all to carry the cross with me to Calvary. Do not forsake me, little ones. I will always help you.

---

[28] The Blessed Mother is blessing our entire prayer group who was present for this message.

We shall continue tomorrow, child. I bless you all, my little children. Go in peace.

We bless you and love you, Lord. Amen.

April 13, 1995 - Holy Thursday

Lord Jesus, do you want to write?

My dear one, come and record my words of love.

Disciples of mine, I, the Lord, am calling you to break bread with me and in turn, share it with your brothers. Daughter, as I dipped my bread in the dish, the one who betrayed me dipped his as well. So many of you, children, feast at my altar and then go and betray me. So many of you approach my altar with unrepentant hearts. You come and partake of my Body and Blood though you be in a state of sin.

Children, I have given you the Sacrament of Reconciliation. Utilize the gifts I have provided. I am the Fountain of Eternal Grace and my love is poured out through my sacraments.

Oh, my children, so few of you came to honor my Last Supper. Again I am going to Calvary forsaken by those I have come to save. Do you not hear the voice of your Savior? I am the Eternal to Eternal God of Abraham, Isaac, and Jacob. Those who do not wish to feast at my dinner table now shall not do so in heaven.

Children, you must open your hearts to my teaching. I AM has come among you to offer you salvation and the eternal banquet. Please accept my invitation of love. Child, I love you and bless you. Go in peace.

I love you and bless you, too, Lord, forever. Amen.

April 14, 1995 - Good Friday

Lord Jesus, do you want to write?

My servant, come and receive my words of love. Children, I, the Lord Jesus

Christ, am calling to you from the Cross. I am calling the lonely, the sick, the hungry, the oppressed. I am calling all of you to come to the foot of the Cross. Children, no matter what your suffering is, I, the Lord, have suffered it. I go before you always, my dear ones.

Each drop of my blood has the name of many souls written upon it. Come and claim your eternal gift, children. Come and claim your inheritance.

Today, dear ones, I desire you to honor my beloved Mother. Many of you cast her aside as if she does not exist. My foolish children, I, Jesus, have given my beloved Mother to you to help you on your journey to me. She is a mighty intercessor before me and the fountain of humility and virtue. Call upon my beloved Mother, dear ones.

Let us continue, child.

Children, you do not realize the love and power of the heavenly court. Call to your angels and pray to the saints. Call upon Padre Pio to assist you. Oh, children, there is nothing greater in heaven than to help you on your journey in righteousness. Today, dear children, I shall again spill my blood for humanity. Who then shall come and follow me?

Thank you, child, for writing. I bless you. Go in peace.

I love you and bless you, too, my Lord. Amen.

April 15, 1995

Lord Jesus, do you want to write?

My dear child, listen to the words of the one who has laid down his life for you.

I am a God of Compassion and Understanding. I am from Eternal to Eternal the Fountain of Mercy and Forgiveness. Children, I desire that you enter the abyss of my mercy. Allow your sins to die and receive new life in me. Rise with me, all those who have ears and all those who have eyes. I AM is calling all of you from Calvary.

Dear ones, heavy is the wood of the Cross created out of the sins of the world.

But I have come to help you. I assure you that I will separate your burdens from your heart and the two shall not mix. For I, the Lord, shall dwell in your heart and I shall give you a heart to endure and persevere.

My child, you are distracted. Picture the woman carrying the water from the well in heavy containers. You cannot do without the water, but I, Jesus, have come to carry the container for you. Drink therefore, children, and do not be discouraged by the weight of the cross. I will always help you.

Dear child, we shall continue tomorrow. Be blessed child of my heart.

Thank you, kind sweet Jesus. I bless you, too. Amen.

April 16, 1995 - Easter Sunday

Lord Jesus, do you want to write?

My devoted children, I am here beside you. Come and receive my message of love.

Rise up, all my children, and allow the glory of the Lord God of Israel to dwell in your hearts. Rise up, O Jerusalem, and hearken to the voice of the Eternal. The trumpets blow and the breath of the Spirit blows where it will, yet you are still in the tomb, for you are sleeping. Children, the rock at the entrance to my tomb is as the door of your heart.

I stand knocking, children. If you do not let me in then you shall be as one dead in the tomb. Without my love the soul will decay with the bacteria of sin. Satan is as a cancer. His malignant way spreads through the hearts and minds of those who push me aside.

Children of Israel, hear my words. I am Jesus, the Sovereign and Omnipotent Lord of Hosts. I have defeated death and sin and I am the eternal welder of men's hearts. Give your hearts to me and I shall make of them a new heart, a heart that serves me and me alone.

Do not look to the idolaters for they are in the tomb and there shall they remain on the last day. Repent, all of you who have ears. Wash yourselves in the abyss of my mercy. You are at the brink of eternal perdition and I have come to rescue you. Children, the choice is yours.

Child, thank you for writing. I love you and I bless you.

Lord, Happy Easter. I love you and bless you, too. Amen.

April 17, 1995

Lord Jesus, do you want to write?

My dear child, I bless you. Come and record my words of love.

Child of mine, examine your faith. Your faith needs to be as the cloak about your shoulders in the cold weather. Your faith needs to be as a glass of water to quench your thirst on a hot summer day. With faith, daughter, all things are possible. With faith, my child, goals are accomplished and dreams are realized.

Children, examine your surroundings and you will find numerous examples of my sustaining love. Look at the rose, children. Does not my Heavenly Father care for this lovely flower? The rose, children, was created in variety that you may know the Lord God loves his creation infinitely. There is no discrimination in heaven. Each of you is as a precious rose to God. Each of you is nurtured and cared for by my Heavenly Father.

Let us continue.

My child, I am trying to teach you that faith is a priceless jewel. All that you ask for in faith shall be granted by my Heavenly Father. Remember, children, to always pray in accordance with the Holy Perfect Will of God. To be outside the Will of God is to be separated from Him Who is Eternal Love. I am Jesus. I am the Way to my Eternal Father. I am the Light of Love and Hope in the World. It is you, children, that need me.

Thank you for writing, dear one. I bless you and love you.

I love you and bless you forever and ever, Lord. Amen.

April 18, 1995

Lord Jesus, do you want to write?

Yes, child, let us begin. I am the Lord, the Holy Spirit.

My child, from where does the harvest come? Will a seed that is planted and left alone become a harvest? No, child, for abundance only comes from perseverance and care. My child, for the seed to become a harvest you must nurture it and persevere in your care of it. Then it shall become a harvest that is fruitful.

Children, if you do not care for the seeds I, the Lord, have planted, you shall have a harvest of weeds. The seed of peace which I, the Lord, have planted must be nurtured and protected by world leaders. Instead, what I have planted has been made a mockery by men. What I have planted is holy, children. Do not therefore take my gifts for granted.

Lord, everything you give us we have to work at.

Child, think of a concert pianist. Does he not pursue his goal and nurture my gift relentlessly? Ah, children, I, the Lord, have given you abundantly and have made provisions for all of you, yet you cast my gifts aside. So few of you acknowledge me and acknowledge my gifts.

Child, tenderly care for the gifts I, the Lord, have given you. How do you expect to have peace in the world when you reject my gifts, the seeds I have planted?

Thank you, little mercy of my heart, for writing. I bless you and love you.

I bless you and love you, too, sweet God. Amen.

April 19, 1995

Lord Jesus, do you want to write?

My child of mercy, come and receive my words of love. My little sparrow, today you are far from the nest of my love. Where is your focus, dear one?

Lord, I'm sorry. I have a lot of things on my mind today. I'm having trouble with everything.

Dear one, to rise above earthly cares you must rise up to me, your Savior. I am the Light in the Darkness. Dear child, I, the Lord, have placed the stars in the sky to illuminate the darkness.

Dear, dear children, there is nothing I would not do for the soul that calls upon me. I have given my life for you already. Open your heart to hear my words.

Little one, let us continue.

In the treasure chest of the heart that loves me, one shall find many gems. There is faith, patience, perseverance, and generosity. The more a soul yearns for my love, the more gifts he is granted. Continue always, child, to desire my will and be obedient to my ways. I will not forsake you, my little sparrow.

Daughter, the Kingdom of Heaven is a grand treasure chest filled with the hearts of those who love me. I, the Lord, Jesus Christ, am calling all my children to lay down your earthly treasures and seek only the treasures of heaven.

We shall continue tomorrow, my dear one. Be secure in my love. I bless you.

I love you, Lord. I love you and bless you, Holy Spirit and Mother Mary. Amen.

April 20, 1995

Lord Jesus, do you want to write?

My precious rose, come and receive my words of love.

My children, you are still sleeping. The Kingdom of Heaven is among you, yet you sleep. I will move through your land and through your homes and through your lives, and I, the Lord, assure you that the audit you receive from me shall be unpleasant. Yes, dear ones, you are accountable and I, the Lord, shall come for the fruits of your labor.

Reflect, my children, and ask for my help. Are you nurturing the gifts I have given you? Are you walking with me or with my adversary? Children, there are only two paths. There is only one choice. The day has come for you to make that choice.

Children, do you believe one in the darkness can dwell in the light? No, my children, he must first leave the darkness. All of creation dwells in darkness, and my Holy Spirit shall guide them back into my Sacred Heart of love. Daughter, you must persevere on the narrow path of salvation.

Remember that I, the Lord, always go before you with the Cross upon my shoulders. Each time you fall under the weight of the cross call to me. I will lift you up and refresh you. I will give you the ability to continue. My child, I know you are weary.[29] Rest in my arms, little one. Allow my love to nourish and refresh you. I AM is giving his heart to you, Creation. Come and receive my love.

Thank you, child, for writing my words. Go in peace, child of my heart. I bless you.

Thank you for your patience and kindness, O Lord. I love and bless you and Blessed Mother. Amen.

April 21, 1995

Lord Jesus, do you want to write?

Come, my disciple of mercy, and record my words of love and hope.

My child, as the earth revolves around the sun, so does the sun revolve around me. I am the Lord, the God of All Creation, from the low to the high. Hear my words, O Israel. My heavenly army shall march through your gates as the mighty trumpets of Zion blow. They shall clear the threshing floor for me, dear ones, as I come in the clouds in glory and fire. My army of angels shall descend upon you, Mankind, as an avalanche, and all creation shall see my glory.

---

[29] I never seem to be without some degree of fatigue these past few weeks and I am not sure whether it's the demands of the newborn or something physically not right.

My daughter, do not stray from my Sacred Heart of love, for my heart is the sun. My heart is the moon. My heart is the existence of humanity. My heart was laid bare on the Cross at Calvary that you Mankind, may live to see my New Jerusalem. I am coming, children, with my mighty army and the heavenly chariots.

I am coming to gather my sheep across the earth and to proclaim to all my authority and kingship. I am Jesus, the Messiah. I am the Alpha and the Omega. I shall surround you, O earth, with pillars of fire and there shall be none to escape my scrutiny.

Be prepared, my children. Ask for the candles in your heart to be ignited by my Spirit of Love and it shall be granted you.

I love you, my child. Your perseverance is pleasing to me. Continue in your efforts.

I love you, too, Lord. I love you, Blessed Mother, forever. Amen.

April 22, 1995

Lord Jesus, do you want to write?

My dear child, record my message of love.

My child, there are many distractions to remove your focus from me. You do not realize the seriousness of the times and my enemy's hunger for souls.

My dear ones, as a vulture preys upon dead flesh, so does my enemy prey upon the sinner. With tentacles of poison he does pierce the heart and change one's direction eternally. But, children, there is none lost who calls upon the name of the Lord. There is none devoured and held hostage by satan who calls upon the name of the Lord. There is none to be defeated who calls upon the name of the Lord.

Children, I, Jesus, have given you my holy name. My name is the name above all names. Evil flees in the face of my name. Say my name often and holiness will cover you and surround you with a heavenly fragrance. Righteousness and dignity will consume you and forgiveness shall illuminate you each time you utter my name.

Dear children, call upon my beloved Mother who will surround you with her mantle of love and purity. Do not be discouraged, my beloved ones, for I, the Lord, have placed the sign of my love upon your brow. I have placed my kiss of love upon your hearts. Be at peace, my child. I love you and bless you.

I love you and bless you, too, Lord. Amen.

April 23, 1995, Sunday - Feast of Divine Mercy[30]

Lord Jesus, do you want to write?

Come, child, you are my messenger of mercy. Record my words.

Today the depths of my mercy have been given to my creation. But there were few to partake of my abundant love. There were few to come to me seeking my mercy. What shall I do with you, O Wicked Generation? You are alive yet dead. Remember, those who call upon my holy name though they are dead, yet shall they live. But none shall live outside my merciful heart. None can approach my altar in the Throne Room of Heaven unless clothed in garments of mercy and righteousness.

Dear child, I have desired this feast of my mercy so that sinners may come to my banquet and share in my royalty.[31] Yes, I desire to share my crown with

---

[30] Earlier in the day at Mass I had a vision of the outline of the U.S. I saw an image of America resting in two large hands and then I saw the hands carry "America" and place her inside a tomb. Our Lord said, "this is where she shall stay until she repents before me."

[31] The Lord is referring to the feast celebrating his Divine Mercy. The origin of this feast is traced to the alleged apparitions of the Lord to Blessed Sr. Helenka Faustina Kowalska of Poland during the 1930s. She took the religious name, "Sr. Maria Faustina of the Blessed Sacrament " upon entering the Congregation of the Sisters of Our Lady of Mercy in 1926. This humble soul had been chosen by our Lord to bring to the twentieth century marvelous messages

all my devoted faithful ones, but you must be covered in mercy and forgiveness.[32] There is none among you that is unblemished. But ask for my mercy and you shall receive my mercy. The depths of my mercy are more than the sands of the earth and so many of you reject my mercy.

Children, you shall thirst and there shall be no quenching it. You shall hunger and there shall be no food, for the arrogant of heart would rather die than to admit his grievous ways. Children, I, the Lord, Jesus Christ, burn with love and mercy. Come and bathe in my goodness. Take comfort in me and me alone. Remember, I am the Eternal Comfort.

Thank you for writing, child. Rest now, my beloved. I bless you.

I bless you, too, Jesus, my love forever. Amen.

---

of his love and mercy for sinners, and particularly for those who have lost hope in God's mercy entirely. The Lord had requested Blessed Sr. Faustina to record his words, and that the first Sunday after Easter be a day commemorating his mercy by prayer, repentance, and veneration of his image of Divine Mercy. It is my understanding that tremendous graces are poured forth upon the world on this day for those souls who petition the Lord with a repentant heart. I have heard it said that the soul who approaches the Sacrament of Reconciliation and receives Holy Communion on this day shall obtain complete forgiveness of sin and punishment, comparable to a second Baptism.

[32] While I am not very familiar with the writings of Blessed Sr. Faustina, my own experience concurs with the general thrust of her messages: God's greatest attribute is his mercy. There is a sentence from a prayer that the Lord taught me that I believe most aptly fits today's celebration: "Let sinners rejoice that thy mercy may cover us and cause our hearts to burn with the fire of thy love." *(Message of August 17, 1994)*. I hope the reader of this volume and *The Heart of God, Vol. 1*, has come to a similar conclusion, that is, no one should have fear to approach the Lord for forgiveness. His only concern is our ultimate well-being - eternal bliss. See message of December 17, 1995 for his promises.

April 24, 1995

Lord Jesus, do you want to write?

My little one, come. I, the Lord, have called to you, dear one. Listen carefully to my words.

Who can comprehend the inexhaustible mercy of the Lord God? Proclaim his mighty works from the mountaintops to the four corners. Little child, why do you doubt in my goodness? Do not doubt in my saving grace. I am a God who provides and sustains. There are those among you who take credit for this but I assure you, children, that should I remove my sustaining hand from you, creation would be a mere speck of dust.

Dear one, continue to write.

Child of my heart, your lack of faith grieves me.[33] Am I not more than a short prayer or phrase? Am I not more than the limits of your thoughts?

Yes, Lord, you are. I'm sorry again for doubting. Please forgive me.

Child, you are weak and wretched, and my mercy consumes you. Do not restrict my gifts by your limitations. I am the Lord God. I do not have limitations. I AM. I AM. I AM.

Child, place your trust in my heart of love and do not take it from there. If your trust remains in my Sacred Heart, it shall grow and flourish as will your faith. I, the Lord, shall always provide for you and help you. Go in peace, little mercy of my heart. I bless you.

I bless you and love you, too, Jesus and Mama Mary. Amen.

---

[33] I was worried about my physical well-being and economic situation. I was calling upon the Lord in my plight but not in the sufficient manner and amount of faith that he was expecting from me.

April 25, 1995

Lord Jesus, do you want to write?

My dear little one, receive my words of love.

I am suffering, dear one. My wounds are deep and I, the Lord, am in a perpetual state of mourning. A dark veil looms over mankind as a dense fog and only by mercy shall this veil be lifted. Mankind is in a cemetery and sleeps with the dead, yet no one who is with me, the Lord God, is dead. Those who walk with me shall be raised from the tomb as I was.

Children, as flesh decays after one's death, so it is that the soul decays if it walks outside my heart of love. The soul is as a flower needing sunlight and water to survive. I, the Lord, solemnly assure you that only I am the Light and Water of the Soul. "Only I AM," says the Lord God of Israel.

Let us continue, child. Do not be distracted.

My merciful heart has upheld humanity but, my children, time is nearing an end. My Eternal Father has lifted up his arm of judgment and soon, dear ones, God's mighty army of angels shall come to deliver justice.

Dear ones, do you think you shall survive outside my merciful heart? There is none among you that has not fallen from eternal grace into the arms of satan. Come back into my heart of grace, my children. You shall perish if you do not.

Thank you, child, for writing. We shall continue tomorrow. Go in peace.

Thank you, Lord, for your patience. I love you and bless you. Amen.

April 26, 1995

Lord Jesus, do you want to write?

My dear children, I am pleased by your sacrifice of love.[34]

My dear one, Wisdom is speaking through you. Child, each sacrifice that is offered to me, the Lord God, is brought to my altar by my angels. Even the sacrifice of praise is carried to my Father's throne and there received into his heart of love.

Listen carefully to my words, daughter. I, the Lord, am among you. I am asking for reparation. Children, you must repair the damage you have caused. I do not wish to force reparation upon you, my children. I am Jesus, the Light of Humanity. I am the Guardian of the Soul and the Way to the Eternal Father. I am mourning, my dear ones.

Oh, my children, the earth is a barren wasteland. She has become a hostage of mankind's terrorist acts against her, and even the mountains cry out to me for revenge. Even the sands of the sea call out to me. But soon, my children, the chariots of heaven shall rule the skies to avenge the earth and then you shall see your King. In the clouds shall I descend, children, with the heavenly host. I am coming with the entire heavenly host, my children, and the earth will delight in my glory.

Have pity, all of you who have ears. Is there none among you with compassion for your suffering King? I will crown each repentant heart with a crown of glory.

Dear children, your perseverance has pleased me. I bless you all, my little ones. Go in peace.

We bless you, too, O Lord. Amen.

April 27, 1995

I am here, my dear one. I am Blessed Virgin Mary and the Mother of God. Children, I have come to bring you to the heart of God and to grant you my motherly intercession. I have come as the Advocate of the Redeemer, who is calling to all humanity. My children, I am calling you to reconcile with God and

---

[34] The Lord is referring to our prayer group and the efforts we are doing regarding the publishing of the first volume.

one another. You must dismiss the divisions within your hearts and within the Church. Cast your pride aside and reach out to your brothers and sisters in the name of my beloved Son, Jesus. I am the Mother of the Lamb and the Queen of the Flock.

Children, many of you are making the effort to please God and to you I offer thanks. But so many of my children have ignored my words and the words of Jesus. How can I help you, children, if you will not open your hearts? The malignancy of satan covers your eyes and your ears, and you do not see nor hear. I am a heavenly messenger sent by the Eternal Light to help gather the flock of the Good Shepherd. So many of you are lost and wandering. Come into my embrace and I will help you. I have roses of love from the heavenly gardens for all my children. Please, my children, you must return to God. Do not procrastinate, my children.

Thank you, child, for recording my words. I shall be with you always. I bless you in the name of the Most Holy God.

I bless you, too, Mother Mary. Amen.

April 28, 1995

Lord Jesus, do you want to write?

My dear disciple, come and record my words. Child of my heart, allow me to use your hand as my instrument of grace.

My child, once I, the Lord, passed through my holy Jerusalem, I was angered by the money changers in the temple. Again, my Jerusalem has become a harlot. Again, my Jerusalem has become a den of thieves. I, the Lord, am referring to all of you who commit abominable acts in my sight. I am speaking to the proud, the rich, the unrepentant. I, the Lord, shall turn over the tables of idolatry in your hearts and I shall give you a new heart. I am rebuilding, children.

Yes, I am Jesus, the Master Carpenter, and I, the Lord, am rebuilding paradise. I am creating a new Garden of Eden and a new Garden of Glory as the dwelling place of my people, Israel. Hearken all of you who have ears to hear. I AM is coming through my holy city. I shall knock down the wicked and build up the righteous.

That is all, my dear one. We shall continue tomorrow. I bless you.

I bless you, too, Lord. Please have mercy. I love you. Amen.

April 29, 1995

Lord Jesus, do you want to write?

My little child, come and receive my words of love.

Dear one, all of heaven is preparing for the feast of my banquet.[35] Place settings are being prepared for my beloved. The day will come when there will be much rejoicing, for I will join you for the heavenly meal. Many of you will not be present though, for you have chosen to reject me and to reject salvation. Dear ones, you cannot receive the gift of salvation if you do not accept me. I am Jesus. I am the Eternal, the One above all others. I AM WHO AM.

Heaven is releasing her great nets upon the entire earth to catch the souls who will be joining me. So many of you will remain in hopeless desolation, for satan will have captured your soul for eternity. Children, are you listening? Have you not heard my calls for conversion and reconciliation? Generation, there shall be weeping and great sorrow. Humanity shall lament her great sins and plead for my mercy.

Children, you are living in the time of my mercy. Open your hearts to receive my gifts. The day of my justice shall come upon you as a streak of lightening. Listen, all of you, to the voice of the Eternal.

Thank you, child of my heart. Go in peace, my little one. I bless you.

I bless you, too, Jesus my Lord. Amen.

---

[35] The reader has gathered by now that the Lord often refers to heaven as a "banquet". I have been told that this term is replete with a rich scriptural and theological tradition. I do know the Lord often refers to the Mass as the "banquet" where heaven and earth meet and thus we are given a foretaste of the "heavenly banquet." See particularly the message of December 7, 1995.

April 30, 1995

Lord Jesus, do you want to write?

I, the Lord, am here, children. I bless you all.[36] Today, my dear ones, we shall talk of the bridge to heaven. It is perseverance, my children.

Yes, the road to me and with me is narrow. It is a road that is paved with sorrow. It is a road less frequently traveled than the road to perdition. But, oh, my beloved, do you realize what awaits you at the end of the journey? I await you. I await you with outstretched arms and my heart bursting with love.

Children, at each intersection on the road to salvation you must choose to persevere, lest you fail to progress. But remember, my little ones, that I, the Lord, go before you always. I am the Lamb of Reconciliation who makes a path for you to the Eternal Father.

There is a bridge to your inheritance, children, and that bridge is perseverance. Here you are, my beloved children, and what have you learned? Try and see the benefits of my wisdom. Do not be in a rush, my children, lest it be a rush to love me. Do not walk ahead of my Spirit of Counsel, children. Children, the bridge to salvation spans the lifetime of the individual. Those who persevere in faith and good works shall find their journey full of rewards from me, the Gift-Giver.

Remember, I, the Lord, desire to bestow abundant gifts upon all of you. Continue, my precious ones, in your efforts to please me and oh, how the fruits of my labor will multiply.

I bless you, all my devoted servants. Go in the peace of my love.

We bless you and love you forever and ever, Lord. Amen.

May 1, 1995

Lord Jesus, do you want to write?

---

[36] The Lord is referring to the members of the prayer group who were present for this message.

My little one, I have been waiting to dictate my words. Receive my message of hope and love.

My dear one, I, the Lord Jesus, am calling for the conversion of humanity to my Sacred Heart. My heart is more immense than the seas of the earth and my graces more abundant than the sands of the earth. "Oh, such gifts shall be given to those who repent and turn back to me," says the Lord God of Hosts. I will wipe away the stain of sin and replace it with my heart of love and reconciliation.

Continue to write, my dear child.

All of heaven and earth is ruled by my Sacred Heart. My heart is the fountain of mercy and forgiveness. Children, I watch in sorrow as you rush to others for forgiveness. I watch as you strive to please another; many of you do so in a sinful manner. Children, you must reconcile with me first and I, the Lord, Jesus Christ, will help you to mend your lives.

Children, I am alive. I desire to be a part of you, to walk with you, and to help you. You cannot comprehend my great love for you.

We shall continue tomorrow, my dear one. Go in peace. I bless you.

I love you and bless you, too, O Lord. Amen.

May 2, 1995

Lord Jesus, do you want to write?

My precious one, allow me to use your hand as the vessel of my mercy. Let us begin.

Many of my children do not believe in the reality of heaven and hell. Your intellect, my children, is robbing you of the truth. You cannot comprehend the majesty of heaven nor can you comprehend the agony of hell. But I solemnly assure you that they are real places and not a product of man's imagination. Children, so great is your deception that you have cast me aside and the very places you will spend eternity.

My dear children, let those who have ears, listen to the Spirit of Truth and Knowledge.

Children, consider the magician. He grants a pleasurable experience by illusion. Yet I, the Lord, have gifts more valuable than these, and I assure you my gifts are no illusion, they are real and for eternity.

Oh, children, your intellect has made you fools, and only the fool has any intellect before me, the Lord God. I AM WHO AM shall flood your hearts with the fire of my love, and your pride and arrogance shall be stamped out and made into ashes. Then, children, what will you say as you stand before me?

I have given you my commandments so that you may be wise in the ways of truth and holiness. But whosoever shall not follow my commandments wears the insignia of satan, and his scars of sin shall stay upon him.

Thank you, dear child, for writing. I bless you. Go in peace, my beloved.

Lord, you are wonderful. Thank you for everything. I bless you forever and Mother Mary. Amen.

May 3, 1995

Lord Jesus, do you want to write?

I do, my little disciple of mercy. Come and receive my message of love. Child, listen carefully to my words and teaching.

Dear ones, self-control is a gift of the Spirit. It is a grace of love. Dear ones, in the face of temptation you must pray for self-control and perseverance. You must pray that you do not sleep and let the great deceiver overtake you. Those of you who have ears, listen. Moderation and the ability to moderate one's behavior is a gift from me. Of your own, you do not possess such a quality. Children, I, the Lord Jesus, desire to bestow many gifts upon you. From the treasure of my heart come these gifts for all who ask.

Children, you go in search of something you desire and many of you make quite an effort to get the item you desire. You do not have to make such an effort for my gifts. All you need to do is ask and you shall receive. I, the Lord, wait to pour out my blessings upon souls. Come to me, children. Come.

Let us continue, my dear one.

Children, if you knew me, you would love me, for I am Love. Come to me all of you in humility and I, the Lord, will grant you the crown of my love. I am your Redeemer, children, and the Gateway to Salvation. There is none among you to inherit salvation on your own. I am the only way. The choice is yours.

Go in peace, my little child. I bless you.

I bless you and love you, too, Lord. Amen.

May 4, 1995

Lord Jesus, do you want to write?

I am here, my beloved. Let us begin. Listen carefully to the words of the Spirit of Truth and Right Judgment.

Dear one, there are many different types of houses in a community, yet they still comprise the neighborhood. I am giving you this example in simplicity. I am referring to my Mystical Body. I tell you solemnly that all those who believe in me are part of my Body and part of my Church. Dear one, I, the Lord, have come among you to unite my Church. Remember child, the divisions within my Church spring forth from the divisions within men's hearts.

Children, you must give your burdens to me. I am Jesus, beloved Son of God. I am the Lamb Slain for your Iniquities and the Eternal Sacrifice of Love. I will refresh you and give you rest. Children, I, the Lord, come always with gifts for those who love me, and my goodness and compassion encompasses those who do not.

I wait as a stranger for my children's love. I wait and watch in sorrow. Children, you seek counsel from those who do not know me. How therefore shall they counsel you? You must be cautious, my little lambs, and pray always for discernment.

Dear one, we shall continue tomorrow. Thank you for your sacrifice of love.

Thank you, Lord, for your love. I love you. Amen.

May 5, 1995

Lord Jesus, do you want to write?

My dear child, rest in my heart of love.

Daughter, the evil one is stalking you and victimizing you.[37] You must increase your prayers. Child, no harm shall befall you, but you must not sleep. You must increase your efforts. I have sent my angels to assist you, but you must always wear the armor of faith. Faith is a pure shield against the attacks of the wicked one. Do not grieve, my little one, but understand how my enemy waits to devour poor souls.

Lord, what are we going to do?

Dear ones, I shall not forsake you. Did I not give you a gift of encouragement today?[38] You must relinquish your life to my care and trust me completely.

Daughter, when you call to me, I, Jesus, run to you. When you call to me, you are calling the Most Blessed and Holy Trinity for we are three, yet one. These things no man can understand, and therefore it is easier to say it is not truth. But soon, my children, you shall see your Savior and you shall see the truth.

Be brave, my children, and I, the Lord, will help you. Remember my faithfulness.

---

[37] There appeared to be more and more roadblocks in my efforts to exercise the directives the Lord had recently given me. Naturally, I find this exasperating.

[38] The Lord had sent me a beautiful rainbow which I didn't ask to receive. I often ask for rainbows as a verification or confirmation to discern if what the Lord has directed me to do is truly coming from him and not the evil one. He sent me this rainbow as a manifestation of his continued presence and triumph over the evil one regardless of how many times the "hinderer" interrupts my efforts to do the Lord's work.

Go in the peace of my love. I bless you and love you.

I bless you and love you, too, Lord. Amen.

May 6, 1995

My daughter, I am here. I am Blessed Virgin Mary and the Mother of God.

My daughter, my hands are clasped in prayer and my eyes are always on God, my Savior. That is what I desire for all my children.

Dear ones, you shall not escape satan's wrath if you do not pray. You must make prayer a central part of your life. My dear children, when you take your eyes off my beloved Jesus, then your heart is quick to follow. Soon you become immersed in materialism, which leads to skepticism, which leads to lack of faith.

Children, call upon me, your heavenly Mother. I will obtain the graces of faith and holiness for you from my beloved Son. I will hold your hand as you journey the road of truth and light. But remember, if you choose the road of darkness and lies, then you go alone. Sadly, that road is heavily traveled.

I have come from heaven, children, to reunite you with God. I am a messenger of the Holy One of Israel.

My Mother?[39]

I am here, dear one. Continue to write.

Children, I am the Mother of the Savior and the Mother of All Creation. I desire only to help you return to God. Be wise, my little children.

Thank you for writing my words. I bless you.

Lord?

---

[39] I was momentarily interrupted by the children during this message and I am now returning to the quiet of my room so I can continue to record the message. The Blessed Mother is so understanding and patient.

I am here, dear one.

I'm sorry for the interruptions, Lord.

Be secure in my love, little one. We shall continue tomorrow. Go in peace.

I love you, Lord and Blessed Mother. Amen.

May 7, 1995

Lord Jesus, do you want to write?

My dear child, I am here. Receive my words of love and truth.

Dear one, patience breeds faith. With patient endurance, the virtue of trust in me is perfected by me. Yes, my child, I, the Lord, Jesus Christ, am happy to bestow such gifts on all those who ask. Dear one, faith does not exist without patience. The heart must be patient while the soul turns to me.

I am the Lord, the One Who Is, the Alpha and the Omega. I am He Who Sustains All of Creation in the Palm of My Hand. I am He Who Breathes Life into My Creation, that they may return all glory and honor to me. But is that so? No, precious one, creation revels in her arrogance, glorifying herself. She delights in the sciences, the sciences which create and destroy. She has lost her dignity and respect for life.

"Generation," thus says the Lord, the God of Israel, "repent and turn from your evil ways, lest I shall come in a storm to strike with my justice. You are not the author of life nor the executioner of life. Only I AM," says the Lord of Hosts.

You treat human life as a cancer destroying both the good and bad at your choosing. You rob the innocents of the right to life because of your selfish arrogance. You are accountable, Generation. The Lord God of Hosts is coming and you, Generation, are accountable. Be prepared. Be prepared. Be prepared.

Lord, have mercy. Lord, have mercy. Lord, have mercy.

Child, thank you for writing. I bless you. Go in peace.

I bless you, too, forever, O Lord. Amen.

May 8, 1995

Lord Jesus, do you want to write?

My beloved disciple of mercy, record my words of love.

My dear one, mankind has robbed dignity from the poor and from the weak. Creation, in your selfishness you have left no place for the poor and lowly. You have cast them from your sight to dwell in the streets. Yet I tell you, the beggar shall be brought to the bosom of the Most High God before the rich. Many of you shall lose all that you have and much more, for surely you have not placed the Kingdom of God first. I tell you solemnly, you must place others' needs before your own if you desire to be my disciple.

Generation, I have seen the hardness of your hearts. I have witnessed your malicious and repugnant lifestyles. I have watched in sorrow as you scorn and mock the poor and the homeless. Surely, I tell you, those who cause despair to the little ones of mine shall suffer eternal hellfire. Children, you must be merciful to those less fortunate. You must be compassionate to those who grieve.

Do you see, my children, how you have become a cold-hearted, uncaring people? There are few among you to represent me, the Lord God. There are few to walk in the light of my love and return glory to me. Again, dear children, I am calling for your conversion.

Be at peace, my little child of mercy. Thank you for writing. I bless you.

I love you forever, O Lord. Amen.

May 9, 1995

Lord Jesus, do you want to write?

Yes, dear child of my heart, let us begin.

As the seed of truth is planted in the hearts of those who call to me, then the flower of righteousness begins to grow. There is no seed that if planted by me, the Lord God, is unproductive. All the seeds planted by my Spirit of Love produce fruit, for the work of my hands is productive. The work of my hands is holy and life giving.

I am the Good Shepherd who has come to gather my flock from the four corners of the earth. From the north and from the south, from the east and from the west, my sheep shall come, for I, the Lord, have called them. My sheep know my voice and from the four corners they will come. Then shall their children and their children's children follow. For the seed I shall plant shall be from generation to generation. The seed that I, the Lord, Jesus Christ, shall plant is my mercy which shall endure despite your sinfulness. My mercy is everlasting to everlasting.

Again there are some of you to deny my mercy. Children, there shall be no shelter for you in the dark hours coming. There is no place to hide except in the depths of my mercy.

My child, I know you are weary. Rest, my beloved servant. I bless you.

Thank you, my blessed God. I love you forever. Amen.

May 10, 1995

Lord Jesus, do you want to write?

My beloved children, thank you for your sacrifice of love.

Why is it, my children, that I, the Lord, place so high a value on faith? Dear ones, faith is the building block of love and I am Love. Does a child not first have faith in his mother's response to his needs? Children, faith begets love and love begets more faith.

Daughter, I, the Lord, Jesus Christ, shall teach you a prayer. Wisdom is speaking. Listen to the words of the Spirit of Love:

> Father Eternal, Majesty Most High, I desire to love you with a
> pure love. Grant me the grace of faith that I may ponder your
> marvelous works. Father, I cannot approach you without

faith. I pray that despite my sinfulness, you will hide me under the umbrella of your love and let your lovely countenance shine upon me, and I shall bless your Holy Name forever and ever. Amen.

Daughter, those with faith will obtain all that they ask in my name.

Children, there are many among you who are lacking in faith and who are confused. Remember I am the One who sees into men's hearts. Be not afraid to approach me, my dear ones. I, the Lord, will always help you.

Thank you for writing, my dear child. We shall continue tomorrow.

My beloved children, come to me.[40] I am Jesus. I am grieving for my lost ones. I need your love, children, for I am sorrowful. Come to me, children, come to me. I bless you all, dear ones. Go in peace.

We bless you, too, O Lord. Amen.

May 11, 1995

Lord Jesus, do you want to write?

My little child of mercy, record my words so that all who read them will be consumed by my Spirit of Love. Listen carefully, my little one.

Time is running out, Generation. The chalices in heaven are filled with the wrath of my Heavenly Father and they are about to spill upon you. Dear ones, my mercy is upon you now. Do not procrastinate. There are many of you, children, to remain outside my heart of love and mercy. How shall you escape the just hand of the Eternal Father if you do not hide in my mercy? Where shall you flee, my dear ones?

Ah, my little ones, many of you are as those sitting in a small vessel as a tidal wave is approaching. You hear the news of the tidal wave, yet you do nothing

---

[40] The Lord is addressing the members of the prayer group who were present for this message.

to escape it. I, the Lord, am offering you a chance to escape the wrath of my Eternal Father and the abyss of hell. You must come to me and repent of your sins. You must convert from your evil ways, lest the tidal wave of the bottomless pit shall consume you. You will drown in the sea of iniquity forever. Children, wake up to my calls.

Continue, my beloved.

Dear ones, I have come so that you may live. I have come among you because I am the Divine Shelter of Mercy. I am the Heart of the Just and Seeker of the Unjust. Hear my words.

Thank you, child, for writing. I bless you and love you.

I bless you and love you, too, O Lord. Amen.

May 12, 1995

Daughter, I am here. I am Blessed Virgin Mary and the Mother of God.

My dear children, I am the Holy Mother of Grace and the Mother of the Divine One. It is because of his love for his children that I have been permitted to come to you in this way. I am appearing in other parts of the world. Although I have different titles, I remain the Mother of the Most High and your loving Mother.

Dearest children, I have come to you because you are divided. I have come to remind you that you are part of the Mystical Body of Jesus. You must unite, my children.

To you, my beloved daughter, our adversary is in your midst. He comes as the destroyer of families and the destroyer of all that is good. Cast him out, my child. Invoke the name of Jesus often and the evil one will flee. Oh, my dear one, heavy the cross upon your shoulders and____, but remember I am here to help you.[41] You must do all that my Son has asked of you. Obedience breeds humility.

---

[41] The Blessed Mother is referring to a dear friend who was present for this message.

Dearest children, I am praying for all of you. I am your Heavenly Mother and the Matriarch of Graces. Come to me, my dear ones. I will guide you to my Son.

Thank you, my little daughter, for writing. I bless you.

Lord?

Dear one, I am here. I am Jesus, the Light of Humanity. Dear one, do not weep. I will help you. I have come to extinguish the darkness and light the candles of my love in every heart. Do not despair. I will help you. I bless you and love you. Go in peace.

I bless you and love you, too, O Lord and Mother Mary. Amen.

May 13, 1995

Lord Jesus, do you want to write?

My dearest disciple, come and record my words of love.

I, the Lord Jesus Christ, have watched as so many of you have been led to the eternal slaughter house by satan. This is where the worm dies not. This is where there is no rest from the consuming fire. Children, do not make the fatal error to think that hell does not exist. It is a place of terror beyond comprehension, for there is total separation from me.

Dear ones, now is the time for conversion and reconciliation with me. I am Jesus. I am the Guardian of the Heart and Soul. Only I possess the soul with love. The evil one can never possess the soul. He can only torture it endlessly. The soul will always cry out for me, the Lord God.

Continue to write, my beloved daughter.

The day will come, Humanity, when the sun shall not rise on the unjust. Know, dear ones, only the righteous shall have light. The day will come when it shall not rain on the unjust. Only the righteous shall receive nourishment. Only the righteous shall receive my gift of salvation.

Again I ask you, children, which side of my mercy shall be your resting place?

Little one, that is all we shall write today. I bless you. Go in peace.

I bless you, too, and love you, Jesus. Amen.

May 14, 1995 - Mother's Day

Happy Mother's Day, Blessed Mother.

Lord Jesus, do you want to write?

My devoted disciple, come. Record my message of love.

Child, when one is lost in a forest, he will look at a compass or to the sun to find his direction. He will seek his way out of the forest. My children, you are all lost in the forest of satan and I, the Lord, am your only way to safety. There is no other way for any of you. You must come to me and repent of your sins.

Daughter, I am coming for the harvest. Many of you, my children, shall be left behind. Oh, my daughter, my children are precious gems to me, yet they do not desire me. I am abandoned and brokenhearted.

Lord, I love you so much. Don't worry, Lord, everything will be all right some day.

My little child, oh, that it would be so. But many shall choose the evil one over me. Many shall choose darkness over light. I, the Lord, shall not force any of my children. All of heaven is grieving, my dear child. My tears are as an incense and all of heaven resounds with my cries.

Time is running out, children. I, the Lord, have grown weary. I pursue humanity relentlessly, yet they hearken not to my calls. Again, dear ones, I am growing weary. What shall you do to console your God?

Thank you for writing, dear one. I bless you. Go in peace.

Thank you, Lord. I bless you, too. Amen.

May 15, 1995

Lord Jesus, do you want to write?

My dear one, come and receive my message of love.

Do not weary, my little daughter. I AM sustains you. I AM sustains all of humanity. I am gathering my sheep from the four corners of the earth. Dear one, I am forming an army of apostles. The apostles of divine mercy shall go out amongst the nations and bring glory to my name. My name is above all other names, dear one.

Listen carefully, my child. Be not distracted.

Dear one, I the Lord shall teach you a prayer. This prayer will heal the sick and anoint many with my love:

> Father Eternal, by the merits of your most obedient Son, our Lord Jesus Christ, we come before you sick and wounded by our sins. Heal us, O Lord, and take our iniquity from us by the passion of our most merciful Savior, Jesus Christ. Heal us of all our suffering both in body and soul, and fill our hearts with the fire of your love. O Holy Master, grant us new hearts. Mend our wounds. Transform us into your image, that by our healing we may bring glory and honor to your Holy Name. For all thy benefits we thank thee and bless thee forever.   Amen.

Dear one, I AM has sanctified this prayer which has been taught you by my heart of love. Remember always my merciful heart. Echo this prayer, dear ones, and many will be healed. Whoever recites this prayer will receive grace from me.

Thank you, dear child, for recording my words. Go in peace with my blessing.

Lord, I love you and bless you forever.

May 16, 1995

Lord Jesus, do you want to write?

My little child of mercy, rest in the shelter of my most Sacred and Merciful Heart. My dear child, write my words.

I am the Divine Healer and I have come among you to vaccinate mankind against the plague of sin. I have come to instill righteousness and holiness in all those who call upon me. I am the Lord, the God of Abraham, Isaac, and Jacob. I have witnessed the disintegration of value, the lack of piety in my most beloved souls, and the moral decay of the family. Generation, have you not witnessed these things as well? Why do you suppose these events occur?

Dear children, one cannot stray from my commandments without consequence. This consequence is chosen by you when you choose to dwell in darkness. The demons of the darkness cause disruption and malice. Children, I am calling you to return to the light of my love.

Oh, my daughter, how I weep for my Jerusalem. She is a city that is quarantined from my love for she is infected with sin. But I am the Divine Healer who from the depths of my most merciful heart has come to heal the sinner. Come to me, my children, and be cleansed from your immortal decay.

Do not be fooled by the evil one. He does not heal, rather he injects the soul with the poison and stench of immorality. I, the Lord, Jesus Christ, have come to heal humanity by my mercy.

Thank you, child, for writing. I bless you, daughter. Go in peace.

I bless you, too, O Lord. Amen.

May 17, 1995

Lord Jesus, do you want to write?

My dear child, allow me to use your hand as an instrument of love. Record my words.

So many of you believe that charity lies in your small contributions to others. Dear ones, permit me to instruct you on the virtue of generosity. Generosity of heart begins with love. Are you giving your love and time to others? Dear ones, generosity is not selfish. The heart that is generous does not give out of excess.

No, on the contrary, the heart that is generous gives more than it is capable of, always trusting me to replenish them.

Oh, dear children, learn from me. I am Jesus. I am the Light of Humanity. I am the Light of the Lost and the Resting Place of the Found.

What good is it to give when you do not miss what has been given? Share, children. Share all that has been given you; I, the Lord, will bless you abundantly. There is not one among you who has given and has not been blessed by me. Be generous with your love and with your possessions, as all things have been given you by me.

Remember I, the Lord, am the Giver of All Gifts. The generous heart is my resting place. Walk with me and reflect me. Do not worry of what you shall eat or what you shall wear or where you shall sleep for the Lord God of Abraham, Isaac, and Jacob shall always provide for your needs.

Thank you, my little one. Rest in my heart of love. I bless you.

I bless you and love you, too, O Lord. Amen.

May 18, 1995[42]

May 19, 1995

Lord Jesus, do you want to write?

Little disciple of mercy, record my words of love. Dear child, listen to the voice of the one who commands the winds and the seas. I AM is speaking. Wisdom is speaking.

My children, so many of you accept your daily tasks with anxiety. Why do you not call upon me? I, the Lord, will lift the burden and refresh you. I will come to you with my heart of love and my Spirit will dissolve your anxiety.

---

[42] I was ill this day and the Lord dispensed me from recording a message.

Dear children, accept your daily tasks with joy. Each task you accept for my sake is a small cross made from the wood of my cross. Join your suffering to mine. Join your sorrow to mine. Join your happiness and your heartache to mine. Share everything with me, my beloved children. I am your Heavenly Father who places your needs in my Holy and Sacred Heart. Children, make a prayer of your daily tasks and offer everything as reparation. If you offer everything to me, then we shall be one heart. Children, allow me to love you and to dwell within you.

Continue, my beloved child.

Children, each thing you do in my name is a step in holiness. Every task you accept with joy for my sake is a step closer to me. I am the Shepherd, children. You are either a sheep that walks with me, or one that roams and is always lost.

Thank you for writing, little one. Go in peace with my blessing and love.

I love you and bless you, too, O Lord. Amen.

May 20, 1995

Lord Jesus, do you want to write?

My little disciple of mercy, record my words of love.

My dear children, the heavens are preparing for my return and the return of the hand of justice. I am returning as the merciful Savior and the deliverer of justice. How can this be, you will ask? I tell you solemnly, for those who reject my mercy it would be better if they had never been born. But for those who hide in the shelter of my mercy, the just hand of God shall not touch them.

Those that approach my mercy will be offered new garments of righteousness and new hearts of flesh. Those who seek my mercy will be hidden in the depths of my most Sacred Heart and in the Immaculate Heart of my beloved Mother. Together we will bring you to the heavenly banquet. Humanity, the heart of my Mother is joined to mine. Our hearts are joined by my bitter passion and by the resurrection of the repentant sinner.

Children, all those who call upon my beloved Mother, your Mother, the Queen, will be led to me. Do not be afraid, my children. Nestle in the Queen's Immaculate Heart, and there shall you find the love of your most holy Mother. There shall you find my love.

Dear children, together with my beloved Mother, I am calling for the conversion of humanity. We are giving you our hearts of love.

Thank you for writing, child. I bless you and love you.

I bless you and love you, too, O Lord and Blessed Mother. Amen.

May 21, 1995

Lord Jesus, do you want to write?

My little one of mercy, come and record my words.

My child, weak are those who do not turn to me. There is no strength other than mine. There is no love other than mine. My precious ones, your delight in earthly things is short and passing. Unless you come to me, your search for lasting delight will be futile.

Daughter, let us continue.

All those who walk in darkness have the cancer of sin spreading through their soul. Do not be deceived by your outer appearance. Though beautiful or homely, all shall return to the dust from whence they came.

How many of you shall stand before me with confidence in your immortal destiny? I solemnly assure you that only those who hide in the abyss of my most merciful heart can approach the Eternal Father in confidence. For I, the Lord, am the shield and the hope to all those who seek refuge in my Sacred Heart. I, the Lord, am the life preserver to all those who are drowning in sin. I am the Way, the Truth, and the Life.

Children, each one of you will face me, whether you believe in me or not. Do you wish to stand in my judgment or in my mercy? Let all those who desire mercy, ask now. There is no time to procrastinate, children. This is the time of mercy. Listen to the clock ticking.[43] The time of mercy is passing many by. It is your choice, children.

Thank you for writing, my precious child. Go in peace.

I love you and bless you, Lord. Amen.

May 22, 1995

Lord Jesus, do you want to write?

My little disciple of mercy, record my words of love. I AM is speaking.

My dearest child, there are different kinds of suffering. There is the physical. There is the emotional. There is suffering caused by anxiety. Dear one, in each situation you must bring your suffering to the foot of the Cross. From the Cross I purchased your salvation and power over diseases.

My dear one, the greatest suffering is the sickness of the soul when the soul is separated from me. There is no greater suffering.

I, the Lord, endured many types of pain for your sake. But most of my suffering is caused by lukewarm souls. They are those souls who know me, yet reject me. These souls cause me the most grief. So many of you reject the cross and therefore reject me. You must embrace the cross, my precious ones. The cross is the way to me and the Eternal Father. The cross is given you by my Spirit of Love who sanctifies and purifies.

Oh, dear children, I, the Lord, am the Divine Sufferer and the Divine Healer. I am the King of Mercy and the Giver of Goodness. There is nothing, children, you can do apart from me. Remember, children, the way to me is the way of the

---

[43] There are times when the only quiet time I receive in order to take a message is late at night when the children and my husband have gone to bed. I was recording this message in the kitchen while I was waiting for something I was baking to be completed. The clock to which the Lord is referring, is the timer, which was ticking loudly and had just signaled, indicating my baking project was done.

cross.

I bless you, daughter. Thank you for writing.

I bless you, too, O Lord. Amen.

May 23, 1995

Lord Jesus, do you want to write?

My precious one, come and record my words of love.

My child, heaven is a place that the imagination of man cannot produce. It is a place created by Love and sustained by Love. I am the Eternal Love. I am the Heart of Heaven, my precious ones.

Do you think the stone or the sand knows me not? I solemnly assure you that all was created to give glory to my Holy Name both on earth and in heaven.

Daughter, if mankind refuses to acknowledge me, then the mountains and the oceans will cry out with acknowledgment. The fish of the sea and the birds of the air will cry out with acknowledgment. I am the Sustaining Force in All Creation. Mankind is not.

Continue to write, my little mercy.

From the innermost depths of the earth, of all that is seen and unseen, I am the Lord, the God of Hosts. I am organizing the heavenly host, my children, and the chariots of heaven shall come. The spears of justice shall pierce the hearts of the unrepentant as they are cast from my sight forever. Before this terrible hour, I, the Lord am offering you my love and mercy. Remember, your wealth and precious jewels are worthless in the face of divine judgment.

Reconcile with me, children. Repent of your sins and I, the Lord, shall heal you.

Daughter, my precious one, I have forgiven you. Go in peace.

I love you, Lord. Again, I'm sorry.[44] *Amen.*

May 24, 1995

My child, I am here. I am Blessed Virgin Mary and the Mother of God. Begin to write, my child.

Daughter, a glorious destiny is planned for all those who walk with Jesus and persevere in faith. God has planned a sacred and holy place for the saints. There are many of you, dear ones, who desire to be saints. In joy I am glad to help you. My Immaculate Heart will house you and keep you distanced from the snares of the malefactor. He shall be crushed, but sadly he shall take many poor souls with him.

Dear ones, the choice to return to God is the only choice, for in going with satan you will lose all your freedom. You will forfeit your eternal heaven and the love of God. Many of you proclaim there is no hell. You say that hell is upon the earth and heaven is upon the earth. This is false, my children. I have come as a messenger from heaven to warn you of satan's ways and deceptions. I have come as a holy candle to light the way for you to return to God. The Savior is waiting for all of you with open arms.

Children, I am pursuing you, for out of the depths of my most Immaculate Heart there burns my motherly love. I am your Mother, children. Love me and hold your hands out to me. I will take you, my beloved, to the heart of God. Oh, so great is my motherly love for all my children.

Thank you, my dear one, for writing. I bless you with love from my Immaculate Heart.

I love you, my most precious Mother Mary.

---

[44] I am expressing my sorrow for some recent sins I had committed. I get disgusted with myself because despite all the gifts the Lord has bestowed upon me, I am still a sinner. His mercy to a wretch like me constantly astounds me. Truly, his mercy is unfathomable. I sincerely wish all of humanity could understand his eagerness to forgive the contrite of heart.

Lord, do you want to write?

My dearest child, I bless you. We shall continue tomorrow. Remember my love. Remember my mercy. I bless you.

I bless you, too, Lord ,forever and ever. Amen.

May 25, 1995 - Feast of the Ascension of Our Lord

Lord Jesus, do you want to write?

My beloved disciple, record my words of love and truth.

Child, there are many fences around the hearts of men. Pride and arrogance are padlocks to the heart. Dear children, imagine a building with a complex security system. You should have to bypass many doors to enter into the building. Children, when I, the Lord, come knocking at the door of your heart, let me not find a security system to prevent me from entering. Cast aside the fences of arrogance and pride and put out the welcome mat of humility and repentance. Then shall I, the Lord God of Israel, come in and dwell within your heart. If your heart is cluttered with worldly distractions, then where is there room for me?

Children, I am a jealous God. I am possessive as I yearn for your love passionately. Children, are there stumbling blocks in your lives? Call upon me and I, the Lord, Jesus Christ, shall make a clear path for you. Together we shall discard the debris of sin and past afflictions, and I, the Lord, will create in you a new and gentle heart.

My little daughter, continue.

Children, your hearts are in heavy chains and I have come to set you free. I have come to unshackle you and refresh you. Take courage in me, my little children. I am the Lamb of Israel.

Dear one, thank you for writing. Go in peace, little mercy. We shall continue tomorrow.

I love you, dear sweet Lord and Blessed Mother. Amen.

May 26, 1995

Lord Jesus, do you want to write?

My dear little child, record my message of love. I AM is speaking through you.

Dear children, my heart is an island of love. Suppose you were on a boat which capsized. Such joy would you have to finally reach dry land and not drown. Dear ones, the dry land is my Sacred Heart and the Immaculate Heart of my Mother. The ocean is satan's playground of sin, and the boat capsizes from the heaviness of the sins.

When there is no reconciliation with me, the weight of the sin increases and you, my children, fall many times under the weight of your sins. It is satan who encourages you to continue in sin, but I, the Lord Jesus Christ, encourage you to be free of your sin. I encourage you to change the weight of sin upon your shoulders to the freedom of the cross. Those who carry the cross are always lifted up by me. Those who reconcile with me remain under my divine protection and have no reason to fear the adversary, for they are clothed in the armor of God. Only those who walk in the darkness need to fear the king of darkness, for he has made you his prisoners.

Call upon me and I shall set you free. I, the Lord, am the King of Light and Love and all those who walk with me need not be afraid. My divine army of angels is always guarding you.

Thank you, beloved of my heart, for writing. Go in the peace of my love. I bless you.

Lord, I love you and bless you, too. Amen.

May 27, 1995

Lord Jesus, do you want to write?

Child of my heart, record my words of love and hope. My dear one, do not despair. Come always to the foot of the Cross and allow Love to refresh you. Allow Holiness to rejuvenate you. I, the Lord, am Love.

I dwell among you, children, to call you to repentance and reconciliation. Oh, children, I am the Suffering One who is still nailed to the Cross each day.

Dear ones, how many of you go to different lengths to communicate with one another? There are telephones and all types of methods of relaying words and thoughts. But I, the Lord, solemnly assure you there is only one way to communicate with me. That is prayer, dear children.

The prayerful one is the one who has placed his life in my care. The prayerful one receives great blessings from me either because he asks or he trusts. Do you see dear ones? If you wish to communicate with me, then you must pray. Not all prayers come from the heart, my children, but I the Lord hear all petitions.

Always pray in accordance with the Holy Perfect Will of the Eternal Father, for his way is perfect. Children, the way of God is not the way of man. Do not deceive yourselves into believing you can predict what I will do. I, the Lord, am All Powerful and All Knowing. Do not try to comprehend me. Prayer requires the willingness to trust me and to wait for my answer. Each prayer is answered, my children. No prayer goes unanswered.

Child, thank you for writing, my precious one. Go in peace, daughter. I bless you.

I bless you and love you forever, Lord. Amen.

May 28, 1995

Lord Jesus, do you want to write?

My precious one, I am here. Record my words of love, child.

Dear children, I, the Lord, am preparing for the feast of deliverance. Yes, this shall be the day when the multitudes shall say, "Here I am, Lord." Oh, dear ones, I am coming soon and I hold the keys to the kingdom. How many will join me? How many will be a part of my feast of deliverance?

Children, I am the Bread of Life. I am the only nourishment of the living, for I am the Light of Humanity. My little sheep, I am calling you. Come across the valley and come to my holy mountain. There shall I, the God of Abraham, Isaac, and Jacob, be waiting for you. There shall I come to meet you in the sanctuary of the Holy One of Israel.

Understand, children, I, the Lord, shall come to meet you. I shall love you just as you are and where you are. My love shall warm your shattered lives. Oh, children, by your sins you have destroyed your lives and your homes. But the Lord God of Israel is a compassionate and loving Father. Come home to me, my prodigal children, and taste the goodness of your Savior.

I know you are weary, my little one. Allow my love to refresh you. Allow my love to guide you on the pathway to salvation. I am the Lamp Post in the Dark Night. Come, children, come.

I bless you, dear heart. Go in peace.

I bless you, too, O kind Lord. Amen.

May 29, 1995

Lord Jesus, do you want to write?

My beloved disciple, record my words of love.

My precious children, I am pleased with your sacrifice of love. My children, imagine the fireplace to be barren and with no coals. Children, the place to give off light and heat would be barren, for the main ingredients are missing.

Listen to my words, child. Wisdom is instructing you.

Dear ones, the fireplace in the home is the same as the heart of a person. Without the right ingredients, they will both be barren of warmth and light. Then, dear children, what purpose will they serve?

Daughter, my love is food for the heart and soul. Without my love the heart shall become hardened and eventually blackened by the decay of sin. Without my love the light of the soul shall not ignite, but the flames of evil shall blaze untamed.

Oh, children, I am Jesus. I am your Holy Teacher who has given you many examples of my love. My love is the brightness of the stars in the heavens. If I, the Lord, should remove the stars and the moon from the sky, then you would be in morbid darkness. But I assure you that without my love and warmth your souls are in morbid darkness as well, for they are as empty fireplaces.

My precious ones, I, the Lord, am carrying you up my holy mountain. I have given you all great tasks, but remember that I go before you always. Children, I am pleased with you. Continue in your efforts and great will be your rewards.

I bless you and love you all.

We bless you and love you, too. Amen.

May 30, 1995

Daughter, I am here. I am Blessed Virgin Mary and the Mother of God.

Children of my most Immaculate Heart, you must learn to live the way of the cross. Just as I stood beside my beloved Son, Jesus, as he walked to Calvary, I shall stand beside those who call on me. I am the Mother of Grace and the Mother of the Holy Church. My Son has planted many mystical seeds during each one of my appearances.

Children, we are calling you to carry your crosses in the army of the Holy One. There is none to escape the cross, children. But I have come to help you embrace the cross, therefore embracing God.

Children, the way of the cross is the way to holiness and purity of heart. The cross breeds humility and obedience. Gentleness and compassion are born in the hearts of those who embrace the cross. My children, virtue and modesty does not exist in your culture. There are very few to possess these great qualities and they are mocked by those who do not.

My little daughter, do not weary of carrying the cross for I am your holy helper. What mother would turn from her child when that child called to her?

No, my dear ones, I shall not forsake you. Be strong, my little sons and daughters, and persevere in your courageous efforts. I bless you and love you all.

I bless you and love you too, Mother Mary. Amen.

Lord, do you want to write?

My little one, we shall continue tomorrow. Go with my blessing. I love you.

I love you, too, Jesus and Blessed Mother. Amen.

May 31, 1995

Lord Jesus, do you want to write?

My gathering of sparrows, thank you for coming to my nest of love.[45]

Dear ones, in the house of my Eternal Father are many mansions. Yes, this is true, but children there shall only be one banquet. I, the Lord Jesus Christ, am calling for helpers to prepare for the banquet. Many of you, children, will be helpers but sadly some of you, children, are only visitors.

I don't understand, Jesus.

Dearest child, open your heart to receive my teaching. In simplicity I shall give the following example: many of you shall eat a meal but only a few of you shall prepare it. Dear ones, time is short. The clock is ticking away and there is no time to procrastinate. Even now, children, my angels are separating the wheat from the chaff.

I am calling all of you to be soldiers of mercy. Go out, children. Tell others of my mercy. Tell others that the Lord God of Abraham, Isaac, and Jacob has sent you. I look out from the cross and I see so many of you refusing my love and refusing my mercy. But, children, my love is so great that I come to you as a beggar, that you, children, would return to me.

---

[45] The Lord is referring to the small band of disciples who were present for this message.

My Cross, children, is made of many small crosses. These crosses I have given to each one of you that we may be of one heart and of one body. Children, come and help prepare the heavenly banquet with me. Those who know me are to reach out to those who do not.

Thank you, my beloved sparrows. Soar on the wings of my love and tell others of my infinite and tender mercy. I bless you all.

We bless you and love you, too, O Lord. Amen.

June 1, 1995

Lord Jesus, do you want to write?

I do, my little disciple. Come and record my words of love.

This is the month of the Sacred Heart and I, the Lord, Jesus Christ, am asking all of you to examine your hearts. It is time, dear ones, for you to put your affairs in order and clean house. Rid yourselves of sin and make a new beginning. My precious children, I, the Lord, am standing at the entrance to your heart. I am always knocking and pleading for your love. Ah, but your hearts are cluttered with material things and that is why you are so unhappy.

Dear ones, I am the Only True and Lasting Happiness. Dear child, when one begins the journey of the heart, then one begins the journey to me and with me. Together we will create a new heart. I say "together," my children, for I have given you free will. I will never force your love.

Let us continue, my dear one. The heart I wish to give you is a heart of love and a heart of compassion. Mercy will be as the blood to run through your heart and it will be spread to all those you come in contact with. Dear children, be not afraid to change. I, the Lord, will always help you, and remember only I am your Consolation and your Strength.

Thank you, dear child, for writing. Rest, my beloved child. I love you and bless you.

I love you and bless you, too, O Lord. Amen.

June 2, 1995

Lord Jesus, do you want to write?

My beloved daughter, record my words of love and reconciliation.

Dear ones, you live as though every window in your home is closed and sealed tight. Yes, it is true that cold air cannot enter but at the same time old stale air cannot leave. Learn from me. I am Jesus, the Lamb of Salvation. I AM is speaking. Wisdom is speaking and strengthening you. Children, what good is it to say, "Jesus, come into my heart" when you are unwilling to change? You must open all the windows, thereby making room for the new and clearing away the old.

I grant many gifts to those who have made room to receive them. You must discard your sin and immoral life styles. You must embrace the Church and the Sacraments. You must embrace humility, that you may fully desire reconciliation. So many of you call upon me only when you are in distress. You treat me as a stranger and an inconvenience.

Oh, children, the time is surely approaching when you shall beat your breasts and beg for my mercy. Though you have ears, Generation, you are deaf. Though you have eyes, Generation, you are blind. I am coming soon, children, to lift up all those who have been patiently waiting for me.
Child, thank you for writing my words. Be secure in my love, my little child. I will always help you. I bless you and love you.

I bless you and love you, too, O God. Amen.

June 3, 1995

Lord Jesus, do you want to write?

My little child, by recording my words you bring glory to my Holy Name. Be not afraid. I will help you. Listen carefully to my words.

Child, for one to glorify me they do not have to do something on a grand scale. They do not have to publicly display the gifts I have given them. No, on the contrary, <u>all</u> things done for me bring glory to my name. The soul that accepts in humility that I, the Lord, am his helper in all things brings glory to me.

Children, it is by your attitude of humility that you glorify me. Follow the examples of my saints. While it is true that some were well known, it is also true that others became saints in silence. Their focus was always on pleasing me and not glorifying themselves.

Oh, my beloved children, though you call yourselves sophisticated, you are truly in the dark ages. Do not become boastful with the gifts I have given you. Utilize these gifts to glorify me, and I will bless you abundantly. I am Jesus, the Resurrection and the Life. I am the Passionate One who is a prisoner of the heart that loves me. Do you see how in love I reveal myself? Yes, children, I am the prisoner of my love for all of you. Come to me, children. I am waiting for your love.

Thank you, child, for writing. I bless you, little one of my heart.

I love you and bless you, too, O Lord. Amen.

June 4, 1995 - Pentecost

Lord Jesus, do you want to write?

My beloved disciple, record the words of the Lord, the Holy Spirit.

My little beloved, why do you despair?[46]   I have given you children and a family to feed and nurture. How much more will I, the Lord, do for you? Be patient, my little mercy, for patience breeds a strong faith.

My beloved, I have come with many gifts for those who are willing to receive my gifts. Today I shall light the candle on the altar of each heart, so that those who love me may desire a stronger union with me. Those that do not know me shall be granted the choice.

---

[46] Due to the fact that I have never seemed to have regained my health since the pregnancy, as well as the stress of other personal situations, I found myself complaining to the Lord and feeling sorry for myself.

This is the feast of the explosion of my love for all creation. I cannot still the fire which consumes my heart. My heart is bursting with love for all of you, children. How can I quench my desires, but that you love me in return and allow me to rest in you?

Carry your crosses, my beloved, and join your suffering to my sorrowful, grieving heart. My love for sinners burns as a torch within me and I desire to share love with you. Oh, dear, consecrated children, I am calling you to spend a little time with me each day. If you desire to spend your eternity with me, then why will you not devote some time to me now? Do you think you shall come as a complete stranger into my Father's kingdom? No, my beloved. Those who desire the Kingdom of Heaven must come in through the door of my heart. I am the only way, beloved.

Child of my heart, I bless you. We shall continue tomorrow. Go in peace.

I love you and bless you, too, Jesus and Blessed Mother. Amen.

June 5, 1995

Lord Jesus, do you want to write?

My beloved disciple, record my words of love.

Child, when I, the Lord, created the earth, I separated man from the animals of the sea. I gave man authority over all things, but to my sorrow man has abused the gifts I have given him. He has made a mockery out of all life, including his own.

The fish are hidden by the powerful waters that conceal them. But is man hidden? No, child, for by the hardness of his heart man commits atrocities and then boasts. Man does not even desire to hide his behavior. There is no modesty or shame in this perverse generation.

Mankind, by my breath the oceans and the land shall be mingled, and they shall not be separate as the poison of your sin mingles with the blood of the unborn. I have warned you, children, yet you have not hearkened to my calls. The abortions must stop. The ocean of water shall become an ocean of blood and it shall spit forth all types of plagues upon the land.

You shall run, Mankind, but there are no hiding places from me, the Lord God, as there are no hiding places for the unborn at the cruel hands of their tormentors. Remember, my children, when the blood of the innocent infects you with my revenge, I, the Lord, shall not hear your cries. Stop the abominations and heed my warnings. My merciful heart is ready to forgive you, if you desire it.

Thank you, child. Rest in my Sacred Heart. I bless you.

I love you and bless you, too, Most Holy God. Amen.

June 6, 1995

Lord Jesus, do you want to write?

My little child of mercy, receive my words of love.

Ah, my precious one, I, the Lord, am your Fortress of Love. I am your Protector and your Inheritance. My beloved, tell others to come and drink from the infinite abyss of my mercy.

Come, children, to the Holy Fountain of Love and Life and drink. I offer my love freely. Children, I am Meek. I am Gentle and Compassionate. My heart is the Heart of the Lamb, who from the Cross saw you all in need of my tender mercy. From the Cross I saw your shortcomings and failures. From the Cross I saw your poverty of spirit and your hardness of heart, yet, dearest ones, I accepted this cruelty as a token of my infinite love for all of you.

Oh, my beloved children, so many of you inflict cruel punishments upon me each time you utter my name in vain. Each time you speak profanity my holy name is blasphemed. Children, I did not give you a voice and a tongue to utter vile and profane language. Think, my children. Be holy as I am holy. Discard your ways and accept mine. I, the Lord, have purchased new garments for each of you.

Dearest child, I know you are weary. We shall continue tomorrow. I bless you.

Thank you, my sweet, Lord, forever and ever. Amen.

June 7, 1995

Lord Jesus, do you want to write?

Child of my Sacred Heart, record my words of love.

Beloved of my heart, I hold in my hand the keys to eternity. Both to heaven and hell do I, the Lord, hold the keys. Ah, child, to enter into heaven one must enter into humility and be clothed in garments of righteousness. One must be made a new creature in my blood which is the Holy Precious Blood of Conversion.

Listen carefully, my beloved child. I know you are weary.

Bridges are built, my child, that you may cross the water in safety. You can cross the water without ever getting wet. Learn from me. I am Jesus, the Holy Teacher. My Precious Blood is the bridge to the soul. The soul is immersed in my blood and all sin is discarded. Do you see, my children? I separate you from your sin and my blood cleanses you.

Come to me, children, and I, the Lord, will clothe you in garments of righteousness. The old garments will I, the Lord, discard and I shall give you new garments made by the angels of heaven. Dear ones, many of you pack up old garments and discard them. This is what I shall do for those souls who call upon me to clothe them in holiness. I shall remember your old garments no longer. All shall be made new in my holy Sacred Heart.
Thank you for writing, child. I bless you. Go in peace, child of my heart.

Lord, I love you and bless you, too, Jesus. Amen.

June 8, 1995

Lord Jesus, do you want to write?

My beloved child of mercy, record my words of love and tenderness. Ah, my precious little sparrow, thank you for your sacrifice of love.

Children, I, the Lord, do not ask very much of you. I desire your time and attention each day for a short while. Am I not the giver of time? Am I not the eternal clock of love? But instead, my children, time has become my adversary.

Time has become my rival in a great sense. Generation, you have lost sight of me. You give me no time, but to sin and abomination you devote all your time. Soon, children, your concept of time shall vanish and this adversary of mine shall no longer exist in the way you are accustomed. You are running, running, running. To appointments and meetings and shopping do you go. Why do you not seek my companionship? I am the only friend and comfort of the soul. Children, am I not worthy of a little of your time?

I assure you that if you place me first, you will reach each destination in your life with joy and serenity. Travel in the light, children, and I, the Lord, will be your holy guide.

I bless you, child of my heart. Thank you for writing.

I bless you and love you, too, Jesus, my Lord. Amen.

June 9, 1995

Lord Jesus, do you want to write?

Yes, my beloved child. Come into my arms of love.

My beloved, my heart has been pierced by the sword of unfaithfulness. This sharp sword has pierced my sacred and grieving heart so many times. Oh, my beloved children, why do so many of you have so little compassion for me? Why do so many of you have hearts of stone?

Listen carefully to my words, little disciple. Each time I am pierced by your lack of love and lack of reverence, so is the Eternal Father pierced, so is the Holy Spirit pierced, for we are One. We are the Triune God of Love on whom you cast your curses and mockeries. Are you so insensitive, Generation, that you care not for the love of God?

It is true, my children, that you esteem men's praises more than mine. It is true, Generation, that you prefer your own house to my house. It is true, Generation, that you prefer the hiddenness of the darkness to the beauty and openness of the light. But I tell you, truly, there is nothing hidden from me, the Lord God. And truly I tell you, that all things shall be accomplished through me, and by me, and within me. I AM WHO AM.

My beloved child, I bless you and love you. Today you have brought me joy for you have surrendered your will and accepted mine.[47] I bless you, my dear one.

I love you forever, my precious God. Amen.

June 10, 1995

Lord Jesus, do you want to write?

My beloved servant, come record my words of love. Dear one, I AM is speaking.

My child, my words are as a cool breeze on a hot summer's day. My words are food for the hungry and light to the blind. My words are a comfort to the deaf and to all those who are oppressed. Children of my heart, I am Jesus, the Lamb. I am the Eternal Victim of Love. I am the Eternal Prisoner of the Heart.

Dear ones, how many times have you prepared a meal for a loved one, only to feel unappreciated? How many times have you prepared a meal for a loved one, only to be forsaken by that person? Understand how I, the Lord, have prepared a delightful and holy meal for you in the Eucharist. I am giving you myself - my Real Presence. I have instituted this meal for you at the Last Supper, but so many of you do not come. So many of you are unappreciative and irreverent when you come to receive me in Holy Communion.

Dear ones, I, the Lord, invite you all to partake of me in Holy Communion. I ask only that you be respectful and appreciative. This sacrament is life-giving, for you receive me and I am the Life.

Child, I bless you. Be patient. Go in the peace of my love.

I love and bless you, too, O Lord and Blessed Mother. Amen.

---

[47] I was nursing my baby at the time and was seriously entertaining the idea of totally switching her to formula because I was more concerned about my weight and wanted to switch to diet pills. I had asked the Lord about this idea and he responded, "I prefer that you not, rather allow the child to be continuously nursed." I complied with the Lord's wish.

June 11, 1995 - Trinity Sunday

Lord Jesus, do you want to write?

My dear little daughter, I have come to dictate my words of love and mercy.

Dear little daughter, the desire of one's heart should be union with me, the Creator. For I, the Lord, the God of Abraham, Isaac, and Jacob, have created all of you to bring glory to my name. In desiring union with me, one glorifies me with love. Love, children, is the perfume of heaven. It is the sweet fragrance of the angels, and of the saints, and of the holy and righteous. Love is in itself a brilliant garment of light for the soul whose heart rests in my heart. Love is the healing and growing force of all creation. Love sustains creation.

Children, I am God; I am Love. I am Eternal; I am Love. I am Sovereign and All Powerful; I am Love. The Holy and Blessed Trinity is Love, Undivided and Perfect.

Daughter, let us continue.

Creation, in itself is the most splendid offering of praise and glory. For who else but the Lord of Hosts could create a mighty and powerful ocean, and a tender and fragile bird?

I AM WHO AM, the Love God of his people, Israel, is offering all of you new garments of love.

Children, please accept my offer. I am Jesus, the Origin of Love.

Thank you for writing, child. Be at peace, my little mercy. I bless you.

I bless you and love you, too, Lord. Amen.

June 12, 1995

Lord Jesus, do you want to write?

My beloved child, record my words of love and hope.

My child, I watch as the earth revolves around the sun by my sustaining grace. But who is it, Generation, that created the sun? Who is it that placed the earth on her path about the sun?

I am Jesus, the Eternal God of Heaven and Earth. Do not accept the teachings of doctors and scientists who forsake me only to follow evolutionary doctrine. Do not accept the current "new age" philosophies. They are lies created by satan and in his self-destructive image. I, the Lord, am the Creator. I am the only One.

Children, your senses are dulled by your egoism and hard hearts. Do you think you are more powerful than me? Oh, foolish ones, the flames of my mercy are scorching you, yet you are ignoring me. Shall you be scorched by the flames of mercy or the flames of hell? Give up your ways and adopt mine.

Children, your paganistic philosophy is saturated with evil. You are trying to be me, to be God and you are not. You are not, nor ever will be the same as me. The poor which are socially unacceptable to most, are acceptable to me, the Lord God. Think, children, think. Place my kingdom and my will before any other.

Daughter, thank you for writing. I bless you and love you.

I love and bless you, too, Jesus. Amen.

June 13, 1995

My beloved, I am here. I am Blessed Virgin Mary and the Mother of God.

Dear child of my Immaculate Heart, I am your Holy Mother sent by God to speak to each heart. My child, my voice is a gentle whisper to the heart. I have come to help each one of my beloved children obtain their precious gift of salvation. I am the hand of love to the poor and the sick. I am the nurse of the soul and my divine Son, Jesus, is the healer. In every step you take, children, towards God, I am by your side encouraging you and interceding on your behalf. I am the advocate of the sinner and I offer each of you a tender caress of a mother.

Dear children, I am the Mother of All Humanity and in my heart there is a place for each of you. My love for you is infinite and through my motherly intercession I obtain all that you need from my beloved Son. Dear ones, in this day and age, you must learn to depend upon my help. I am leading you to the heart of God which is love and mercy. I am the tender companion to the soul.

Dearest child, thank you for writing my words.

Mama Mary, is that all?

Yes, beloved child, I bless you.

I bless you, too, my beautiful Mother. Lord, do you want to write?

No, my little child. Rest. We shall continue tomorrow. I bless you and love you.

I bless and love you, too, Lord, Holy Spirit, and Blessed Mother. Amen.

June 14, 1995

Lord Jesus, do you want to write?

My beloved children, your enthusiasm to do my work is refreshing. I welcome all of you into my heart of love.

My beloved child, I shall instruct you on the Holy Sacrament of Penance. Dear one, I, the Lord, have instituted this sacrament as an avenue of grace. I, who am Love, have provided you with a ship of hope in your ocean of despair.

Oh, precious children, how foolish you are at times. I, the Lord, wait to cover you in my mercy and compassion. Each time you approach me in this sacrament, I place a drop of my Holy Precious Blood upon your heart. Your sins are forgiven and forgotten. I remember them no longer.

Dear children, I watch as you try to dislodge yourselves from satan's web. You become his prey because he uses your sins to victimize you. Each time you reconcile with me in this sacrament, satan has less ammunition to threaten you.

Beloved children, my heart burns with mercy and love for the sinner. I wait for you, children, with wondrous gifts of love. Do not be afraid to approach me in this sacrament, but rather be wise and utilize the tools of grace I have provided for you.

Thank you, my dear disciples. Your efforts have pleased me. Continue on the path of holiness. I bless you all.

We bless you and love you, too, Lord. Amen.

June 15, 1995

Lord Jesus, do you want to write?

Child of my heart, receive my words of love and mercy.

Dear children, the fragrance of the heart that loves me is the fragrance of holiness. It is the fragrance of the desire of the soul to be one with me. Complete union with me occurs in heaven but I permit the soul to rest in me therefore preparing your final journey. Yes, children, the time to prepare for heaven is now on earth. There is no time to procrastinate.

My children, I, the Lord, am giving you the chance to prepare yourselves, for the great chastisement is soon to be. But you are as those in the days of Noah, you are as those who were warned of the flood but did not listen. You are as those who were invited into the ark to escape the flood, but continually mocked these warnings.

Children, I, the Lord, am again offering you a hiding place aboard the ark of my mercy. My mercy shall protect you in the coming days but alas, most of you still refuse my help. Children, your foolish arrogance has blinded you to the truth. Call upon my infinite mercy, my children.
Thank you, little one. Rest, my beloved child. Do not despair.

Thank you, my blessed and merciful God. Amen.

June 16, 1995

Lord Jesus, do you want to write?

My beloved child, record my words of love. Listen carefully to my words. I am the Lord, the Holy Spirit. I have come to illuminate mankind and to separate the wheat from the chaff.

Children, there shall be a tidal wave of mercy upon the earth. This great act of mercy will enable the soul to realize his state before me. The soul who is in darkness will be given the opportunity to come into the light.

My little child, do not despair. I will always help you. I am your Comfort and Consolation. The soul that comes from the darkness into my arms of love shall be cradled by me as a mother tenderly cradles her infant. I, the Lord Jesus, shall care for you as a newborn. I shall carry you until you are able to walk. Do you see, my precious ones, how patiently I, the Lord, wait for souls? Ah, beloved, there is a crib in my Sacred Heart for each tender soul. Come to me, children, and receive nourishment from my heart of love.

We shall continue tomorrow, my child. I love you and I bless you.

I love and bless you, too, Lord God. Amen.

June 17, 1995

Lord Jesus, do you want to write?

My beloved disciple, record the words of the One Who Is.

Oh, beloved one, I desire you to examine your faith. Faith is as a small seed planted by me during Baptism. Each cross you are given strengthens your faith and grants the grace of humility and perseverance.

My daughter, listen to the words of the Holy One of Israel. I AM WHO AM is speaking.

Dear child, as I, the Lord, Jesus Christ, speak to you, I am speaking to all my beloved children. I am the Giver of Faith. I am the Eternal Fountain of Love, and therefore, trust. Yes, my beloved, you cannot love without trusting. Recall my instruction to you. The infant learns to love his mother because he has trust. Where one has trust, the small seed of faith planted at Baptism can grow into a mighty tree. One who has faith produces by his faith the fruits of Christian life. One who has faith and trust in me, obtains all that he asks for in my name according to the delight of the Eternal Father.

Dear one, we shall continue tomorrow. Persevere, my little lamb. I am with you always.

Jesus, thank you for your patience and love. Amen.

June 18, 1995 - The Feast of Corpus Christi

Lord Jesus, do you want to write?

My beloved child, allow me to use your hand to record my words of love. Focus on me, little one. You are distracted.[48]

For one to become a saint, one must trust in my tender mercy and guidance. For those who possess this goal, I, the Lord, become their Holy Teacher and Guide. They become apprentices of my sorrowful passion and I, the Lord, Jesus Christ, personally instruct them in the different virtues required.

Beloved, the road to sainthood is not paved with gold, nor is there self-glory. However, there is a final reward, for I, Jesus, am the Reward and Consolation of the Soul. I am as the pot of gold at the end of the rainbow, yet I, the Lord, creator of the rainbow, shall uphold the journey of all those who hide in my merciful heart.

Children, desire to be saints. Pray for this great treasure chest of eternal gifts. Remember, I, the Lord, am the Eternal Gift-Giver and I desire to bestow great gifts on souls.

Oh, beloved of my heart, if only you could understand the depths of my merciful heart and how my heart burns to transform sinners into saints. Of yourselves, my children, you can do nothing. Call upon me and I, the Lord will help you.

My child, my beloved one, rest. Renew your strength. Partake of me in the Eucharist frequently, my little ones, that my life will grow in you.

---

[48] There was a lot of noise coming from the next room, which began to occupy my attention.

I bless you, child. Go in peace.

I bless you and love you forever, Lord. Amen.

June 19, 1995

Lord Jesus, do you want to write?

My beloved child, receive the words from my Sacred Heart of Love. Do not despair, little mercy of my heart. Remember, I am helping you to carry the cross.

Child, when one makes reparation to my Eternal Father, then a thorn is plucked from my brow and a rose is placed instead in my crown. I am asking for reparatory acts on behalf of those who do not pray. I am asking for reparation as a way to amend your lives and to make a sin offering on behalf of the non-believers. These poor souls grieve me so. They believe in a purely scientific and visual world, which cannot under any circumstances explain me or my creation. Many of you, children, are the jokers in a pack of cards. You go along with the ride but there is really no purpose or place for you.

My beloved ones, listen to my calls of love. Where I, the Lord Jesus, go, there is a place and purpose for all of you.

Children of my heart, to amend your lives means to change your lives and only the Spirit of Love can help you. Only the Lord God can help you. Bring to me all the darkness in your lives and I will illuminate you with my Holy Precious Blood.

Thank you for writing, my little heart beat. Go in the peace of my love. I bless you.

I bless you, too, O Lord. I love you, Mother Mary, forever. Amen.

June 20, 1995

Lord Jesus, do you want to write?

Child of my heart, come and record my words of love. Dear one, I AM is speaking. Let Wisdom instruct you.

My children, love is as a circle. Love begins with me, evolves in me, and has its completion in me. I am the Divine Origin and Sanctuary of Love. Love is not selfish, my children, nor is love demanding. Love is not critical but rather love is encouraging. Love is a salve to the wounded and hope for the hopeless.

Come, little one, let us continue. Oh, my precious one, when you plant a seed and then give it water, it is I, the Lord, who causes the seed to grow and blossom. Plant the seed of love in all those you encounter. Plant the seed of my presence in all those you encounter, and eventually, they shall come full circle into the light of my love.

Dear children, it is crucial that you pray for one another. Allow your love for me to radiate to others in your life that they will see me in you. As you pray for others, they shall be blessed and so shall you. Do not lose hope in any seed planted, for I, the Lord, am the Divine Gardener. Love will nourish and sustain the seeds planted by you. Love will consume all of humanity.

Child, I know it has been difficult for you. Persevere, my little lamb, and I, the Lord, will help you. I bless you, my child.

I bless you, too, O Lord. Thank you. I love you. Amen.

June 21, 1995

Lord Jesus, do you want to write?

My beloved disciple, record my words of love.

My beloved children, so many of you have low self-esteem and are disgusted with your lives. I tell you, my children, do not place an emphasis on your outer appearance. Dear ones, why do you lack dignity? Surely, it is because you value man's opinion and not mine. Surely, it is because you pursue earthly riches and not heavenly ones.

Children, I have created all of you in my image and therefore, I offer you dignity and self-respect. I love each of you to the depths you cannot comprehend, and I, the Lord, respect you. How therefore do you not have respect for yourselves or for one another? By whose standards do you assess another? With cluttered hearts how can you see clearly, my children?

Oh, my beloved children, if only you focused on me instead of worldly things, I, the Lord, Jesus Christ, would grant you all that you need. I am the Treasure Keeper of Dignity and Self-Respect. If I value you so, my dear ones, why do you have such disrespect for life? From the moment of conception a soul is given by me and consecrated to me. I AM breathes life into every creature. Do not destroy what I, the Lord, have created.

Daughter, my beloved, thank you for recording my words. I bless you.

I bless you, too, O Lord, my beloved, and Holy God and Father. Amen.

June 22, 1995

My child, I am here. I am Blessed Virgin Mary and the Mother of God. I am the Mother of Saints and Angels, and the Queen of Peace.

Children of my heart, you must include prayers for world peace each day. My little army of children, I know I have asked a great deal of you. All that you give shall be blessed and returned to you by my Beloved Son.

Dear children, God does not wish to take things away from you. On the contrary, God is asking for gifts of love. God is asking you to share with him and with one another.

My beloved children, so many of my little ones are hungry. They are lacking the necessities. Many of you have been blessed abundantly by my Son. It is so that you may share with the poor. It is not God's way that while one may have several pair of shoes, another will be barefoot. To those of you who have children, would you permit one to starve while another is overfed? I beseech you, my beloved children, to search your hearts and give, give, give! Give generously, that your Heavenly Father may return all that you have given and abundantly.

My beloved child, thank you for writing. I bless you and love you.

I love you, Mama Mary. Amen.

June 23, 1995

Lord Jesus, do you want to write?

Child of my heart, I am Jesus, the Eternal to Eternal, Heart of Love.

Do you see my merciful heart, my beloved? My heart is aflame with love for sinners. My heart cannot contain itself. I have infinite graces and love that I desire to bestow on each of you. Each soul that approaches my merciful heart is welcomed and adorned in my mercy. My mercy covers the sinner as a cloak.

Oh, beloved of my heart, your falls and imperfections glorify me. Accept your limitations, my child. I, the Lord, do not look for perfection in you. I accept you as you are with your blaring wretchedness. My mercy shall consume you and I, the Lord, shall make a brilliant diamond from the coal of your sins.

Do you see, my beloved, there is nothing I cannot do for the soul who trusts in my mercy?

Lord, you are so kind and good. Please hide me in your merciful heart.

Come, beloved child. My mercy shall consume you as a fire. Be merciful to others, my beloved. Learn from me.

We shall continue tomorrow. I bless you and love you, child.

I bless you and love you, too, Lord. Amen.

June 24, 1995

Lord Jesus, do you want to write?

My beloved child, do you see my patience and great love for you? Child, the purpose of each situation is to bring you closer to me. Yes, it is necessary to walk through the fire of purification each time, but know that I, the Lord, Jesus Christ, am always with you.

Child, each time you do something wrong, call upon me to counsel you. I am the Holy Spirit of Right Judgment and Counsel, and I, the Lord, will speak to your heart. If you desire the truth, then wisdom shall be granted you. Your heart shall be illuminated that you will know the very nature of your sin.

Many of you, in your feeble attempt to examine your lives, only see what you desire to see. But I solemnly assure you to grow in my light and love, you must grow in your knowledge of the truth. You must learn to see yourselves as I, the Lord, see you. Then, and only then, can you honestly confess your sins and be reconciled to me. How can you repent of a sin when you know not the full nature and effect of the sin? Call upon me. I am the Lord, the Spirit of Wisdom. I will teach you my ways and truth shall enclose your heart in the love of God.

I have forgiven you, my precious one. Seek my counsel often, child, and I, the Lord, will enlighten you. Many of you have eyes but truly you do not see. If you only see some things but see not what is important, then truly, you are blind. Call upon me and I, the Lord, will teach you to see.

Thank you, beloved child of my heart. Go in peace, my little mercy.

I love you so much, Lord. I bless you. Amen.

June 25, 1995

Lord Jesus, do you want to write?

My beloved child, rest in my Sacred Heart. When one falls under the weight of his sins, then he is forced into a decision. He will either call upon me to help him stand or he will submit. When I, Jesus, say, "submit," I am speaking of one's willingness to sin and to continue in sin. This generation is so blinded by pride and hardness of heart, that it no longer recognizes sin nor satan's infiltration.

I, the Lord, extend my hand to the sinners. I will help you to rise above sin. I will help you stand each time you fall. Remember how I, the Lord Jesus, fell beneath the weight of the Cross three times? In everything you do, children, remember, I, the Lord, go before you. I am the Way, the Truth, and the Life. I am the Risen Lord who has come to help sinners rise above their sins and into the light of my love.

Child, take hold of the hand of salvation. My hand is extended to each of you.

My blood was shed for each of you.

My beloved child, thank you for writing. Rest in my merciful heart. I love you and bless you.

I love you and bless you, too, O Lord. Amen.

June 26, 1995

Lord Jesus, do you want to write?

My beloved child of mercy, record my words of love. Be not discouraged, my little lamb, though your cross be heavy. I, the Lord, am helping you to carry the cross. Your cross, my beloved, is stained with my blood. The wood of the Cross breaks into small splinters to indicate the many beatings and bruises inflicted on my sacred flesh. Each time a splinter pierces your flesh, think of me being nailed to the Cross for you.

I am referring to all of you, my little children. Yes, I realize that all through your lives you receive small splinters from the wood of the cross. For never does the full weight of the cross rest upon your shoulder. Only I, the Lord, suffered that pain.

Dear ones, oh, see the mercy and compassion of God, your Savior. How each tear penetrates his Sacred Heart. How each hurt causes his wounds to bleed. Yes, Love bleeds for you. Love cries for you. Love desires to heal you. I am Love. I am Jesus, the Sovereign Lord of Love. I am the Creator, Redeemer, and Sanctifier. I AM. I AM. I AM.

Sweet child of my heart, persevere on the road to Calvary and I, the Lord, shall help you. I bless you, child of my heart. Go in the peace of my love.

I bless you and love you, too, O Lord. Amen.

June 27, 1995

Lord Jesus, do you want to write?

My little one, your faithfulness has pleased me. Do you think that because one is faithful, one is without sin? No, my child. Only I, the Lord, am without sin; only my beloved Mother is without sin.

Child of my heart, you must relinquish control of your life to my care. Do you see the areas of your life you withhold from me? I am grieving, child. Do not hold anything back from me. I am Jesus, the Divine Welder, and you, my little child, are the metal. Be pliable, my little lamb. Allow me to use you as I desire. But I solemnly assure you that I, Jesus, shall not forsake you.

Continue to write, beloved child.

You are my rebellious one, child, and yes, I do speak this term to many of you. Search your hearts, you know who you are. You are my precious Peter.[49] I extend my hand to you and as you are standing above the water, you fall from your lack of faith. Believe in my power totally, child, and you shall never fall. The temptations that cause you to fall into sin today, shall not move you when you trust me completely. Do you see how I am willing to rescue you each and every time you fall?

My beloved child, I am the Ship of Mercy, come to rescue the drowning victim. But sadly, many of you still refuse my help. I, the Lord, am the only help of the soul.

Thank you for writing, my beloved child. You shall see me very soon, child of my heart.

I love you, Jesus, my Savior. Amen.[50]

---

[49] The Lord is comparing me to the Apostle Peter who evidently was a bit strong headed and rebellious, which I am, too. In addition, despite so many of my experiences with the Lord, I, at times, like Peter, fail to place enough trust in him.

[50] At the termination of this message the Lord said in a wonderfully lighter tone, more in terms of a playful banter, that he was here in my room and my room was a mess! I should clean it up as well as his altar (a small table consisting of several statues, rosaries, and votive candles). Then he said quite seriously but very lovingly: "now do you see how intimately I wish to be

June 28, 1995

Lord Jesus, do you want to write?

My precious children, thank you for responding to my invitation of love.

Dear ones, why do you think I, the Lord, am asking for reparation? Do you think you can ever offer enough reparation to alleviate the sins of mankind? Only I, the Lord, can repair your broken aching lives. Only, I, the Lord, have made complete reparation for your sins.

Children, my wounds are aching for your love. Each time a child presents a drawing of love to his parent, that parent's wounds are caressed. Each time one of you says a kind word to another, love nourishes the soul. I am the Ultimate and Eternal Fountain of Love and each act of reparation is an act of love.

No, children, you can never completely atone for your sins for I, the Lord, have accepted this painful task. Be a witness of my love by offering my love to others, therefore returning love to Love. Love is a circle, my children, beginning with me and ending with me.

Children, reparation is the humble offering of love from the soul to his Creator therefore acknowledging the sovereignty of the Creator.

Children, again, I thank you for your sacrifice of love. Be blessed, my disciples of mercy. Go in peace.

Thank you, Lord. We love you and bless you too, Amen.

June 29, 1995

Lord Jesus, do you want to write?

My beloved disciple, record my words of love. I AM is speaking. Wisdom is speaking.

_____

involved in your lives? Tell others."

I am the Lord, the Holy Spirit. How many of you call upon me in your daily lives? Do you not know that I am one with the Son and one with the Father? I am God. I am the Third Person of the Blessed Trinity and I am God.

Dear ones, I am the Author of these messages. I am the Inspiration and Author of Scripture. No man can say the name of "Jesus" without my inspiration, for the name of "Jesus" is so holy that without my assistance man could not utter it. I am the one who is ever by your side when you call upon the name of the Lord.

Let us continue. Dear child, you are distracted.[51]

Oh, little mercy of my heart, I am the Lord, the Spirit of Love. I am the Heart of Heaven and the Heart of all Creation. Imagine me, my beloved one.[52]

Lord, what does this mean?

My heart is alive, beloved, and it beats with love and mercy. It bleeds for the sins of humanity. My blood continues to spill upon the earth. This is the era of cleansing of humanity, for this is the era of mercy from the Infinite Heart of Mercy.

Thank you for writing, my child. I love you and I bless you.

I love and bless you, too, Lord. Amen.

June 30, 1995

Lord Jesus, do you want to write?

My beloved disciple, record my words of love.

---

[51] The children in the next room were making a commotion which caused me to divert my attention.

[52] At the time of this statement, I imagined Jesus holding a bleeding heart in his hands, which were above the earth. Drops of blood were hitting the earth. I inquired further as to its meaning.

Children, I, the Lord, am again asking you to examine your lives.[53] Many graces have been given to all those who have asked. Sadly, my little ones, many do not believe they will receive when they ask. Many have no faith in my goodness and compassion. Is there one among you who is as good and as compassionate as I am? No, my beloved children. Yet when you are asked for something, you will give it if you are able. Then how much more shall I, Jesus, give to those who ask?

Listen to my words, beloved child. In each situation you encounter, I, the Lord, am the only answer. Remember, children, you can do nothing apart from me.

The month of the Sacred Heart is coming to a close and I, the Lord, am still waiting for most of you. I am a Prisoner of the Tabernacle because I am the Prisoner of Love Eternal. I am the Only Guardian of the Heart and the Soul. I am a Prisoner of the Blessed Sacrament because, I, Jesus, am a prisoner of my love for each of you. Open your hearts to the call of your Savior who has died so that you may live.

Thank you, daughter, for writing. I love you and I bless you.

I love and I bless you, too. Amen.

July 1, 1995

Let us begin, dear one.

I am Blessed Virgin Mary and the Mother of God. I come today with tidings of joy because of the inexhaustible mercy and goodness of God.

You, my dear children, are living in the era of mercy where the incomprehensible God of Hosts has illuminated this earth with his light and love. Never before has there been such an outpouring of Mercy's gifts. The Holy Spirit majestically spreads his wings of love and covers all of humanity in his caress. But humanity hides from God's mercy and does not recognize my beloved Son, Jesus, your Savior.

---

[53] The Lord in early June had requested that we examine the manner in which we are living and he is reminding us again. See message of June 1, 1995.

Dear children, I am your Holy Mother who is consumed with grief because of your rejection of God. There is only one way for there to be peace in your world and that is if the world returns to the merciful heart of God. If humanity does not heed my warnings to prayer, fasting, and reconciliation, this world shall be justly condemned by the one who has the authority to judge it. There is only one judge and he is sovereign, mighty, and eternal. He is the Lord, the King of kings, Emmanuel.

Come, my beloved children and I, your holy Mother, will escort you to the merciful depths of his tender heart.

I love you, child. Thank you for writing.

Thank you, Mama, I love you, too.

Lord?

I am here. We shall continue tomorrow. Go in peace with my blessing.

Lord, thank you for sending us your gracious Mother as a messenger for you and intercessor on our behalf. Amen.

July 2, 1995

Lord Jesus, do you want to write?

My little one, come and record my words of love.

Do not despair, little mercy of my heart. I AM WHO AM will always help you. When you fall under the weight of the cross, as you look up, there shall I, the Lord, be. I shall be looking at you with my hand extended to help you. Reach out to me, beloved children. You cannot stand alone. The weight of the cross is different for each of you, but my presence and my love is faithful. Come to me, children, when you are heavy laden. I will anoint you with love and Love will refresh you. Love will caress you and Love will strengthen you, for all those who truly partake of the cross are my followers. Many of you do not understand the way of suffering is the way of the cross. Children, your time on earth is short and many of you are asked to offer reparation for others. Many of you are asked for reparation for your own sins as well as your parents' and children's.

You must trust in me completely in any situation you face and I, the Lord, will always help you.

Thank you, child, for writing. I bless you and I love you.

I love you and bless you forever, my Lord and my God. Amen.

July 3, 1995

Lord Jesus, do you want to write?

Come, my beloved child, and record my words of love. Listen to my words.

Many of you go through your day without acknowledging me. It is I, the Lord, who has watched while your sleeping bodies rest, waiting and hoping you will call to me. Alas, it is not so. I, the Lord, am calling for my faithful servants to be more devoted to me. I, the Lord, am igniting the flame of passion in each of you, children, that you may choose the narrow path to heaven and not the wide path to perdition. There is no return from hell, my beloved children. The great abyss of light prevents it.

Ah, beloved, I have granted messages of mercy because of my tender love for each of you. So few have acknowledged me. So few have repented and asked my help. I, the Lord, Jesus Christ, have again manifested my love to you through my different prophets. Those who mock and scorn one of my prophets, truly does he mock and scorn me. I AM is speaking to all humanity through simple, humble servants. Who among you shall listen and heed my message? My love is extended to all of you.

Thank you for writing, my dear one. I bless you and love you.

Lord, I love and bless you, too. Amen.

July 4, 1995

Lord Jesus, do you want to write?

Yes, my little student, record my teaching.

Do you see, dear one, how I, the Lord, Jesus Christ, have referred to you as "student"? You are in my school of learning and I am your Holy Teacher. I AM is speaking. Let wisdom instruct you.

Each time I inspire your heart, wisdom grows within you. You grow in my light, for my truth grows within you. As long as you remain in my school, children, you shall gain a holy and righteous education. Become one of my beloved students and thereby receive dignity. Receive knowledge and wisdom. Receive peace, my peace. My peace cannot be obtained through material possessions, nor through people. It is a gift given to those who choose me and walk with me. It is a gift given to all those who desire to be taught by me, the Lord God.

Many of you are well educated according to your own standards. But I solemnly assure you that unless you are in my school, you have no wisdom. Wisdom is not granted those who do not partake of me. Knowledge is useless without wisdom, my children. Be wise of the things of God. Be repentant and humble. Call upon me and I will teach you.

Persevere, little one. I will help you. I bless you and love you.

Lord and Blessed Mother, I love you both, forever. Amen.

July 5, 1995

Lord Jesus, do you want to write?

My beloved disciple of mercy, receive my message of love. I AM is speaking. Patience and Compassion is speaking. I am the Lord, thy God, from Everlasting to Everlasting. I am the Master of the Humble and Contrite. I am the King of Mercy and Justice. I am God of the Just and the Unjust.

Listen carefully, little child, be not judgmental nor critical of others. Acknowledge your own faults before you acknowledge others. Be a friend and protector to your brother and neighbor, yet do not judge them. For who is able to determine the weight of one man's sin as opposed to another? "Only I am," says the Lord God of Hosts. Be ever gentle in your reprimand of your children and friends. Reflect me. I am Jesus and I am the Gentle and Compassionate One. Respond to every situation with love and patience. Respond to another's plight as you desire me to do. If you are not judgmental, you shall not be judged by my eternal Father.

Children, avoid situations that will plummet you into darkness and into the snares of evil. Pray, children, pray.

Dear one, we shall continue tomorrow. Go in peace.

I love you and bless you. Amen. Thank you, Lord.

July 6, 1995

Lord Jesus, do you want to write?

My child of mercy, renew your strength in my heart of love.

Dearest one, I, the Lord Jesus Christ, am the head of my Church. I am the High Priest who makes an offering of myself to the Eternal Father. I make this offering of both my humanity and divinity at the Holy Sacrifice of the Mass. I am the hidden one, my children, as I am concealed in the Holy Eucharist. Do you see how I, Jesus, love? I hide my glory from you that you will love me as an act of your will. I hide myself so that you, children, can choose to love me or not. I love each of you to depths you cannot comprehend.

Oh, children, so many of you come to the sanctuary as victims. I say "victims" because your pride and arrogance hold you hostage. Many of you refuse my sacraments and the graces they will afford you. Do not make the mistake to think I will not forgive you if you are sincere. Do not put a limit on my mercy and compassion. Yes, I am a just judge, but I, the Lord, am a Merciful and Compassionate Father.

When you partake of the Sacrament of Reconciliation, it is as if you were coming to a fountain of cool, refreshing water after thirsting. You will be fulfilled, for you will drink from the fountain of my mercy and thirst no longer.

Thank you, beloved child, for writing. Go in peace with my blessing.

I love you, Jesus, Holy Spirit, and Mama Mary. Amen.

July 7, 1995

Lord Jesus, do you want to write?

My beloved child, I AM is speaking. Love and Wisdom is speaking.

Children, I, the Lord, do not ask very much of you. Understand, my little ones, that what I ask of you, I have given you. I provide you with all that you have and therefore what I ask of you is already mine. Children, I desire time and your attention. I desire willingness and humility.

My beloved children, how many of you believe you are in relationships that are one-sided? Where one gives and one receives, there is an absence of love. Oh, children, hear the voice of your God. I am not some object of another world that you seek through a telescope. On the contrary, I, the Lord, am Love. I desire a loving and intimate relationship with each of you. All that I ask of you is time. Let your concept of time not be my adversary. If you give me a few moments each day, you will see "our" relationship grow. You will grow in me and I, the Lord, will grow in you. Our relationship will be one of sharing and mutual love. I will water the seeds of love I have planted in your hearts with my heart of love. You shall be fulfilled, my beloved. Come to me, children, and allow me to share in your lives.

Thank you, child of my Sacred Heart. I bless you.

I bless you and love you, too, forever. Amen.

July 8, 1995

Lord Jesus, do you want to write?

Come, my little lamb, and record my words of love.

Dear ones, discouragement is as a great tree that has fallen across a highway. After traveling at a certain speed for awhile, suddenly, the fallen tree blocks your way. I, the Lord Jesus Christ give this example to you in simplicity.

What are you to do? Oh, my beloved child, call upon me to help remove this obstacle from your path. Ask me to change your discouragement into encouragement. I stand waiting for all of you to come into my arms of love. Children, remember that all of your weaknesses are my strengths. I, the Lord, shall turn your shortcomings into virtues and your wickedness into self-examination. I, the Lord, will change any obstacle in your life into an improvement in strength and perseverance. All darkness shall be turned into light by me.

I am Jesus. I am the candle in the hearts of those who love me. I am the soul's only true and everlasting love. I am God.

Little one, this is all we shall write today. Go in the peace of my love. I bless you.

I bless you, too, O Lord. Amen.

July 9, 1995

Lord Jesus, do you want to write?

Little child of mercy, allow me to use your hand to record my message of love.[54]

Dearest children of my Sacred and Holy Heart, I, the Lord, am in your midst. I am the Guardian and Caretaker of Humanity and Love's Best Friend.

Children, I am calling for your love and loyalty. If your allegiance is not to me, then it is to satan. Children, if you desire your immortal home to be with satan, then continue as you are. Your current lifestyles will guarantee you an eternity in hell. If you desire your eternity to be heaven and endless bliss, then you must turn back to me. You must turn from your ways and accept mine.

Many of you say that I, Jesus, am repetitive. I solemnly assure you that my repetitive call to you is an act of love and mercy. But as many times as I humble myself to beg for your love, there will be those who forsake me. The time is soon approaching that every person on the face of the earth will have heard my

---

[54] The Lord is speaking metaphorically and not literally. He has never taken over my writing where the written page results in a handwriting that is completely different from my own.

call. I shall come as your King and your Savior, and I assure you I shall be a stranger to none.

Thank you, child of my heart, for writing. Go with my blessing. Be secure in my love.

I love you and bless you, too, forever. Amen.

July 10, 1995

Lord Jesus, do you want to write?

My little child of mercy, record my words of love.

Beloved children of mine, I am Jesus, I am the Gentle and Compassionate One Who Is. I am the Alpha and the Omega. I, the Lord, am calling you to be charitable. I am not only referring to financial charity. If that were so, then what chance would the poor have to achieve this virtue?

Children, love is not selfish. Love always places others' needs before your own. Love places no limitations on another's needs. Love never puts an end to helping another. Love endures.

Ah, beloved child, do you see my patience with you? I, the Lord, do not limit my generosity to you. I, the Lord, do not limit my availability to you.

Oh, foolish Generation, what building can stand if the foundation is not of concrete? Will it remain when the storms come? No, my beloved. Listen to my teaching. Let love for me be the basis of each relationship you have with others. Then, truly, you will shine with the light of my love.

Little one, thank you for writing. Go in peace. I bless you.

I bless you, too, O Lord, my God. Amen.

July 11, 1995

Lord Jesus, do you want to write?

My beloved child, record my words of love.

Dear child, do you see how my mercy consumes you? Do you see how I lift you up each time you fall? Dear one, you cannot comprehend me. Do not attempt to place your human limitations on me. I AM WHO AM.

Child of my heart, you must strive to grow in obedience. I, the Lord, honor obedience. Be ever on guard of satan's efforts to seduce you into disobedience of my will and my commandments. He will continuously try to confuse and disillusion you. He will cause you to believe you are without sin.

Children, the time has come when you must pray unceasingly to the Holy Spirit. If you do not, you will be stalked as a lion stalks his prey. And, my children, you will be caught. Yet it is by mercy and grace that I, Jesus, shall rescue you. Yes, my love for each of you is so strong that I wait and watch as a mother hen. My heart grieves each time one of you turns from me to find comfort somewhere else. Yet, children, unless you come to me, the comfort you have received is only temporary. I am the only Permanent Source of Love and Comfort.

My beloved, rest. I know you are weary. Remember always my great love for you. Be secure in my love, child. I will not forsake you.

Lord, I love you so much. I'm sorry for my sins. Please forgive me.

I forgive you, dear one. Be at peace.

July 12, 1995

Lord Jesus, do you want to write?

Little child of my heart, receive my message of love. Do you see my merciful way, little one?

Children, I watch as you suffer in sin. You cannot go against my commandments and not suffer. I, the Lord, have given you my laws to keep you free of mortal shackles and humiliations. But each time you are disobedient to my will, you become entangled in the net of sins. One sin leads to another, and to another, and soon, my precious children, you are as those drowning. It is as if the ship you are on is sinking and you cannot find a life-preserver.

Children of my heart, I am the only way for the soul to stay afloat. Yes, I am the harbor master and I, the Lord, am calling all of you to shore. Would you rather set your feet upon solid foundation or be drowning in an uncontrollable ocean?

Dear children, if you take an honest look at your lives, you will see how they are infested with sin. You will see yourselves in darkness. And yes, children, those who are in darkness have much to fear. When the waves of despair come up about them, they shall drown if they do not call to me.

Little one, we shall continue tomorrow. Be at peace. I forgive you.

I love you and bless you, Lord. Amen.

July 13, 1995

Child, I am here. I am the Blessed Virgin Mary and the Mother of God. I am the Queen of Angels and the Queen of Prophets.

Child of my Immaculate Heart, the shackles of suffering are about you. I know that it is difficult, my beloved, but please accept this that you may share in my Son's Cross. His Cross is a heavy humiliation upon the heart but share this with him, my beloved child, and you shall also share in his joy.

Children, my Son has called you to be his disciples.

Let us continue, dear child.[55]

When one is truly a disciple of my Son's, then the Eternal Father grants him a crown of thorns as well. God permits a share of the suffering as well as a share of the glory. Oh, children, become disciples of my Son. I am calling all of those who love God to make a stronger commitment to him.
I am your Holy Mother, beloved children, and I will always be beside you to help you. Do not fear the words of another man, rather seek God's approval. Do not judge those who judge you, my children. Leave that to your Heavenly Father

---

[55] I was interrupted during the message. I had to attend to it before resuming the message. The Blessed Mother is extremely patient and understanding with me.

who has the right to judge. Be not afraid to stand up in faith for my beloved Son, Jesus.

I bless you, child. Thank you for writing.

I bless you and love, too, Mama Mary.

Lord?

Rest, beloved, we shall continue tomorrow.

I bless you, too, O Lord. Amen.

July 14, 1995

Lord Jesus, do you want to write?

My beloved child, come into my arms and record my words of love. Daughter of my heart, I, the Lord, am teaching you to be as an infant in my arms. Yes, I, the Lord, am your nursemaid. Do you see, child, that I, the Lord, am your creator? I have brought you to my breasts that I may feed you the milk of righteousness. From my Sacred Heart I nurse you as my tender mercy consumes you. Lift up your eyes to me frequently, little one, as I yearn for your love.

Little child, some of your suffering is self-inflicted. I see you in your distress and anxiety hoping you will turn from that emptiness to me, the fullness of life. If you trusted me completely, there should be no reason for anxiety. It is a useless smokescreen and distraction to keep the soul from focusing on me completely. Ah, beloved of my heart, I am consumed with pity for you. You are the weakest of all my creatures and yet I am willing to cradle you at my breast. I desire to nourish you with love. Come to me, little children, I am Jesus, the one who loves you with an infinite and everlasting love.

Thank you, child, for writing. Go in peace.

Thank you, Lord, for your love. May I become a more trusting disciple. Amen.

July 15, 1996[56]

July 16, 1995

Lord Jesus, do you want to write?

My beloved disciple, thank you for your sacrifice of love. When a soul comes from the darkness into the light of my love, the heart becomes a sanctuary of praise. Even though you are unaware, the heart sings its melodious praise to me, the Lord God. For you see, my children, I cover the heart with my blood, thereby giving you a new heart. The new heart I, the Lord, give you beats with mine and together we become as one heart.

Children, come and give me your heart and I will give you my eternal heart. I will give you my eternal love. Ah, child, blessed are those who desire to love me. Blessed are those who desire to follow me. Blessed are those who trust in my tender mercy. Blessed are those who seek my counsel. Blessed are those who desire the truth. Blessed are those who strive for the Kingdom of Heaven.

Child, my heart is one of infinite love. It is a heart that you cannot comprehend. It is a heart that cries for my children's affection. My heart cannot be satisfied by a mere glance or an occasional prayer. My heart can only be satisfied by the fullness of your love.

Dearest child, thank you for writing. I love you and bless you.

I love you and bless you, too, Lord. Thank you for your patience. Amen.

July 17, 1995

Lord Jesus, do you want to write?

My devoted child, come and record my words of love. I AM is speaking. Wisdom is speaking.

---

[56] I was ill this day and the Lord dispensed me from receiving a message.

Mankind does not recognize the signs of the times. You continuously look for something to happen yet you do not recognize the events occurring each day.

Listen carefully, child. How is it, dear ones, that you know to put gasoline in your vehicle, as it cannot run without it? How is it that you know to eat and to drink, lest you will perish? How is it that you know to arrive at a certain time to begin your daily chores? Yet with all the things you do know, my beloved children, you are blind and deaf to reality. You do not see nor hear the truth of this day. The bells toll to announce the beginning of services, yet you continue to sleep on the outside steps. You are worse than those in a coma, for you have been given choices which you fail to realize. You are worse than those who are critically ill, yet mortally healthy, children.[57]

I, the Lord, do not abide by your concept of time. Time is my adversary, for you favor your self-centered time more than time spent with me. I am the Lord. I am the Eternal Clock of Love and Life. Come to me, children, if you desire life. Do not have other gods before me. I do not care for adversaries in the hearts that profess their love for me.

Thank you, beloved child. Go in peace with my blessing.

I love you and bless you, too, O Lord.

July 18, 1995

Lord Jesus, do you want to write?

Dear child, record my words of love. I AM is speaking. Listen to the words of the Holy One of Israel.

Generation, Generation, the war has begun to end all wars. This is the war that I, the King of all kings, has declared upon the kingdoms of darkness. This is the

---

[57] The Lord is speaking of our spiritual condition and the lax attitude mankind has developed regarding it. Despite the many overtures the Lord has made to us through his chosen prophets and visionaries of today, the world continues to ignore its diagnosis. We are in a stupor, and the prognosis is extremely dim unless we change our lifestyles and focus on him alone.

war that I, the General and Lamb of the Throne, shall claim the sweet victory. Yes, the fragrance of victory shall permeate the heavens as I, Jesus, return with my army of glory.

Continue, my little child. Persevere in your efforts to acquire heaven. Dear one, would you desire citizenship in a place you despise? This is where you are heading, my children. You are headed for eternal citizenship in hell, a place that will devour your skin and gnaw at your bones. Those who do not believe such a place exists are arrogant fools. Their pride and hardness of heart blinds them to the truth. Many of you are so arrogant that you refuse to believe in something unless you see it for yourself. You are incorrect to believe you have the ability to reason. For the Truth begs for your love and you reject the Truth - you reject me. I am the Truth.

Thank you, beloved child. Go in peace, little one of my heart. I bless you.

Thank you, Lord. I love you, too. Amen.

July 19, 1995

Lord Jesus, do you want to write?

My beloved disciple of mercy, thank you for your sacrifice of love and praise. Beloved disciples, today I, the Lord, am rejoicing for you have harkened to my call of love.

Dear children, so few respond to my invitation. So few desire heaven. So few desire love. Oh, how I grieve, my children. I, the Lord, shall ask all of my devoted children for an increase in your commitment to me. Please, my children, increase your prayers. Increase your efforts to serve me and I, Jesus, will help you. Increase your prayers for my lost children, for the day has come when there is an unending flow of souls into the depths of hell. Never has there been such a decay of morality and values. My commandments are ignored and ridiculed. My precepts are made a mockery. Children, you must desire holiness and righteousness. These virtues sanctify the soul with my perfume, and my incense consumes them. You must desire to change your ways and to accept my ways.

Yes, there is an unending flow of souls into the depths of the kingdom of darkness. Come to me, children. Desire the kingdom of holiness which is my kingdom, and I, the Lord, will clothe you in new garments. I will cover you with the perfume of sanctity and you shall dwell in the light of my love.

Thank you, dear children, for your devotion and love. I bless you all.

We love you forever, Lord, and bless you, too. Amen.

July 20, 1995

Lord Jesus, do you want to write?

My devoted child, record my words of love. I AM is speaking. Listen carefully to my words. From the Throne Room of the Lord God of Israel comes this message to his people.

Harken your ears to my calls and lift up your eyes toward heaven. The chariots of the Lamb are being assembled, the King of all kings leading his mighty army. This is an angelic army of majesty and glory. I, the Lord God, shall return in a bright flash of heavenly power and glory. The earth will tremble at my majesty and power. Every creature, of the land, of the air, and of the sea, shall observe my return in glory and they shall utter praises to the Lamb.

Dear children, I, Jesus, have been preparing you for my return. I have been preparing you through my prophets and visionaries. Those I have spoken my words to are as pinpoints of light in your dark humanity. They are to tell others and prepare the way of my return. Woe to those who mock the ones I have chosen to spread my messages for it is I who is mocked.

Dear child, we shall continue tomorrow. Thank you for recording my words of love. I bless you and love you.

I bless you and love you, too, O Lord. Amen

July 21, 1995

Lord Jesus, do you want to write?

My beloved child, record my message of mercy and love. I AM is speaking through you and using your hand as a vessel of grace.

Dear child, do you see my patient instruction to you? I stand at your side reinforcing my love and faithfulness. I place my mercy at your disposal each and every day. I guard you as you sleep hoping you will wake and call to me. Yes, I, Jesus, am the one who hides in the dark shadow of your room each night as you sleep. I, Jesus, am the one who paces with you each step you take. You are never out of my sight.

My precious, precious children, I, the Lord, am educating you by my messages of mercy. I am revealing my merciful way to you, that you may desire me. Oh, children, if you knew what awaits those who turn from me, you would be filled with grief and horror. Pray, my children, pray. Pray unceasingly for your lost brothers and sisters.

Those of you who claim to be my disciples, forget not your charity and generosity to the poor. Do not put a limit on the help you give others. Remember my generosity to you.

We shall continue tomorrow, my little sparrow. Go in peace. I bless you.

Thank you, Lord. I love you and bless you, too. Amen.

July 22, 1995

I am here, my child. I am Blessed Virgin Mary and the Mother of God.
Dearest children, my motherly heart is grieving for you. I am grieving those who are lost and who have not found their way back to the grace of God. Children, my Son's graces are available to all those who ask. This is the day of the greatest outpouring of God's mercy.[58] Why do you linger in the shadows of the evil one when God has his hands extended to all of you? My motherly heart longs to call your attention to reality.

Children, the truth is not the reality of scientists and doctors. On the contrary,

---

[58] The term "day" does not refer specifically to this day but rather to the fact that we are living in an era of great mercy.

the truth is not visible to man. The truth is God. God alone is the truth and reality of creation. If you do not believe this then you are without wisdom. You are without knowledge. What good is your knowledge of worldly things when you do not know God? God, who is Creator, sustains all life. You cannot produce life nor sustain life without the grace of God. There is absolutely nothing you could do without the grace of God.

Children, be still and listen to the calls of your Heavenly Mother who loves you to a degree you are incapable of understanding.

Thank you, my beloved child, for writing. I bless you always and love you.

I love you and bless you, too, Mama.

Do you want to write, Lord?

No, child. Meditate on the words of my Mother. We shall continue tomorrow. I bless you. Go in peace.

I bless you, too. Amen.

July 23, 1995

Lord Jesus, do you want to write?

My little child of mercy, do you see how my compassion consumes you and lifts you above your earthly mortality?

My beloved children, my compassion covers you, and in turn, I desire you to reach out to others. There are always those who are less fortunate then you. If you truly desire to be my disciple, then you must face each challenge in your life with full trust in me. There is no situation that is impossible for me. I am the Lord, the God of Abraham, Isaac, and Jacob.

Dear children, can you comprehend the vastness of the universe? Then why do you try to comprehend me, the Creator? I am more than the universe which you cannot comprehend. I am more than your eyes can see. I am the Creator of the visible as well as the invisible. Those who think they can comprehend me are consumed by their own ignorance. Their first name is ignorance as is their last name! Until they humble themselves before me they shall possess the name of ignorance.

Children, only I, the Lord, am the giver of wisdom to those who desire to know me. Wisdom does not come from a book or a newspaper. Wisdom and intelligence comes from heaven - from me. Do not be so foolish as to believe you possess these qualities without my help. **All goodness comes from me, the Lord God.**[59]

Child, remember my compassion. I will always help you. Go in peace, little one.

I love you, Lord. Give me the grace to be your true and faithful disciple. Amen.

July 24, 1995

Lord Jesus, do you want to write?

My beloved child, I have come to dictate my message of mercy. I, the Lord Jesus Christ, have instructed you to title these messages "The Heart of God." I have opened my heart of love and mercy on the Cross. I continue to open my heart in the Mass. The Eucharist is the Heart of God. The Eucharist is one and the same with my heart.

Children, every grace is poured forth on those who come to Mass. My heart envelops those as mercy and love consumes and heals the sinner. Take courage, all of you, in the Heart of God. My heart is the reason for your existence. My heart is the reason I, the Lord, have prepared a heaven for you. Each word that I, the Lord, speak is consumed with love and mercy. All those who have ears, listen to the voice of your God. When I speak, it is the Heart of the Most Holy and Blessed Trinity that is speaking. It is the voice of the Father, the voice of the Son, and the voice of the Holy Spirit. So infinite is my Sacred

---

[59] This sentence is highlighted in bold because of the manner of emphasis that was conveyed by the tone of the Lord's voice. Shortly after this comment, the Lord said, "You cannot go from the ground to the roof without a ladder. I am the ladder and every rung on the ladder is a step that you must call out to me as you take each step."

Heart that no man nor angel can comprehend it. The fires of my love and mercy burn eternally.

Child, thank you for writing and sacrificing this time for me. I will help you with everything, my child of mercy. Go in peace.

I love you forever, my God. Amen.

July 25, 1995

Lord Jesus, do you want to write?

My little child of mercy, I AM is speaking. Listen to the words of the Holy One of Israel.

Children, the earth has become a barren wasteland. It has become a garden of weeds where the very essence of goodness has been suffocated by sin. My children, the earth has the virus of sin consuming it. I, the Lord, am the only cure of the poisoning of humanity. Can you deny, my dear ones, the abominations of immorality that are a part of your everyday lives? Can you deny that your greed and pride has transformed you into a cannibalistic people? You devour the innocent to obtain more possessions.

Dear little one, let us continue. There is blood upon you, O Earth. The blood of the unborn covers you, and I, the Lord, have warned you repeatedly: stop the abortions! The choice of life or death is not up to you. It is my decision and mine alone. Thus says the Lord, the God of Israel, "I am watching you, Generation. There shall be a bloodbath upon the entire world if my warnings are not heeded."

I am weary, children. Return to the sacraments. Return to my commandments. Return to righteousness. Do not remain a part of the abominations lest you shall be crushed by them.

Thank you for writing, my beloved child. Rest in my love. I bless you.

I bless you and love you, too, O Lord. Amen.

July 26, 1995

Lord Jesus, do you want to write?

My beloved child, come and record my words of love. I am the Holy Spirit, the Lord. Hear my words.

My Jerusalem has become an abomination in my sight. You are infected with every type of deviant behavior and atrocity. Oh, Generation, so quick are you to pass harsh punishments on others. You do not recognize your own sinful behavior. There is not one among you to survive outside the merciful heart of God. There is not one among you that has not committed violent and harsh abominations in my sight. Oh, Generation, the day is soon to be upon you when you shall see yourselves through my eyes. Many of you will perish immediately as your fear of your own immorality and sinfulness consumes you. Those of you who continue to mock me will lie prostrate before me on that day.

Generation, you have canceled my commandments and instituted your own. I assure you that with each step you take away from me, you dig your immortal grave. Each day more and more souls are lost to the flaming pit, as those who remain make a joke of it. Ah, children, I assure you there shall be no laughing as you embrace your last day. Each of you will stand before me alone.

Thank you for writing, child. I bless you, my little daughter. Go in peace.

I bless you, too, Lord, forever. I love you. Amen.

July 27, 1995

Lord Jesus, do you want to write?

My child of mercy, let us begin.

Children, my mercy is greater than all the grains of sand in the universe. My heart burns eternally with the torch of mercy and love for each one of you. Oh, children, I, the Lord, desire you to know how infinitely precious you are to me. If there was only one among you to desire me, I should go to Calvary again. But alas, my death on the Cross is meaningless to most of you. My kingship and authority over all creation is meaningless to most of you. My heart grieves the most for those who know me yet reject me. Those who know me but cast me aside for material wealth are the ones that wound me the most.

Come and console me, children. Come to the tabernacle and spend time with your Savior. I spend eternity loving you and calling you. Children, you cannot imagine my grief over those souls who are eternally lost from me. Yes, I cradled you in my arms when you were infants. I watched you grow as my love sustained your way. But then when you were old enough to understand your choice, you chose to reject me. You chose to walk away from me and into the arms of satan. It is the king of darkness who holds you hostage.

My children, I desire all of you to know me. If you did, then surely you would love me as I am, the Origin and Fountain of Love.

Thank you, beloved child, for writing. I bless you and love you.

I bless you and love you, too, O Lord. Amen.

July 28, 1995

Lord Jesus, do you want to write?

My beloved child, my mercy consumes you. You are the most miserable and wretched of all creatures, yet my love for you sets my heart aflame.

My children, there is none among you who is free of sin. There is none among you who has not repeatedly yielded to temptation. Children, you are quick to judge another's weakness, yet you do not see your own. You are quick to criticize another when he falls, yet you fail to see your own falls.

Children, each time you fall I, the Lord, am waiting to gather you up into my arms. I shall lift you up and place your feet upon a new foundation. Each time you trust me in the face of temptation, you receive grace to overcome that temptation. Children, you cannot rise above your human weaknesses and frailties without my help. I am the one who strengthens and makes able the weak. Remember, I am the helper of the weak and the physician to the sick. I am the Lord, the one who is all powerful and everlasting.

Dear children, I, the Lord, do not expect more than you are capable of. Reflect this to others, my little ones, and you shall instill dignity and self-respect in those around you. Is there one among you who has the right to criticize another? Learn, my children. Learn from me. I am Jesus. I am the one who judges with mercy and compassion. You, children, do not possess these attributes and have no right to be critical.

Thank you, child of my heart, for writing. Persevere, my little one. I will always help you.

I love you, Lord, forever. Amen.

July 29, 1995

Lord Jesus, do you want to write?

My beloved child, come into my arms and receive my strength. Receive courage.

Dearest child, many times much courage is required in order for one to surrender to my will. It is not always easy to bypass your ways and accept mine. However, when a soul desires union with me, he is given the courage and strength by me to accomplish this. At times it is difficult to live in the world yet not be a part of the world.

Children, I am a Compassionate God and a Tender and Loving Father. I see you as you are. I, the Lord, am the only one who knows your true potential. When you learn to accept your human weaknesses and trust me completely, you shall soar as an eagle. You shall soar above human bondage, for you shall soar with the Spirit of Freedom and Faith. Do not put your faith in people or in possessions. These things are fragile and weak. They are limited by their own weaknesses.

Children, listen to my teaching. I am Jesus. I am one with the Father. I am one with the Spirit. I am God and I am Holy. Place your trust and faith in me alone. Seek my counsel first in any situation. I will always guide and protect those who call upon my name.

Thank you, child, for writing. We shall continue tomorrow. I bless you.

I bless you and praise you, O Lord, forever and ever. Amen.

July 30, 1995

Lord Jesus, do you want to write?

Come, my little child, record my words of love.

Children, the turmoil that exists in your lives is a direct result of your distance from me. I am the Lord God. I am the Forgotten One, the one who died so that you may live. I, Jesus, assure you that my wounds are still bleeding. My blood will mingle with all the seas of the earth. Remember, children, when the floods come and the rains hold you captive, my blood will cover you as well. My blood is spilling upon the earth to heal the sinner and to restore holiness to the unholy. Many of you shall run from my attempts to call you, but only the putrid grounds of hell await you. Come to me, children. Allow my blood to cleanse you and restore you to righteousness and virtue.

Beloved child, grave times are surrounding mankind. Catastrophes shall come from the East and West, North and South. These catastrophes shall come as I lower my arm of chastisement upon you. Thus says the Lord, the God of His People Israel, "I shall unleash the oceans from their mighty captivity; the waters will come and your false idols and technologies shall be washed away." Yes, I, the Lord, shall show you the uselessness of your false idols, for they shall not protect you when you cry to them. They shall not hear you. Unless you repent before me, I shall not hear you either.

O Lord, please be merciful.

Have I not offered my mercy? I am rejected. Therefore, so is my mercy rejected. Open your ears to my call, Generation.

Thank you, child, for writing. Go in peace, child.

I love and bless you, too, Lord. Amen.

July 31, 1995

Daughter, I am here, I am the Blessed Virgin Mary and the Mother of God. I have come as a messenger of the Most High to deliver words of mercy.

Dearest children, the day of mercy is upon you, but soon it shall pass away. Then the day of judgment shall come. Many of you, beloved children, are unprepared. You have not reconciled with God nor have you ever made the attempt to convert.

Children, these warnings are messages of mercy. You have been given a time of grace by the Eternal Father. Those who continue to ignore the heavenly warnings have made a mockery of the most Sacred and Blessed Trinity. You cannot mock God and live in the grace of God.

Children, when a substance burns, it becomes ashes. It is then no longer existent. This is what shall become of those who continue to scourge and betray my Son. Their sins shall burn them and they shall become as ashes while they stray from the grace of God.

Why do you not listen, my children? Your earthly pleasures have cast illusions all about you. Your hearts have become as coal. They are black and twisted, for you no longer desire the love of God. The catastrophes are coming, my little ones. Come and give me your heart and hand. I, your Heavenly Mother, will lead you back to God. Do not delay. Pray for God's mercy constantly. Pray, pray, pray.

Thank you, child of my heart. I bless you.

I bless you forever, Mama Mary.

Lord?

We shall continue tomorrow, dearest. Go in peace.

I love you, Lord. Amen.

August 1, 1995

Lord Jesus, do you want to write?

My little child, come into my arms and receive strength. Receive courage.

Each of you, my children, is weak and frail. You are as delicate flowers in the midst of a storm. The storm I, the Lord, am referring to, is satan. He attacks you by tempting you in your weakness. He uses your loves to weaken you and then he eagerly overtakes you. In essence you are held hostage by your temptations. You become the victim of your lusts and pleasures, instead of becoming the master of your desires.

Oh, how weak is the flesh and how easily the flesh yields to temptation. To overcome your weaknesses, you must desire to do my will at all times. No matter the cost to your earthly body, you must desire to do my will first. Then, and only then, will you be able to overcome your temptations, and the evil one shall no longer be able to dull your senses with material possessions. Yes, cravings for various things can be put to rest, but only by grace received from me.

How do you obtain strength, my children? Prayer and faith are the means by which the soul flourishes and receives strength to overcome the temptations of the flesh. You must persevere in your prayers, my children. Do not give up if the answer you are seeking does not immediately come. All prayers are answered according to the Holy Perfect Will of the Eternal Father.

Continue in your efforts, my child. Thank you for writing, child. I bless you.

I bless you and love you forever, O Lord. Amen.

August 2, 1995

Lord Jesus, do you want to write?
Yes, little mercy of my heart. Record my words of love and hope.

Dearest children, do not permit the evil one to lure you into a false security. Do not call yourselves humble or righteous. Only I, the Lord, am the one to judge. Do you see, my beloved, that you can be lost from me by your claims to holiness?

Oh, how my adversary stalks those who pray and fast, especially the ones who do so in the public eye. Satan will cause you to have pride about your spiritual condition and it is here that you are in the greatest danger. To be truly humble you must seek my approval at all times, never once trying to impress another. Do not care whether you are called holy by others. This can also become a great trap of the malefactor.

Be always on guard of your ego. The danger comes when one feels he has no ego or pride, then truly he has been baited by satan and has been caught. Be quiet in your opinion of yourself and of another. Bring your self-examination to me and I, the Lord, will guide you.

It is in your confusion and pride that you are so easily caught. Be covered with grace at all times. Let the grace you receive at reconciliation cover you with wisdom and discernment. Be on guard. Be on guard. Be on guard.

Thank you, beloved child, for writing. Go in peace, little one of my heart.

I love you and bless you, too, Jesus. Amen.

August 3, 1995

Lord Jesus, do you want to write?

Little child of my heart, record my words of love. I AM is speaking!

Dear children, there are many obstacles on the pathway to holiness, but I, the Lord, will help you overcome these obstacles. Though they be obstacles, they are in reality anchors for you to hold on to. Children, along the path to me are trials and tribulations, yet I have provided a way for you to endure. I have provided you a stopping place along your life-long journey. While you stop to live this tribulation, your soul grows closer to me. It is however your choice, children, to acknowledge your soul's closeness with me or to deny it. When you close your heart to me then you are choosing to withhold your soul from my loving embrace. But those who open their hearts to my love shall be consumed by my tenderness and compassion. I shall dwell in your heart and you shall dwell in mine.

Each one of you has been given free will by the Eternal Father. In this way you have the choice to love your God or not. You have the choice to choose goodness and reject evil. You have the choice to follow the commandments or follow the false ideologies of the evil one. Choose wisely, my beloved children.

Thank you, daughter, for writing. I know you are weary. I love you.

I love you, too, Lord. Thank you for your patience! Amen.

August 4, 1995

Lord Jesus, do you want to write?

My little disciple, come and record my words of love which are life. My adversary is stalking you, beloved. He stalks the rays of light upon this dark earth. Have no fear, little ones, for I am always by your side. I am the Eternal to Eternal Mind and Heart. Remember, children, there are no secrets hidden from me, the Lord God.

Let us continue, little child.

All things of value are put into the eternal fire by the Eternal Father. Yes, all things of value are repeatedly fire-tried. Their perseverance is pleasing to the heavenlies. My children, try to persevere through each and every trial. In every situation you are to keep your eyes on me. Though you be suffering, remember that I, Jesus, have gone before you in all suffering. I, Jesus, stand by you as your understanding friend and father. Tell me, children, can you honestly say that you have a more loyal and devoted friend? How can you? I am God and I am Love. I am he who holds my hands out to all my children. I have not come to call the righteous. On the contrary, I have come to call the sinners, the ones who are weak and confused. I am standing at the intersection of the road to eternity. You must choose to stay to the right with me or choose the side of hell. I will not force you.

Than you, daughter, for writing. Go in peace.

I love you and I bless you, Lord, Amen.

August 5, 1995

Lord Jesus, do you want to write?

My beloved child, open your heart to hear my words. Be on guard, my little ones. Be on guard. You are stalked by the predators of the soul. They play upon your weaknesses and insecurities. When they see a drowning victim, they will not offer a life preserver, on the contrary, they will swim to that person offering consolation and safety, and then they shall have captured you. Your head is held underwater by the king of perdition. For you there are no more choices, he has always been waiting for you.

I, Jesus, wait for you, too, my little ones. I am the life preserver to all those who are drowning in satan's ocean of deception. The evil one leads you to believe you may place your feet upon a solid foundation each time you desire. Yet, sadly, at the last moment you realize that was all a lie of the evil one, and you drown in his ocean of lies.

Walk with me, children, and no matter where you walk, I will be with you. Though you be stalked as prey by satan's demons, they shall not trap you, for I, the Lord, go before you always. There is no secret and dark hiding place from me, the Lord God. If you are mine, then I will always find you.

Thank you, little mercy of my heart. Go in the peace of my love. I bless you.

I bless you and love you, too, O Lord. Amen.

August 6, 1995

Lord Jesus, do you want to write?

My little disciple of mercy, come and record my words. My beloved one, I shall teach you a prayer of gratitude, which is praise. When the soul acknowledges its inability to function without my help, then the soul offers gratitude to me, the Lord God. Listen carefully, child, say:

> Gracious God, humble and generous in thy affections, compassionate and loving in thy responses, consumed with love and mercy for the wretched, I come to offer you nothing but praise. I come acknowledging you as Lord and God. I come seeking your counsel and wisdom. But most of all, my gracious God, I come to adore you and praise your Holy Name. May the name of the Lord be blessed and adored, forever and ever. Amen.

My beloved one, gratitude comes when one truly accepts his lowliness and insignificance. Will the world cease to exist without your presence? Will there be a collapse of life without your presence? Understand, dear children, that your very lives are gifts from me, the Gift-Giver. I will you into existence, and I, the Lord, breathe life into you each day. There is nothing you could do apart from me. Learn to be grateful, my children. Gratitude is praise, my beloved ones.

Thank you, for writing, my dear one. I will always help you. I bless you and love you.

I bless you and love you, too, O my God. Thank you. Amen.

August 7, 1995 [60]

August 8, 1995

Lord Jesus, do you want to write?

My beloved child, come and record my words of love.

My beloved children, in each situation you encounter, I am present. But as I, the Lord, am present, so then does the evil one try to distract you and loose your focus from me. Children, how easily you are distracted by earthly pleasures. How easily your focus is turned from holy to unholy. You truly do not realize the closeness of my adversary at all times. I, the Lord, have given you many tools to help you on your journey to me, which is a journey in the light. I, the Lord, shall give you an example in simplicity.

Imagine leaving an infant alone on a bed. Soon he will begin to roll until he at last is one step away from the edge. Ah, but this infant is unaware of his proximity to doom. It is here that the parent will once again place the infant in the center of the bed. You, children, are as infants. With each step you take, I, the Lord, watch over and guide you. When you come to the "edge" in your lives, I gently prod you in the hope you will accept my assistance, for I have

---

[60] I was in the hospital for tests and the Lord had dispensed me from receiving a message this day.

given you free will as an act of love and compassion. Many of you refuse my guiding hand, and yes, you will fall. Children, call upon me and accept the help I freely give in love.

Thank you, beloved daughter, for writing. I love you and bless you.

I love you and bless you, too, O Lord my God, forever, Amen.

August 9, 1995

Lord Jesus, do you want to write?

My beloved one, record my words of love. Dear one, Wisdom is speaking. I am Jehovah. I AM is speaking.

My children, there are many entrances into a building. There are many ways to reach the same destination, but I solemnly assure you there is only one way to the Kingdom of Heaven. There is only one door. I, Jesus am the Door to the Eternal Heaven. I am the Only Way. Many of you do not accept this teaching. Woe to you, children, for on that day, the day that each one of you will encounter, you will see that I, Jesus, am Master and Lord. I am the one you have mocked, despised, and crucified. I am He who mourns day and night in every tabernacle. I am He who is the Eternal Prisoner of my love for you, and yes, children, you will all see me. You will all know the truth, for I am the Truth.

My little children, to those who are faithful, you know me for you are mine. To my faithful ones, I, the Lord, am strengthening you and preparing you for battle. The battle for souls is intense, but I, the Lord, shall be victorious. Oh, foolish children, search your hearts and listen! I am He who is the Gentle Voice of the Heart. I am the Eternal to Eternal Voice.

We shall continue tomorrow, my beloved child. Rest, little mercy of my heart. I bless you.

I bless you, too, O Lord. I love you, Lord. Amen.

August 10, 1995

Lord Jesus, do you want to write?

My beloved child of mercy, I have been waiting for you. Record my words of love.

Precious children, for each one of you, I, the Lord Jesus Christ, have offered my life on the Cross. I saw each one of you then as I do now. I was infinitely in love with you then as I am now. Children, my love is eternal. My love is faithful and spans the generations. I am the Alpha and the Omega; the Beginning and the End.

Children, do not equate my power to your own lives. You only see a glimpse of my power in your lives. I am the Lord God. You cannot comprehend me. I am the Infinite Source and Revelation of Love.

Ah, beloved, the Eucharist is truly my heart of love. I am the Prisoner of Love in the tabernacle, and then I am the Prisoner of Love in the Holy Eucharist. The Eucharist is one and the same with the Holy Trinity as I am one and the same with the Holy Trinity. Come and allow me to nourish and refresh you. Partake of me with reverence and compassion.

So many of you come to Mass only to mock me. I tell you, children, I, the Lord, am the High Priest at Mass. Reflect on my presence at each Mass and be reverent. Be respectful. It is upon the Lord, your God, whom your gaze rests. I am he who stands at the altar.

Come, children, and give me your hearts. I have given you mine.

Thank you, dearest child, for recording my words. I bless you, little one.

Lord, I bless you, too, my God. Amen.

August 11, 1995

Lord Jesus, do you want to write?

My beloved one, come into my merciful heart. I AM is speaking. Wisdom is speaking.

Let us continue, my beloved child. My love for sinners is so consuming that my mercy covers them as a flood. Come children, call upon me and live in my mercy. Children, it is my mercy that quenches the soul's desire to cast away sin. It is my mercy that cradles the newborn in faith in my arms of love. Oh, children, in every step you take, I, the Lord Jesus Christ, am present. I am either encouraging you or discouraging you. However, unless you ask me to leave, I faithfully remain by your side.

Ah yes, though my heart is consumed with love for sinners, many ask me to leave. Truly, the heavens are shaken each time a precious soul is lost. Children, realize that I, the Lord, adore you and have lifted you above all of my earthly creatures.[61] I have given you both a heart and a soul. I have poured my gifts upon you. I am waiting to lavish even more gifts upon you. Children, open your hearts to receive my gifts. Are my gifts not priceless treasures of love? There is no other heart as loving and merciful as mine. You shall not find comfort and love in the world. I am the only true and lasting source of comfort in the world.

Rest now, my devoted child. I know you are weary. I bless you and love you.

I bless you and love you, too, Lord Jesus, forever. Amen.

August 12, 1995

Lord Jesus, do you want to write?

My beloved child, let us begin.

I AM is speaking. I am the Lord thy God, from Everlasting to Everlasting. Listen

---

[61] I had asked the Lord about the meaning of the word "adore" for surely he doesn't mean to imply that the Almighty God bows down to us. The Lord said that the term is used in a very limited way, not in the sense that I interpreted it nor is man to be "glorified," for all glory is reserved to the Lord. Nevertheless, the Lord is saying that his love for humankind is so overwhelming that he has adorned each of us with faculties and gifts above all other creatures so we might freely reciprocate our love for him. Sadly, we endowed beings, who are so lovingly admired, fail to acknowledge even the existence of our Creator, Gift-Giver, and Source of Love and Happiness itself.

to my words.

The heart, my children, is as a vault. What is in the vault remains hidden from the outside world. What is in the vault cannot be removed unless permission is given. O children, learn from me. I am Jesus. I am the Keeper of the Great Vault of Love. I am freely offering my heart to you. I am waiting to give each of you the precious gift of faith. Once you receive this gift, it is stored in your heart as a priceless gem is stored in a vault. My beloved children, there is no one who could remove your faith. You must truly desire to lose your faith and, even then, shall your faith only become hidden deep in the chambers of your heart. Once you have been given the gift of faith, you must consider it the most precious possession you have. For without faith one cannot enter into the kingdom of heaven. Without faith one cannot come to know me, the Lord God.

Children, each day you should pray for an increase in faith. Faith in me is not limited because I, the Lord, am Infinite. I am waiting to bestow many gifts on all those who ask. Come, children, come.

Thank you, beloved of my heart. I bless you.

Thank you, my beloved God, forever. I bless you, too. Amen.

August 13, 1995

My beloved child, I am here. I am the Blessed Virgin Mary and the Mother of God. I am the Mother of Mercy.

Children, I am your heavenly Mother sent as a messenger of the Most High God to entice souls to return to his heart of love. I have come as the adversary for righteousness, and as the tabernacle for sinners. Children, my motherly mantle protects you from the savage one as well as shields you from divine justice. I, your Mother of Mercy, plead for each one of you to obtain mercy and pardon for you.

This Generation has committed abominable crimes, that of which the killing of the unborn is the most serious. Many of you are so consumed by earthly pleasures that you are sleeping. Instead of being alert and heeding my calls and the calls of my beloved Son, you sleep and therefore you make a mockery of God.

Children, unless you repent and convert, you shall not escape the hand of justice. The choice is yours. I am a messenger of the heavenly kingdom and my grief and mourning is great. Each day many, many are lost to the abyss of hell, never to return.

Children, call to me. Consider me your one, true Mother Most Holy. Many of you have never known your earth mothers and you are reluctant to call upon me. I assure you that my motherly love transcends all other love except for the love of God. Come to me, children, I am waiting.

Mama Mary, thank you. I bless you and love you forever.

I love you and bless you, too, dearest child.

Lord?

My beloved child, we shall not write today. Meditate on these words from my beloved Mother. I love you and I bless you.

I love you and I bless you, too. Amen.

August 14, 1995

Lord Jesus, do you want to write?

My devoted child, come and record my words of love.

Children, I, the Lord, the God of Abraham, Isaac, and Jacob, have heard the groaning of my people and of the earth I have created. I have heard the cries of my faithful ones at the hands of persecutors, both physical and moral. I have heard the cries of the innocent victims savagely betrayed.

Do you not despise the world in which you live? You are a hardened and uncivilized people who slaughter for sport. You are no different from the cannibals. You have ears, yet you do not hear. You have eyes, yet you do not see. The sins of the earth are upon the earth, who cries out for vengeance. For the sins of mankind weigh heavily upon the heart of the earth, who cries to me for revenge. Mankind, your sins have come upon you. There shall be plagues. There shall be groans of hunger in places that have not experienced such sufferings. The earth shall become as a womb, wherein, you, the unborn of holiness shall have no place to flee. Unless you repent and convert, you are as dead. You shall become as part of the plague to cover the earth.

Call upon my mercy, child, and be born into holiness. Be consumed with my love and mercy.

Thank you, dearest child, for writing. I bless you and love you.

I bless you and love you, too, Jesus. I love you, Holy Spirit. Blessed be God forever! Amen.

August 15, 1995 - Feast of the Assumption

Lord Jesus, do you want to write?

I do, my beloved child. Receive my message of hope.

My beloved child, do not doubt in my goodness. My goodness overshadows the entire earth. My goodness is the reason the sun rises each day.

Yes, there are storms, but always does the sun shine again. There are lessons of learning all about you. There is something to be learned by every creature and every event. Ask what it is that I, the Lord, desire you to learn and you shall be granted wisdom. The light of my love shall shine as a brilliant candle upon your heart, and wisdom will set you apart from all the others.

I, the Lord, desire you to have faith in all situations. There is no situation that I am unaware of. All of creation rests and restores itself in the palm of my hand. I am the eternal love of each and every heart. Oh, children, you who are restless, come and rest in me. There is no other resting place. Oh, children, you who are lost, come back to me, and you shall be lost no longer. I am the Way, the Truth, and the Life. I am the author and sustainer of all life. I am the breath of the breathless and the speech to the speechless. Receive my words of love into your heart. I, the Lord, shall increase your heart and increase your faith. Remember, faith is a priceless gem.

Thank you, child, for writing. Go in peace, my little disciple of mercy. I bless you.

I bless you, too, my God and my King. Amen.

August 16, 1995

Lord Jesus, do you want to write?

My beloved daughter, do you see my patience? I have been waiting an eternity for you. Let us begin.

I am the Lord, the God of your Fathers, the God of Abraham, Isaac, and Jacob. My Sacred Heart has willed the earth and all of her inhabitants into existence. Life has developed because of Love and Love has nourished and sustained all life. I am Love, children, and my heart is the heart of all creation. Each beat of my heart causes: the sun to rise and set, children to be born, and those who are alive to continue living. I watch you, children, as you rely more and more on technology and less and less on me. Who can withstand the power of the Lord, thy God?

Each day I watch as you depend on alarm clocks to wake you up. Oh, foolish children, if I did not breathe life into your sleeping bodies each day, no alarm would wake you. Yet you continue to ignore me, giving thanks to your false gods of comfort. Many of you are arrogant, even to mock me, should you be without electrical power. For many of you, the earthly comforts you possess now will be turned into an eternal millstone which shall cause you discomfort forever. Think, children, think, if you do not choose me now, you shall be separated from me forever. Foolish children, do not be so blind as to believe you can comprehend eternity.

Rest, beloved child. Thank you for writing. I bless you and love you.

Thank you, O Lord. Have mercy, O God, forever. Amen.

August 17, 1995

Lord Jesus, do you want to write?

Child of my Sacred Heart, record my words of love. I AM is speaking. Wisdom is speaking.

Dear children, you are as fish in a pond. The fisherman comes and casts his line and how easily you are caught. Satan is the fisherman of souls. He uses your pride and greed as well as material possessions to lure you from the pond of holiness. Oh, children, remember also that I, the Lord, am the fisher of men's souls. I come for each of you with my arms outstretched. I come holding my heart in my hands for each of you.

Dear children, there is no place for you to hide. Your are either with me, or you are against me. You can either be a victim to satan's devious ways, or you can become a warrior of the Most High God. How does one become a warrior in my army of souls? Truly, I tell you that repentance and prayer shall lead a soul into my camp. Truly, I tell you that prayer and humility will transform an ordinary soldier into a magnificent and holy warrior. Make the decision, my children. The choice is yours.

Come children, come, and follow me. I am Jesus. I am the Great Shepherd who has come to gather my flock from the four corners. Listen to my calls of love.

Child, I bless you. Go in peace, little mercy of my heart.

I bless you, too, O Lord, forever. Amen.

August 18, 1995

Lord Jesus, do you want to write?

Little one of my heart, I am here. Record my words of love.

Children, you are separated. You are as numerous as the sands of the sea yet each of you is upon a different shore.[62] Children, I, the Lord, am referring to discrimination. Understand, my beloved ones, that I am a God of the Heart and not of the flesh. I love each of you equally. There is no discrimination in

---

[62] The Lord is saying that although we all share in humanity, each one of us is unique and different from each other, even persons of the same race. Hence, there are no grounds for discrimination since in God's eyes we are not classified by a particular race or to be categorized according to any typing other than those who uniquely love God.

heaven. What good is the flesh of a man if his heart is as stone? His hardened heart shall be as a weight to hurl him into the abyss of perpetual darkness. The color of one's flesh shall have nothing to do with one's eternal destiny.

Let us continue.

Mankind, if your heart is with me, then you are mine and you shall have your eternal reward. My Heavenly Father has prepared a place for all those who are devoted to me. It is your heart that shall find you a place at my dinner table, not the color of your skin.

My children, there is none among you free of prejudice. It is your nature. Come to me with a humble and contrite heart and I, the Lord, shall teach you to love. You shall learn to love with my heart, for my love shall grow in you.

Thank you, child, for writing. I bless you, little mercy of my heart. Be at peace.

I bless you and love you forever. Amen.

August 19, 1995

Lord Jesus, do you want to write?

My beloved disciple, come and record my words of love. Open your heart, child, to hear my voice.

My children, I, the Lord, speak to each heart. I sing the heart lullabies each night and songs of greeting as you arise each day. I watch you as you sleep, counting the moments until you arise in the hope you will remember me. But so many of you forget me. So many of you break my heart each day.

Children, in my humility I, the Lord, am revealing my heart to you. Many of you will use these revelations to mock me even more. Woe to those who mock my sensitive and merciful heart. I reveal myself in this way in the hope that some of you will return to me. Remember, children, I shall not force your love and loyalty. The heart that I, the Lord, wish to give each one of you beats with my heart. I wish to create a heart of holiness in each of you. If mankind would return to my heart of love, there would be peace. There would be love and generosity. Violence would be washed away by my Sacred Blood. The earth would become a kingdom of love and peace.

Sadly, many of you, in your selfishness and greed, would rather have your idols and possessions than the fruits of the kingdom of God. Your choices are more devastating to the soul than arsenic is to the body. Wake up, my sleeping children. Wisdom is calling you. The Lord thy God is calling you.

Child, I bless you. Thank you, for writing my words. Go in peace.

I bless you and love you, Jesus and Mother Mary. Amen.

August 20, 1995

Lord Jesus, do you want to write?

My beloved disciple, your perseverance to record my words has pleased me. Come, let us begin.

Child, I am the Lord, the Holy Spirit. I am the Spirit of Love and Humility who has come with the eternal message of salvation.

Children, salvation is a gift of mercy. There is nothing you could do to merit such a gift. I am the Spirit of the Most High God. I am one God, Mighty and Eternal. I have placed an invisible door by each heart. Those with faith will understand that is the doorway to me. For I, the Lord, have said "knock and it shall be opened for you." Oh, beloved children, see the destruction all about you. This in itself should be enough of an admission that you cannot live without me. My commandments are not old-fashioned. They are not valuable to some and worthless to others. My commandments are the foundation to your mortal and immortal lives. Without a strong foundation, your lives shall crumble. Look about you and see the lives that are crumbling everywhere.

Daughter, I, the Lord, have come with gifts of mercy for all. I have come because I have had pity on all of you. I see your self-destructive ways, and I, the Lord, have had pity upon you. Do not turn your back on my call of love.

Thank you, child, for writing. Go in the peace of my love.

I love you and bless you, too, O Lord. Amen.

August 21, 1995

Lord Jesus, do you want to write?

Little child of mercy, come and record my words. I am the Lord, the God of Abraham, Isaac, and Jacob.

Children, learn from me. I am Jesus, the Innkeeper of the Heart. I am He who rests in the heart of the ones who love me. As the sea faithfully meets the shore, so I, the Lord, faithfully meet those who call to me. As soon as one utters my name, I am present. When you call my name children, understand that you are invoking the most Holy and Blessed Trinity of the Lord God. Do not use my name as part of your everyday conversation. For in your self-centeredness and ignorance, you constantly make a mockery of me.

Do not use the phrase "O God" unless you have the intention of prayer or praise. Children, my children, when you are in conversations why do you not defend my Holy Name to those who mock me? Those who defend their God and his commandments shall be defended by me. Do not be afraid of the thoughts of others. Can the thoughts and opinions of another purchase salvation for you? No, my precious ones. Therefore say I, the Lord of Hosts: "Worry only of my opinion. Seek my approval at all times. I, the Lord, shall help you."

Thank you for writing, little one of mercy. Go in peace. Amen.

I love you, Lord. I bless you. Amen.

August 22, 1995

Lord Jesus, do you want to write?

Child, I am here. Record my words of love.

Children, the oceans are trembling, for the oceans recognize the signs of the times. The earth is getting ready for the perilous days ahead. Children, the signs of these days are upon you, yet you fail to see them. When the winter approaches, many of you change the tires on your vehicles. You place snow tires on your vehicles that you may be prepared for the harsh weather. But I, the Lord, have spoken to my prophets. I have given many messages that you may prepare, yet you hearken not to my words. If you have difficulty managing through a harsh winter without snow tires, then how much more difficulty shall you have when the winter of judgment comes upon you? There are only a few of you who are prepared. I have sent my Noahs to call you aboard the ark of my mercy, lest you drown. Yet my people are mocked and ridiculed. If you do not prepare for my return, then the ark of my mercy shall sail away from you to seek another.

Children, the signs are all about you. I have not concealed them. On the contrary, they are all about you according to Scripture. Will you be as weeds that I have no use for or as precious fruit that I will bring to my Heavenly Father? The wise hear my voice. The wise hear my voice. The wise hear my voice.

Thank you, child, for recording my words. Go in peace.

Thank you, O God, for your patience and mercy. I love you.

August 23, 1995

My beloved child, I am here. I am the Blessed Virgin Mary and the Mother of God. I am Queen of Apostles and Saints. I have come to embrace this earth in my motherly mantle. I am a servant of the Most Holy and Blessed Trinity. I have come to make an *urgent* appeal to my children.

Children, I am your Mother, the one who loves you despite your harsh and cruel torments of my Son. Do you see, my little ones, that each time one of you mocks my Son, Jesus, a sword pierces my heart? Each time one of you comforts my beloved Son, it is as if I received a bouquet of roses.

Oh, my little ones, what I would not do for the children who wish to return to God. I will come to you in your darkness and guide you into the waiting arms of Jesus. I, your Mother, will obtain for you the grace of conversion. Children, when you light a candle on the altar to revere my Son, you also bring great joy to my motherly heart. Oh, my children, I have come to you so many times pleading for your return to God. Where is the reparation we have asked for? Where are your prayers and your efforts to serve the one who serves you eternally?

Children, time is dwindling and I have come to prepare you. I will not force you to love my Son and honor me. Remember, I am a messenger of the Eternal Father and your eternal Mother.

Thank you, child, for writing. I love you and I bless you.

I love you and bless you, too, Mama. Amen.

Lord, are we going to write?

We shall continue tomorrow, beloved daughter.

I love you, Lord. Amen.

August 24, 1995

Lord Jesus, do you want to write?

Come, my little student, and record the words of the Master Teacher. I am He Who Strengthens and Consoles. I am he who watches over all of you as a mother hen.

Ah, my little flock, you are growing slowly. I have cared for you and nurtured you as a farmer carefully and tenderly waters the seeds he has planted. Who is it that causes a small seed to grow into a magnificent tree? I am He, the Eternal Farmer.

Ah, but even the tree needs sunlight and water to grow. Children, to grow in holiness, you need the sunlight and water which only I, the Lord Jesus Christ, can provide. It is the Spirit of God who comes to help the weak grow strong, to make the seed become a great tree. It is the tree that bears fruit that returns glory and honor to my Holy Name.

Children, examine your lives. See if the blood that runs through your veins is love. Think love. Breathe love. Be reflections of me. Love is never selfish. It is always generous, always yielding to the other's needs.

Truly, I tell you, many of you have hearts of stone. You openly pretend to love and invariably you despise and resent. I am the Lord who sees into men's hearts. If you desire to love, you must love with the heart of love. You must love with the Heart of God, which is my Heart. I am the Eternal Source of Love.

Thank you, little mercy of my heart. Go in peace, daughter.

I love you, O Lord, forever. Amen.

August 25, 1995

Lord Jesus, do you want to write?

Come, little child of my heart, and record my words of love. I AM WHO AM is speaking.

Children of mine, the earth in its entirety is as a jigsaw puzzle. All the pieces are connected, and without all the pieces the puzzle is incomplete.

In your arrogance, children, some of you have claimed superiority to others. Those who exalt themselves now shall be cast down forever. Do not lift yourself above another, for I, the Lord, have not done so. I have not created a superior race. On the contrary, each of you is from the dust and shall return to the dust. Many of you are spending too much time worrying and in disagreement with others.

I tell you, children, compared to eternity, your life span is shorter than the blink of an eye. There are those who have come before you and those to come after you. Though I have given each one of you different external characteristics, do not be fooled. Each of you has the same color blood, the same color as mine, which was poured out for all of you.

I, Jesus, did not die on the Cross for one race or one religion. Remember, children, I am a God of the Heart who loves each one of you infinitely and tenderly. Why do you waste your precious time squabbling with your brother? I tell you solemnly, each of you will someday stand before me. Each of you shall be accountable to me, the Lord God.

Thank you, child of my heart, for recording my words.

Thank you, Father, forever. Thank you, Holy Spirit. Amen.

August 26, 1995

Lord Jesus, do you want to write?

My little child of mercy, come and record my words of love. I am he who pours forth oceans of mercy upon the earth.

Children, your arrogance has blinded you to the truth of my love. I, the Lord, did not create man and then place him in the ocean. Nor did I take the fish and place him upon dry land. Children, I, the Lord, am a God with infinite love and respect for life. I created the womb to be a shield for the unborn. But you, wicked ones, have taken knives and have lacerated the safety of the womb. Again, I, the Lord, the God of Israel, am warning you to stop the abortions. If you do not heed my warning, then every womb of safety and comfort you have in your lives will be lacerated by catastrophes. You shall become as a woman giving birth to triplets, there shall be no time for you to recover before the next catastrophe strikes.

Because of your abominable and grievous ways, you are deciding your own punishments. Many have blamed me as the stench of your iniquity has sickened you. I tell you solemnly that you are to blame.

You have cursed the heavens and have cursed me, thereby making a mockery of all that is righteous and holy. Those who have no regard for the sanctity of the womb shall find themselves in the eternal womb of hell, enclosed forever by their unholy principles and lifestyles. Again, I implore you to heed my warnings and repent of your ways.

Thank you, child, for writing my words. Be secure in my love. I bless you.

I bless you forever, O Lord. Amen.

August 27, 1995

Lord Jesus, do you want to write?

My devoted disciple, come and record my words. My words are water to the thirsty and food for the hungry. Yes, many thirsty and hungry children shall read these words and be comforted in my embrace.

Daughter, open your heart to the Spirit of Counsel and Right Judgment. The Spirit of God has come upon the earth to separate the pearls from their shells. Oh yes, my beloved, while the shells are surely visible, the pearls are always hidden. Be hidden as well, my dear children. Be hidden from the things of the world and cast your glance to the heavens to await my return. Be looking and watching for my return and you shall be rewarded by my Heavenly Father.

Let us continue, my dear child.

Each pearl that the Spirit finds shall be rewarded greatly. Ah, but for those who are not pearls, they shall lose all that they have. It is wise to remain hidden from the things of the earth. The wise man is knowledgeable of the things of God; he does not need to make a spectacle of himself to the public as the Pharisees did. No, on the contrary, the wise man is hidden, as is the pearl, but the Heavenly Father sees all things for nothing is hidden from him. Do not be loud and joyful when you speak of the world. Rather, be humble and silent, imploring my mercy day and night, night and day.

I AM WHO AM, am a God of Mercy. There is no other.

Thank you, my beloved daughter. Go in peace, little disciple of mercy. I bless you.

I bless you, too, O Lord. Amen.

August 28, 1995

Lord Jesus, do you want to write?

My beloved child, thank you, for your sacrifice of love. Record my words. I am the Lord, the God of Abraham, Isaac, and Jacob. I am He Who Sustains all Creation by grace.

Grace is a gift, my children, to you from my merciful heart. Grace comes down from heaven as a shower upon the soul, that the soul is purified and strengthened.

Children, each prayer is answered from the depths of my merciful heart. I see you, children, in your daily struggles and I pour forth my grace upon you. Grace is as one brightly lit candle in a dark room, thus allowing you to see. With grace, the soul receives light to be able to see spiritually. Grace enables one to have spiritual eyesight and spiritual hearing, thus strengthening the physical as well.

Children, I, the Lord, Jesus, shall give you an example in simplicity. Imagine a box of cereal. The physical box is only cardboard and it holds no value. However, it is the cereal within the box that provides nutrition when eaten. Grace is inner nutrition provided by me, the Lord God.

Yes, it is true that you all have ears and eyes, but I solemnly assure you that if the soul cannot see or hear, then one is truly blind and deaf.

Thank you, dear one for writing my words. Go in peace, little disciple of mercy.

Thank you, O God of my heart. Forever I love you. Amen.

August 29, 1995

Lord Jesus, do you want to write?

My beloved child, record my words of love.

Remember, I am the only source of love. Who can count the grains of sand upon the earth? There is no man to complete such a task. But I solemnly assure you that the Eternal Father knows how many grains of sand are upon the earth. Why does man place a limit on an unlimited God? Why does man say he alone is powerful when he cannot even know the grains of sand upon the earth?

Oh, foolish children, your spectacles of pride have caused you to be blind to reality. Children, listen to my words. Wisdom is speaking. Creation is crumbling, for they are worshiping false gods. Those of you who depend upon your computers for strength and guidance shall fall upon your knees as you realize your stupidity. Those of you who have completely invested yourselves in material possessions and technology shall become bankrupt. When one does not have a spiritual foundation, one will crumble in adversities. Children, I am Jesus. I am the only source of strength and comfort. The more you rely on earthly comforts, the less you rely on me. Then surely you will fall as you are pushed closer to the abyss of hell each day. Many of you still continue to mock me and to mock my beloved Mother. Yet, who is it that holds all of the earth in the palm of his hand? I AM says the Lord God of Hosts.

Repent, Generation, repent. I am waiting to heal you.

Thank you, child, for writing. I bless you.

I bless and love you, too. Amen.

August 30, 1995

I am here, beloved child. I am Blessed Virgin Mary and the Mother of the Savior.

Children, the season of mercy is ending, and the season of justice is beginning. The Eternal Father shall purge the earth of all sin and only the holy and righteous shall be left standing. It is as my beloved Son, Jesus, has so often told you: "Be as a sturdy vessel in faith, that you will not sink when the storms come."

Children, your faith shall be tested as never before. If your foundation is not of the Holy Spirit, you shall not survive the dark days approaching. You are all called by my beloved Son, Jesus, to come aboard the ark of his divine mercy. If you do not accept this invitation, then you shall perish when the storms of justice descend upon you. Many prison terms as you know it cannot begin to compare to the suffering inflicted upon those in hell. It is the eternal prison where death is a constant desire.

Children of my Immaculate Heart, you must dedicate your lives to the service of God. This is the era where the faithful are being called to commitment to their God. You must not procrastinate. The clock is ticking, children. Time is slipping away from you rapidly. Consecrate yourselves to the Sacred Heart of Jesus and to my Immaculate Heart and begin to live a life of holiness.

Thank you, for writing, my beloved daughter. I love you and bless you.

I love you, too, Mother. I bless you, too.

Shall we write, Lord?

We shall continue tomorrow, dear one. Go in the peace of my love.

Happy anniversary, Lord.[63]

And to you as well, beloved.

Amen.

August 31, 1995

Lord Jesus, do you want to write?

My beloved disciple, come and record the words of the Master Teacher. I AM is speaking. Wisdom is speaking.

Children of my Sacred Heart, my mercy has afforded you the ability to make choices, for true love never is forceful. True love is always encouraging and never critical. I, the Lord, have given each of you the ability to choose the good and to discard the bad. I have placed my Heavenly Court of Angels and Saints at your disposal so that each one of you can succeed on your journey to me. Utilize the gifts I have made available to all of you, children. "Ask and you shall receive."

My beloved Mother is eagerly awaiting to escort you to my heart of love. Dear children, when you choose to walk away from me, then you turn your back on all that is righteous and holy. Satan waits for you as a spider waits for a fly. The web that satan weaves begins with your refusal of my love. Then you are nothing more than prey for the malefactor's feast. Let me solemnly assure you that it is more difficult to return from darkness each time you consent to be in darkness. You are deceived and made ignorant by satan's treacheries, and they blind you to the truth.

Children, I, the Lord, shall return soon and each of you shall see the true state of your soul. Then, surely, there will be weeping and cries for mercy. I am he who waits an eternity for each of you.

---

[63] It was the sixteenth monthly anniversary of the messages and I am congratulating the Lord for his perseverance and patience with me.

Thank you, beloved one, for writing. Go with my blessing.

Thank you, my beloved Lord. Amen.

September 1, 1995

Lord Jesus, do you want to write?

Yes, beloved child, record my words.

Dearest children, why have you let time become my adversary? I watch as you rush from one place to the next, never even thinking of me. Yet I, the Lord, think of you constantly. Do you not realize that I am the one who holds your hand from one destination to the next? Imagine a small child learning to cross the street. The parent will hold the child's hand while safely crossing to one side, and similarly, on the return. Do you think I, the Lord, would do any less for you? Do you think I would not be beside you each time you cross the street of a new horizon?

Oh, silly children, do you believe you are more capable than I am? Open your hearts to the truth. You have created a society that is void of love because you have cast me out. There cannot be love unless the Spirit of Love is present.

Listen to my words, beloved student. In many places there is a drought. But I solemnly assure you that the absence of love in your lives has begotten a more serious drought. You cannot repair your outer circumstances if you do not repair your heart. If your heart is not with me, then it is against me, and the drought you are experiencing is much more serious than a lack of water. If your heart is not with me, then you are experiencing a lack of grace. Be wise, my children.

Thank you, daughter, for writing. I bless you.

I bless you and love you, too, O Lord. Amen.

September 2, 1995

Lord Jesus, do you want to write?

My beloved child, record my words of love.

In heaven there are many mansions, my child. This is where the hearts that love me shall dwell. No, children, heaven is not as the earth. You cannot comprehend the beauty of heaven. It is truly a place created by love and sustained by love. I am He who has prepared a home for each of you. Though there are many mansions in heaven, there is only one door. I, Jesus, am the door to paradise.

Many of you go through your lives believing there are many doors to heaven. But I solemnly assure you there is only one door. There is only one way. I am the Way, the Truth, and the Life. All of you shall stand before me some day. You shall not stand before another. I, the Lord, shall ask you why you worshiped false gods. I shall ask you why you neglected the poor and needy, and the ones who are forced to beg each day. The ones who are forced to beg now shall not have to beg later. They will be given everything by me, for on earth they had nothing. Those who are wealthy and feast on the misfortune of others shall be denied. They shall hunger for all eternity. Remember, I, the Lord, have told you that your choices are for eternity.

Children, when an infant wakes up from a nap he looks for his mother and father. Be as infants, my children. Seek me first.

I love you, Jesus.

I love you, too, beloved child. Be blessed.

I bless you, too, O Lord. Amen.

September 3, 1995

Lord Jesus, do you want to write?

My beloved disciple, come and record my words of love and life.

Children, in order for you to be in a state of grace, you must be reconciled to me. You must confess and repent, and I, the Lord, shall shower you with the grace of forgiveness. Thus, you will be healed. Many of you only seek physical healings. Truly, I tell you, unless your soul is healed by forgiveness, your physical body can never be well.

If you were to bandage a wound that had not been cleansed, the wound would not heal. In fact, it would grow worse. So it is with the accumulation of sin. Sin does not disappear from the soul just because you place a bandage of silence or complacency on it. On the contrary, my beloved children, sin multiplies as a cancer and suffocates the soul. The soul which was in light is plummeted into darkness. With grace received by confession of one's sins, the darkness is lifted and the soul is fragranced by the light of my love.

Ah, beloved ones, if you could see the beauty of a soul that is alive in my love, it is brighter than the most brilliant diamond, for it radiates with my love. I, Jesus, am the Eternal Light of the Soul. With deep sorrow I watch souls that are plunged into eternal darkness. Be humble, my dear ones. I, Jesus, am the only helper of the soul.

Thank you, devoted child. Be blessed, little mercy of my heart.

Be blessed, Lord of my heart. Amen.

September 4, 1995 - Labor Day

Beloved children, I am here. I am Blessed Virgin Mary and the Mother of God. I am the Mother of the Church and the Queen of the Eternal Heaven.

Children of my heart, I have come into this home to thank you for your efforts and cooperation to bring my children back to Jesus.[64] As your beloved Mother, I personally wish to bless and thank each and every one of you.

I have come as the messenger of the Eternal Light. My Son is bleeding, my

---

[64] The following message was dictated by our Blessed Mother at the home of a recent disciple where several members of his prayer group were in attendance. These disciples are very active in spreading God's love for each person in their workplaces. In addition, they have been very committed for a number of years to holding a weekly cenacle of prayer on Sundays, commencing at 2:30 p.m. The cenacle follows the format outlined by Father Stefano Gobbi, founder of the Marian Movement of Priests. The Blessed Mother speaks of her appreciation for their efforts in spreading her cause.

beloved ones. I cry and mourn to see my Son's blood splattered upon the dry ground of hardened hearts. Can any one of you open your heart and allow my Son's love to dominate you? Be docile, my beloved children. Be as clay in the hands of the master potter who desires to use each one of you as a vessel of glory.

My dearest children, if you truly wish to serve my beloved Son, Jesus, you must cast aside all criticism. You must learn to love with his heart and not your own. You can accomplish this by consecrating yourselves to my Immaculate Heart and to the Sacred Heart of Jesus.

Children, if you truly desire to be my Son's disciples you must serve the poor. When you serve the poor then you serve the Eternal Savior who died on the Cross as a servant. Remember, the King of All Glory came as a servant. Be a servant to others, my sweet ones, and open your hearts to the cries of others. Then truly you shall hear Jesus.

Thank you, my devoted children, for your efforts. I bless you and love you all.

We bless you and love you, too, Mama.

Lord, shall we write?

Continue in your efforts, beloved students. We shall continue tomorrow, little one of mercy. I bless you all.

We bless you and love you, too, Lord. Amen.

September 5, 1995

Lord Jesus, do you want to write?

Yes, beloved daughter. I AM is speaking. Record my words of love.

Dearest children, rains of mercy are flooding the entire earth. Many of you shall say, "how can this be so?" I solemnly assure you that the earth is resting in the palm of my hand.

Children, I have sustained the earth and all of her inhabitants despite the sinful abominations committed upon the earth. How, therefore, can you say I am not a God of mercy? It is you, children, who have become as cannibals. Is there one among you who has never committed a violent act or had a violent thought? Yet, it is by mercy that you arise each day. What if the sun and the moon were to flee from your midst? But no, my beloved ones, my heart which is so infinitely in love with each of you, does not permit this to happen.

Remember, my beloved children, it is mercy that sustains you. I, the Lord, have looked into each heart hoping to find a willing soul. This soul would be granted the grace to love, and to love without limit. For I, the Lord, am the All Powerful and Unlimited God. From dust I created you, to dust you shall return. I shall sustain you each day, this is my merciful way. Call upon my mercy, beloved ones, for my heart of mercy is an infinite fountain of love.

Thank you, dearest child, for writing. Be patient, little child of my heart.[65] I love you and I bless you.

I love you and I bless you, too, O Lord, forever. Amen.

September 6, 1995

Lord Jesus, do you want to write?

My beloved children, thank you for your sacrifice of love.

Each sacrifice of love removes a thorn from my brow and a rose is placed in my crown instead. Oh, beloved ones, learn to love with my heart. Let there be no jealousy for your brothers, for I, the Lord, love each one of you equally and infinitely. You cannot comprehend perfect love. You, my children, can only love with an imperfect heart. You are limited in your humanity. But am I, the Lord,

---

[65] For the past eighteen months I have been getting more ill. It seemed I never regained my health since the commencement of my pregnancy. Despite the physician's assurances that my symptoms appeared to be minor, I was becoming more apprehensive as to whether they were so minor since no medication seemed to give me relief. I was growing more anxious over this and asked the Lord as to whether my concerns were justified.

limited? No, beloved. When you learn to love with my heart, your boundaries and limitations will increase greatly as your love for others will increase greatly. Listen to my words, my beloved ones. I, the Lord shall teach you a prayer:

> Infinite God, source of love and comfort, source of all creation, blessed be your Holy Name. Teach me your ways, O God. Reveal your heart to me that by your love, my heart shall burn as a candle upon the eternal altar. O Father Eternal, set a flame in my heart. Teach me your ways. Teach me to love with the Great Heart of Love. May the name of the Lord be blessed forever and ever. Amen.

Children of my heart, remember I am a God of the Heart, not of the flesh. Allow me to use each of you for my glory. Cast aside the attachments you have to self-glorification.

Thank you, beloved child, for writing my words. I, Jesus, love and bless you all. Go in peace.

Thank you, Jesus. We love you and bless you, too. Amen.

September 7, 1995

Lord Jesus, do you want to write?

My little disciple of mercy, come and record my words. My words are life.

Do you see my patience, my little daughter? I wait as an outsider until I am called, and sadly, many of you never call to me. What would it feel like if your child were to arise in the morning without acknowledging you, would you not be hurt? If the same child continued to ignore you day after day, and year after year, would you not grieve?

Children, if you who are imperfect and who have imperfect hearts, are able to experience grief, than how much more is my grief? No, my dearest children, you cannot comprehend my grief. Children, when someone you love passes away, you stand at their coffin one time and say goodbye. But I, the Lord, stand and watch over the coffins of those who have cast me aside for all eternity. Ever before my face is the eternal burial ground for the lost. Throughout your lives you exercise free will and many of you choose to ignore me. Why then do you wonder at the hour of your death the place you shall spend eternity? You have all been told but many have not listened.

Beloved one of my heart, I am addressing the heart of each of you. You do not read my words without my heart joining to yours. Call to me, little ones. Call to me and receive the many gifts I desire to bestow upon you.

Child of my heart, go in peace. Thank you for writing my words.

I love you, Jesus. Amen.

September 8, 1995

Lord Jesus, do you want to write?

Little one of mercy, come into my arms and record my words of love.

Children, I, the Lord, have given each of you a heart that your heart may be joined to mine eternally. My Sacred Heart rules in heaven and on earth. Yes, child, heaven was created and sustained by my heart to serve my heart. All creation was made to serve my heart of love.

Yes, child, though you be dust, I, the Lord Jesus Christ, am infinitely in love with you. I am the one who cradles you in my arms and who hides you in the infinite depths of my merciful heart.

Children, where is your treasure? Is it in a bank, or in a home, or perhaps in some fine jewelry? Ah, beloved, who shall guard your treasure after death? Will it still be your treasure after you die? What good is a treasure if it is only valuable for a short period of time? Think, my beloved ones. Allow me to be the treasure of your heart. I assure you that your joy will be far greater than it was while you cherished your material treasure. For I, the Lord, am the treasure that is everlasting to everlasting. I am the Treasure that the Heart is Always Seeking.

Children, unless you come to me, you truly have nothing. I am the one who created you in love and by love. If you choose earthly wealth over my wealth of love, then you have also chosen to follow the evil one. Remember, you cannot serve two masters.

Thank you, dear one for writing. Go in peace, little disciple.

I love you, Lord, forever. Amen.

September 9, 1995

Lord Jesus, do you want to write?

My devoted disciple of mercy, record my words of love. Listen carefully to my words. I am the Spirit of the Eternal Heart, from Everlasting to Everlasting. I am the God of Abraham, Isaac, and Jacob. I am God and I am One.

Daughter, a great tree has many branches. When it rains, one branch does not say to the other, "I shall drink all the water and you shall have none." Nor does one branch say to the other, "I shall absorb all the sunlight and you shall have none." No, dear one, on the contrary, the greatness of the tree comes from sharing. The many branches share the gifts I, the Lord, have provided for the benefit of the entire tree. It is this mutual support and sharing that contributes to the greatness of the tree.

I, the Lord, desire you to learn from my teaching. My Mystical Body is as a great tree. Each of you has been given different gifts by me to be shared. If my Mystical Body is to be strong, then each of you must be mutually supportive of the others. However, there are many of you who have abundant comforts, while others have nothing. Do you see, my beloved children, if you were to share your blessings with others who are less fortunate, then your blessings as well as the receiver's blessings would be multiplied? Oh, how fruitful is the generous and compassionate person. The generous one always finds favor with the Eternal Father who rejoices to multiply his blessings. The more that you give, my children, the more that will be given to you.

Beloved child of my heart, thank you for recording my words. Go in peace, little disciple of mercy. I bless you and love you.

I bless you and love you forever, my God. Amen.

September 10, 1995

Lord Jesus, do you want to write?

Yes, my beloved one, come and record my words. I AM WHO AM is speaking. I am the God of your Fathers, the Eternal Light and Mind. Listen to my words.

Children, when you leave your home you take a key, that you may return through the front door. I, Jesus, use this example in simplicity. Your home on earth is only for a short amount of time. Yet I solemnly assure you that your home in heaven was prepared that you may dwell there eternally. Yet, children, there is only one door and one key to heaven. I, the Lord, am the door and my mercy is the key.

Why do you go about your daily lives unconcerned that you do not have the key for your future home? This is not sensible, my beloved ones. I, the Lord, have told you that your stay on earth is shorter than the blink of an eye compared to eternity. Yet most of you spend all your time devoted to your earthly comfort. Soon all comfort shall slip away from you. The wise man, however, shall search his pockets and there he shall find the key to his eternal home because the wise man has emptied his pockets of all earthly attachments, therefore being only attached to me. Once his pockets have been emptied, I, the Lord, placed the key to heaven inside them, and surely, the wise man knows where to look for such a key.

Dear children, when I, Jesus, say "pockets", I am referring to the heart. Let your heart not be cluttered with things of this earth, children. Make room in your heart for me.

Daughter, thank you for writing. I love you and I bless you.

Lord, I love you and bless you, too. Amen.

September 11, 1995

Lord Jesus, do you wish to write?

My dearest child, come and rest in my arms of love. I know you are weary, my little lamb. Persevere in your journey to Calvary, my child.[66]

Record my words. I am the Lord, the Holy Spirit. I am the Alpha and the Omega, from Everlasting to Everlasting.

Dear children, each difficult event in your lives is a stepping stone to me. If you desire to follow me, then you must embrace the crosses I send you. Never, my children, do you have to carry the cross alone. My beloved Mother desires to help each one of you carry the cross. Children, I cannot emphasize the importance of the cross enough. I, the Lord, chose the means of my death. I, the Lord, chose the Cross as the gateway to salvation. As I, Jesus, embraced this Cross for your sake, I ask that you embrace the cross for my sake. Though the Cross I perished upon was only wood, I have exalted this wooden Cross through all time.

I do not use gold and silver, and priceless jewels, for the work I do. On the contrary, I use humble and simple things and exalt them into priceless jewels. Do you see, my children, how it is that the beggar shall acquire heaven long before the wealthy? Yes, while it is true that the wealthy can acquire all they desire on earth, it is the beggar who shall acquire heaven. Who then is really wealthy, my beloved ones? You must learn to think and see with your heart, for I, Jesus, am a God of the Heart.

Thank you, daughter of my heart. I bless you and love you, dear child. Be secure in my love.

Thank you, Jesus, my special Lord. I love you. Amen.

---

[66] Today, after a series of tests done in the hospital, I discovered that I have ovarian cancer. This was why I never seemed to regain my health since my pregnancy. The news knocked me for a loop and I was feeling extremely downcast and drained physically. The Lord teaches me the lesson that this event is not without meaning and benefit to me. He and his beloved Mother will accompany me throughout this trial. Knowing that they are always present does console me.

September 12 - 22, 1995 [67]

September 23, 1995

Lord Jesus, do you want to write?

My beloved children, I am here. I will dictate my words of love. [68] My beloved ones, what man can place a value on faith? Faith is the absence of fear in all situations. Faith is knowing that a cool breeze will refresh you on a hot sweltering day. Faith permits the soul to say, "Abba." Call me "Abba," children.

My beloved ones, I am Jesus. I am the one who stands at every heart. Many of you have heard me calling, yet you mock me and disregard my pleas for your love. Yet, I still desire for you to call me "Abba."

When one has faith, all that he asks of the Eternal Father shall be granted him. But, my children, you do not understand how your concept of time is my adversary. You must persevere and be persistent in your prayers. Faith develops slowly, my children. It begins as a piece of coal. When the man sees the coal he realizes that it is only an outer appearance. With a small amount of faith he understands that the piece of coal is only a covering for a deeper and more priceless beauty. With a small amount of faith he will change the piece of coal until it becomes a magnificent diamond. But this is as faith is; faith is not limited, my children. Faith is unlimited because I am unlimited. When you

---

[67] During the next ten days I was in the hospital undergoing more tests and ultimately having a hysterectomy done to remove my ovaries. The Lord dispensed me from taking the daily messages during this period.

[68] Understandably, the process of receiving a message requires my full concentration in both listening and simultaneously recording it. Because of the difficulty of just keeping alert and focused due to the amount of pain medication I was receiving during my time of convalescence, the Lord allowed me to have another "scribe or disciple" present who would do the recording while I transmitted vocally the words of the Lord.

ask the Eternal Father for something in faith, though you may be asking for a piece of coal, the Eternal Father shall always give you a diamond.

I use this example to illustrate how the simplicity of the cross cannot be comprehended by man. Though the cross may have an unattractive outer appearance, it is truly a most priceless gem.

Children, I, Jesus, go before you in every situation. I, Jesus, go with you and behind you in every situation. Never do you walk alone. Ask, children, for the faith to see the cross through my eyes and these graces shall be granted you. Ask for the courage to look beyond the situations in your lives, that you may see the great value they actually merit. Remember, I, the Lord, will always help you.

Thank you, my child, for recording my words. Be not afraid of the cross, the cross is my gift to you. The cross is life!

I bless you. Go in peace.

Thank you, Lord. We bless you, too. Amen.

September 24, 1995

Lord Jesus, do you want to write?

My devoted children, thank you for your sacrifice of love. How many of you, children, truly understand the meaning of sacrifice? A sacrifice is the act of separating one's self from something that gives pleasure. When one sacrifices something, then one willfully agrees to forfeit an attachment.

Children, when you desire to forfeit an attachment for my sake, then I, the Lord, find rest in your heart. I find rest in your heart because you have uncluttered your heart for my sake. The greater the attachment you have to a material comfort, the greater the sacrifice it becomes. Many of you are quick to view another through binoculars of pride. You say he should sacrifice more, or she should sacrifice more. Many of you make a public display of your sacrifices. You give a coat to someone who has none, yet five more are hidden in your closet. Do not look at another and say he or she should do more. Only the Eternal Father knows the hearts of each one.

When you offer a sacrifice, children, be silent, and the Eternal Father shall hear your silent voice as a frequent melody. Remember, my little ones, if you are poor and you give, then you have given much more than the wealthiest of all men. If you give only from your excess, do not boast that you have sacrificed, for truly you have not.

There are many types of sacrifices, children. The sacrifice of praise is when one turns away from something he cares for to spend time with me, his God. And that, my children, is an act of love. Each act of love removes a thorn from my brow and places a rose on my brow instead.

Children, remember my death on the Cross. Has there ever been a greater sacrifice of love? Think of me, my children, and do not be greedy with the time you spend with me. Am I not worthy of your attention?

Thank you, my devoted children, for the time you have spent with me. I bless you and I love you.

We bless you and we love you forever, Lord. Amen.

September 25, 1995

Lord Jesus, do you want to write?

My beloved children, today my precious Mother shall dictate my words of love.

My children, I am here. I am the Blessed Virgin Mary and the Mother of God. I am the Mother of Saints and the Queen of Angels.

My beloved children, as far as the East is from the West, this is how far many of you are from God. A great abyss separates you from the love of God. That abyss is your pride and hardness of heart. Many of you, children, are swimming in satan's ocean of deception. Truly, you believe you are floating above the water, but I tell you, you are wearing blinders. It is not that you are floating above the water, it is actually you are drowning in the abyss of evil. My visits have become more frequent because day and night, and night and day, I pursue you relentlessly. I seek your love and your return to God.

There are many manifestations of your distance from God, my children. First, the soul trembles with loneliness for the soul was designed to rest in God. Once the soul is separated from God, physical decay is imminent. You cannot be a light in the world if your soul is in darkness. For those who have been asked to make a stronger commitment to Jesus, my beloved Son, do not be afraid of the cross. For those who carry their crosses now, a special place at the heavenly banquet has been reserved. Do not fear the nails of illness nor the beatings from the whips of pain because it is into my arms you shall be when it is time to rest.

My beloved children, I am making an appeal once again for your deeper commitment and devotion to my beloved Son, Jesus. Thank you for recording my words.

Children, there is no greater love than the love of God and the love of your heavenly Mother. Do not be afraid to trust your lives to our care. I bless you and I love you, dear little children.

We bless you and love you, too, Mother Mary.

September 26, 1995[69]

September 27, 1995

Lord Jesus, do you want to write?

My beloved children, I am here. I am the God of Abraham, Isaac, and Jacob. I am the mysterious, unseen God of your fathers. Though I am unseen, I have offered you my heart by means of many different revelations. I am a God of intimacy. I am the One who Sustains and Cherishes All Life. Even the clouds are intimate with their surroundings. Even a lion in the plains of Africa is intimate with his surroundings. Even the sea with her mighty majesty is intimate with the shore countless times each day.

My dear children, I have revealed my love to you in many different ways but the most intimate revelation of my love is on the Cross. I looked at you, Humanity,

---

[69] I was not feeling very well this day, so the Lord dispensed me from taking a message.

with all of your sins, with all of your frailties, and I loved you. The Cross is a revelation from my most merciful heart. Each time one of you comes to the foot of the Cross, it is as if you were saying, "be intimate with me, for you are my God." When one comes to the foot of the Cross, though he comes with an empty and painful soul, he leaves filled with gifts from me, the Gift-Giver.

Children, I am Jesus. I am the Alpha and the Omega. I am the Infinite Revelation of the Eternal Father's love and mercy. Do not be afraid that you will walk away empty handed when you come to the foot of the Cross.

My children, I am the invisible God and my ways are invisible to man. The gifts received at the foot of the Cross are priceless and cannot be received any other place.

Remember, my beloved ones, each one of you, when you go through that door which is death's door, you will see me. I am the One who has loved you for all eternity. I am the One who has died on the Cross so this day will belong to you. Each time one of you comes to me in the Blessed Sacrament, you come to the foot of the Cross. Make time in your lives for me, children. I do not demand that much time from you, but remember I, the Lord, am the Giver of Time. Time is a gift from me. So again, my beloved ones, I will wait for you in every tabernacle; on every cross I will wait for you.

Thank you for recording my words. I bless you, dear little children. Thank you for your sacrifice of love.

Thank you, Lord, and we bless you for your wonderful generosity. Amen.

September 28, 1995

Lord Jesus, do you want to write?

My beloved children, I am here. I am the Lord, the Holy Spirit.

My beloved children, I am weary. I have called for your love so many times, yet you continue to ignore me. Foolish children, do you believe there was only one Judas? Do you believe there was only one to betray me? Ah, my children, you sleep. Search your hearts, my beloved ones. Each one of you has betrayed me with a kiss. Each time you come to receive me in the Eucharist and you come with sin in your heart, you betray me with a kiss.

I, the Lord, have provided the means for you to approach me in grace. I have given you the sacrament of reconciliation. I have empowered my priest to carry out my desire to have each of you reconciled to me. What do you fear, my children? Do you think I'm unaware of your sins? It is not the priest that grants you forgiveness, children. I am the one who wraps my merciful arms around each of you and showers my forgiveness upon you. Make use of this sacrament, my children, before you partake of me in the Eucharist. Come to me with a humble and contrite heart. Come to me hungry. Come to me thirsty. I am the Bread of Life. From Everlasting to Everlasting, I AM. Partake of me and you shall never hunger, nor shall you thirst.

Thank you, my devoted disciples, for your sacrifices of love. Be secure in my love. I bless you all. Go in peace.

We bless you, too, O Lord, and love you forever and ever. Amen.

September 29, 1995

Lord Jesus, do you want to write?

My beloved children, what a joy you have brought to my grieving heart tonight.[70] Though it is so easy to turn away from me in your weakness, you have remembered me, your God. My heart is rejoicing because of your gift of love.

My children, it is the one who spends the time with me when he is exhausted and ill, that is truly my most devoted servant. Many of you come to me and say, "Here I am, Lord. Your servant is here, Lord." It is during your times of convenience, and sometimes even boredom, that prompts you to approach me

---

[70] It was extremely late at night and both my husband and I were feeling ill, he from sheer exhaustion and worry, and me from the effects of the chemotherapy. Nevertheless, we made the effort to record the Lord's message which he so deeply appreciated.

in this way. But I, Jesus, solemnly assure you that my most devoted servants come to me in times of exhaustion and inconvenience. When I walked among you and I was called to someone's home to heal the sick, do you think it was only during times of convenience that I went? No, my beloved, I, Jesus, came upon the earth to be a servant to all.

Many of you say, "Master, I am your servant and I will do all that you ask of me." But I say, "Search your hearts!" Will you walk away from a television program to do my work? Will you put off a delicious meal to do my work? In the face of exhaustion will you say, "Lord, I am tired but I am here; what will you have me do?"

Remember, my beloved ones, the servant is not greater than the master. If you truly wish to be my disciple, then you must place me first.
Remember, children, I am a jealous God. I am possessive of your love.

Thank you, my beloved ones, for writing. Your perseverance has pleased me greatly. I bless you and love you. We shall continue tomorrow.

We bless and love you, O Lord, forever. Amen.

September 30, 1995

Lord Jesus, do you want to write?

Children of my heart, I am here! I am the Spirit of Love and Right Judgment.

Children of my heart, I have given you feet that you may stand on the earth below you. I have given you hands that you may touch all that I have created. I have given you eyes to bear witness to my supremacy and domicile. I, the Lord, have provided every avenue for you to live comfortably in the world I have created. But there is another world, my children, that is the world of the spirit. Do not think I have abandoned you and left you to only live upon the earth. I have provided you with many ways to live in the world of the spirit, which is, in fact, the real and everlasting world. I have provided my commandments to strengthen the soul, that the soul may soar freely in the world of the spirit. All those who ask are given the gift of prayer which is the highest form of communication with me.

My foolish children, there are satellites in space to communicate television and radio to those below. You have unlimited communication abilities and yet there is no communication between you. No matter your technology, there will never be communication between you. First, you must communicate with me. Consider me as the only true and necessary satellite.

The way to me is simple. I am a Simple and Humble God. I have given every heart a voice and the very instant your heart speaks to me, I hear you. Can your technology stop a hurricane or a flood? Those with ears, listen to your God. Prayer can stop a hurricane. Prayer can stop a flood. Prayer can end a war.

So again, I ask you, children, which world is truly the significant one? Is it the one of the earth or is it the world of the spirit, the world that I dwell in? You see, my children, the world of the spirit is reality and those people who choose not to dwell there are living a fantasy. The choice is yours, my beloved ones.

Thank you for recording my words, my beloved children. Tell others of my love. My heart burns with love eternally. It is my love that created you and brought you into existence. You cannot comprehend my love. Tell others of my mercy. You are my disciples, children. You are my voice as John the Baptist was my voice in the wilderness of sin. Be not afraid of the persecutions and scourges because I, Jesus, go before you always.[71] I will always help you, my beloved disciples. Be secure in my love. Go in peace.

Thank you, Lord. Send us the Spirit of Love and Prayer that we may always reflect your message. Amen.

---

[71] When the disciple who was present and I were reviewing the message, a discussion arose questioning the meaning of the previous two sentences. Suddenly, I had stopped conversing with the disciple and received a message from the Lord that answered the inquiry. The Lord had just told me that we, the disciples, are like his original disciples when he told them similar messages which now we were to repeat to our world as they did in their time. This is not to say that the reception of these messages by others were to be any different than when they were delivered in his era. We are to be prepared for the difficulties ahead.

October 1, 1995

Lord Jesus, do you want to write?

Little child of my mercy, come and record my words of love. I am the Lord, the Holy Spirit. I am the Guardian of the Heart.

Oh, beloved children, if you could see the heart as I, the Lord, do, you would see a golden key. This key is the key to either heaven or hell. Yes, truly I tell you that it is the heart that unlocks eternity and determines your final destination. Many of you continue to believe that your earthly stature plays a role after your death. Many of you shall stand before me at that hour and remind me of the important position you held upon the earth. Such arrogance, my beloved ones! Even at death's door many of you will be seeking ways to bribe me and to hide behind the faults of others.

Children, I, Jesus, solemnly assure you that when you stand before me, you shall stand alone. Your heart shall be your only alibi to your life. Your heart shall save you or betray you. You have your entire earthly life to prepare for heaven. During your life you will be given many opportunities to be generous and charitable. Will you make use of these opportunities or will you disregard them? You will be given many chances to make amends and to offer reparation for your actions. Will you make use of these opportunities or will you ignore them?

Children, consider that you are in the university school of the Spirit of the Lord God. If you do not do the assignments sent to you throughout the year, then when the time comes for the final exam, you will fail. Little by little, my children, you work your way to heaven. There is nothing you could ever do to merit heaven. The gift of salvation is just that - a gift of infinite love and mercy. Open your hearts to receive my gift.

Child, thank you for writing. I know you are weary. Rest in my love, child. I bless you and love you.

I bless you and love you, too, Jesus. Amen.

October 2, 1995

Lord Jesus, do you want to write?

Come, my beloved child, and record my words of love. You are a vessel of grace, my dear daughter. I, the Lord, shall touch many hearts through you.

Dearest child, allow me to use you as I desire. Coal can be used in the furnace, but as you well know, it can create a diamond. Do not put a limit on my use of you, my daughter. Allow grace to freely flow. Grace is the river that shall flow through you to others. Oh, beloved one, so few truly desire to serve me. So few give their hearts to me. I, the Lord, the Creator of All, am only given bits and pieces in return.

Children, if you give me your whole heart, oh, how much shall I, Jesus, give you in return. Our hearts shall beat as one. Am I not worthy of your complete love and attention? Oh, but sadly, I love each of you so very much that I will even accept the small crumbs of affection you cast my way. Do you see my humility? Do you see how I, Jesus, am a prisoner of my love for you? The heart that gives itself to me completely crowns me with sweet roses. The heart that belongs to me completely is also crowned with roses by me.

Oh, my beloved ones, I, Jesus, am asking you to share everything with me. Those who share my suffering, will share my glory. Every thorn shall eventually become a rose until eventually there shall be no more thorns in heaven. Ah, but I wait patiently for this great transformation. All darkness shall disappear and the light of my love shall consume humanity. Mercy shall consume humanity.

Go, my beloved one. Return to your family. I thank you for recording my words. I bless you and love you.

I bless and love you, too, O God. Amen.

October 3, 1995

Lord, do you want to write?

My dearest children, I am here! I am the Eternal Candle Upon Each Heart. I am the Alpha and the Omega, from Everlasting to Everlasting, I AM.[72]

---

[72] There was a long pause between Jesus' initial announcement of his presence and the beginning of his instruction. During this time I was testing the

I shall teach you, my beloved ones, about my faithfulness. I, the Lord, am more faithful than the mighty ocean. Do you ever doubt that the tides will not meet with the shore? How many of you wonder whether or not the sun will rise and set that day? How many of you wonder if there will be more or less than 365 days in a year?

I, the Lord, am giving you examples of faithfulness. I give you these examples that you may understand that it is by my faithful hand that these examples are a reality.

My little children, yes, you can measure the seconds within an hour but can you measure the seconds that it will take a small wave to become a tidal wave? You know the amount of days in a month but do you know how many days it will take for the birth of a new star?

Children, it is my faithfulness that sustains all creation. You cannot even comprehend my creation. Though you have eyes, you are limited in what you see. Though you have ears, you are limited in what you hear. Why is it that you cannot hear a dog whistle or you cannot see an atom? Truly, I tell you that those with faith understand that this is all my handiwork. Truly, I tell you those with faith are trusting in my faithfulness. Many of you cry to me, children, you have an earthly parent that is not trustworthy. I, Jesus, say this to you, do not

---

spirits by invoking the question, "Do you bow down to God the Father? " Jesus replied affirmatively. In addition, since September 24, the Lord, in deference to my illness and the difficulties associated with simultaneously listening to his voice and writing the message due to much pain medication, permitted a disciple to be always present to record the message while he spoke the message through me. It was during this pause that the magnitude of what was happening really occurred to me. I suddenly began sensing my own limitations and proneness to "step outside and look" at myself while the Lord was to speak through me. I questioned whether I was truly able to be so selfless as to allow Jesus the latitude to use me entirely as he sees fit. In short, I petitioned the Lord that my humanness and pride not hinder the message in any way and that I not lapse into being a participant observer (and thereby scrutinize what is being said) while the message is being delivered. Jesus replied, "you are a vessel of grace, allow me to speak freely through you. "

put your faith in another person; it is not your nature to be faithful. It is only my nature to be faithful. Be tolerant and merciful to those around you. There is none among you worthy to be placed upon a pedestal. If you elevate another human being, you will always be disappointed. Come to me, therefore, and you shall never be disappointed. I, Jesus, am the only true and faithful friend of the soul. Come to me and I will give you rest.

Thank you, devoted children, for recording my words. I bless you and I love you. Go in peace.

We bless you and love you, too, Lord. Please help us to be faithful to you. Amen.

October 4, 1995

Lord Jesus, do you want to write?

Children, I am here. I am Jesus. I am One with the Father and One with the Holy Spirit. I am the Blessed Trinity. I AM. I AM. I AM.

Beloved children, I have set the concerns of the entire earth before my face. I have listened to the groanings of the elderly and I have listened to the whimperings of the young. The only abyss that separates you from me is the hardness of your hearts.

Yes, there is a great gulf between heaven and hell, and that gulf shall never be crossed. Do not procrastinate, my children. The gulf that separates you from me can disappear within a beat of the heart. I, the Lord, look into every heart over and over again. I wait patiently at the door to each heart. A humble and contrite heart is what I wait for. I yearn to lavish love and mercy upon each of you. I yearn for the day that you will invite me into your heart and into your life. Though I, Jesus, knock and knock, many of you are quick to shut the door in my face.

Dearest children, many of you will only call to me during catastrophe. I am greatly saddened by this, children. I am offering my friendship. I am offering my heart. I am a God of Love and Peace. Offer your lives to me, children, and I, Jesus, promise you will not be disappointed.

Thank you for recording my words, beloved children. I bless you and I love you.

I bless and love you, too, Lord.

October 5, 1995

Lord Jesus, do you want to write?

Come, my devoted disciple and record my words of love. My words come from the eternal fountain of love which is my heart. Listen carefully to my words, little daughter.

Do not dwell upon your weaknesses. Bring your weaknesses to me and I, Jesus, shall purify them in my blood. I shall combine your weaknesses with my wounds, and you shall be given strength. Every weakness shall glorify me and shall be transformed.

Oh, my children, why do you try to hide from me? Approach me honestly. Approach me in humility. Do not be afraid or embarrassed by your limitations. Your limitations are my strengths. Your trials and tribulations become my battles of victory. Each time you come to me and say, "Lord, I am weak, help me," I rush to your side. I do not turn away from you because of the type of weakness you may possess. On the contrary, the weaker the soul, the more that my strength will be manifested. So many of you are out of control with certain things or issues in your lives.

Come to me, children. Be not afraid. I saw you from Calvary. I loved you from the Cross just as much then as I do today. Do not let sin overtake and consume you. There is no problem "we" cannot solve together. There is nothing that cannot be accomplished with my help. I am the Unlimited God of Love and Mercy. If you would give me a chance, surely you would love me. Again I, Jesus, call for your hands and your hearts.

Thank you, child, for recording my words. Be not afraid, dear one. I will always help you. I bless you.

I bless you and love you, too, O Lord. Amen.

October 6, 1995

Lord Jesus, do you want to write?

Dear children, I am here. I am the Consolation of the Heart and the Eternal and Everlasting Food of the Soul.

Children of my heart, I have created you after my own image. This does not mean that you look like me, rather that in a three-fold way I have placed my life within you. I have given you flesh. I have given you a soul, and I have given you a Spirit which is the Spirit of the Heart.

Foolish children, there is great grief in heaven because of the emphasis that is placed upon the physical body. I am a compassionate Father. I am well aware of your need to be physically attractive to others.

We shall continue, children.[73]

It is a fallacy, my children, to believe that you are not beautiful. Though I understand your needs, I, Jesus, solemnly assure you that it is the beauty of one's heart which manifests itself on a physical level. My sweet ones, your vanity causes you great suffering. I have children in hospital beds because of self-inflicted starvation. Yes, I have set your concerns before my face, but I assure you that I am the only solution to your problems. Satan has deceived you into believing it is the physical body that requires most attention, but it is not. It is the heart which requires the most attention. If it were not so, I would have told you. If it were not so, then what would be the purpose of the flesh to grow old and die?

The things that come from me are pure and simple, and they are not hidden. But all of you must pray constantly to the Holy Spirit for discernment and wisdom. If you are only wise of the things of the earth, then truly you are ignorant. The man who is wise delights in the things of God and anguishes over

---

[73] There was an interruption during the message due to an important phone call from the office of my doctor. Jesus told me to respond to the call and that he would wait. The Lord is very considerate and respectful of our needs.

the things of the earth.

Foolish Generation, with all of your technology, you are truly blind to your problems. Contrary to what you arrogantly believe, the solution does not lie in the palm of your hand. It lies in the palm of my hand, yet you continue to reject my offers of love. Soon the gates of heaven shall open and the chariots of justice shall swoop down upon the earth as a vulture seeks her prey. If you are not prepared in your heart, you shall be as the vulture's prey. It is time, children, to stop focusing on your outer appearances and begin focusing on your inner ones. I do not expect you to do this alone. Remember, I, Jesus, am the One, True, and Faithful Friend of the Soul. Call to me and I will help.

Thank you, dear children, for recording my words. Teach others as I have taught you. Stand firm in your faith and I will strengthen it. Be not afraid of what you will speak, for the Lord of Hosts shall touch your tongue with the fire of his love. I bless you. I am always with you. Go in peace.

We bless you, too, Lord, and pray that we may be always imitative of your humility and open to the Holy Spirit of Love.

October 7, 1995

Lord Jesus, do you want to write?

My beloved child, come and record my words of love. I am Love. I am he who waits in every tabernacle throughout the entire world for souls. I am he who hungers endlessly for your love.

My beloved children, I am present in every thought and in every breath you take. I, the Lord, am present in each beat of your heart. I, the Lord, watch over you as you sleep each night and then, faithfully, I recall you to life each day. Oh, I am so grieved by those who do not recognize my intimate ways.

Children, I, the Lord, have created each of you with a specific purpose: that purpose is love. My desire is that you love me. My hope is that you accept me as your Lord and God. My heart aches for your love day and night, but love does not force itself. Love never criticizes or presumes.

Children, though I desire your love, it is more important that you freely give your love to me. Be as a little flower that turns upward to face the sun. Be as a tree who points its leaves towards heaven when the rains are coming. Turn your hearts towards me and I, the Lord, will change your life and your direction. I will grant you the gift of holiness and I will clothe you with new garments. "Together" we will achieve victory. "Together" you shall find the fulfillment of your desire.

Thank you, beloved one, for writing. I bless you. Go in peace.

I bless you and love you, too, O Lord. Amen.

October 8, 1995

My beloved children, I am here. I am Blessed Virgin Mary and the Mother of God.

My beloved children, thank you for your devotion to my Son. The reign of mercy which has been granted you by the Eternal Father is almost over. Soon the hand of justice shall be pointing to each of you. The time shall come upon you as swiftly as day becomes night.

I know the cross is heavy for many of you. In a way, many of you are carrying crosses for others as well. It is in this difficulty that you must truly persevere in your faith. It is on your journey to Calvary that you must not abandon Jesus. Many of you have obeyed my motherly calls for your conversion and reconciliation with God. I urge you, children, to go to Mass. The graces you receive at Mass are more valuable than you can imagine.

Many of you allow many things to crowd your lives and you do not make time for my Son. When you do not attend Mass, it is as if you have left him to be crucified. I appeal to you again but remember, my children, it is "you" who need God. There is nothing you can do without God.

Thank you, my beloved children, for recording my words. Go in peace with my blessing.

Lord, do you want to write?

No, my child, we shall continue tomorrow.

Thank you, Lord and Blessed Mother, we love you both so much. Amen.

October 9, 1995

Lord Jesus, do you want to write?

Yes, child of my heart. Receive my messages of love. As the heart sustains the body, I, the Lord, sustain all creation.

Listen carefully, my little one. Why do you despair, my little lamb?[74] Yes, the time has come for you to walk to Calvary with me. With each step you take, remember my wounds. Remember the scourges and humiliations I received at the cruel hands of Pilate's men. Do you know how many times I was slapped in the face and kicked in the ribs? Do you know that the thorns penetrated my brow and caused the blood to cover my face? But throughout my ordeal I, Jesus, thought of you. Throughout my suffering I, Jesus, dreamt of the day that you would acknowledge me as Lord.

Now, my little one, I have given you and your family a great cross. But remember that I, Jesus, am closer to you than ever before. Learn to think of me in your suffering as I, Jesus, have always thought of you. Be not afraid of the cross. The cross shall not harm you; in fact, the cross is the tool of sanctification.

Persevere, my little lamb, and trust in my sustaining care of you. I, the Lord, will not forsake you. I love you, child. Go in peace, little mercy of my heart. I bless you.

I bless you and love you, too, Lord. Amen.

October 10, 1995

Lord Jesus, do you want to write?

---

[74] I am still in the throes of conflict between the assurances by the Lord that my "illness is only temporary," with that of the prognosis by the physicians.

Children of my heart, I am here. I am the Father of Humanity.

Ah, beloved ones, where do you think your strength comes from? Where do you think the heat of a fire or the chill of an ice cube comes from? Where do you think a rainbow comes from?

In heaven, my beloved, there are many mansions. There are many storehouses of treasure. In these storehouses I, the Lord, keep gifts for each of you. I keep food for each of you. I keep grain for the farmer, and rain for the trees, and water for the oceans, and sand for the desert. When the land is plentiful, it is because I, the Lord, have opened the storehouses of heaven for you. I do not ask for payment. I do not come to you for gold and silver. All I ask for is your loyalty. I ask for your love and obedience to my commandments. When you follow my way, look how much I give you in return.

But as great as my generosity is, so then shall my anger descend upon those who mock me. I shall shut the storehouses of heaven and they shall not open for you. I shall shut my ears to your cries. Have you not shut your ears to my cries? There shall be plagues and famines and diseases. There shall be one catastrophe after another, and heaven will have shut her gates to you.

Yes, I am a merciful Father, but I am also a just judge. Who shall withstand my judgment? It is while you are in times of plenty that you should be praying for mercy. It is while heaven pours forth her benefits upon you that you should be in constant prayer. Do not procrastinate, my children.

Do you want to say any more, Jesus?

No, child. I have said enough. We shall continue tomorrow. Be secure in my love. I love you. I bless you.

I bless you and love you, too, Lord.

October 11, 1995

Lord Jesus, do you want to write?

My beloved one, come and record my words of love.

Child, mankind is dwelling within a tunnel. Slowly, the waters of sin shall rise above and begin to enter the tunnel. There shall be no place to hide on that day. Everyone shall be consumed by the waters of sin. For those who are reconciled with me, my beloved faithful ones, the waters shall be as a baptism. For those who are not, the waters shall drown you. They shall be the deluge of justice from the Hand of Justice.

Child, what does the man who is with me have to fear? Who can harm him if I, Jesus, am his ally? Surely, there is no one. Why do you fear the cross so, my child? The cross will never harm you. Even if the cross were to kill your human body, surely the cross would save your soul.

Children of my heart, you are reckless with the care of your soul. Sadly, you take better care of an automobile than you do with your immortal soul. I have given you wisdom and common sense, but your pride and hardness of heart blocks my love. Again, I, the Lord, am calling to you, children. Do not be caught in the tunnel when the waters come, if you are not with me. The call for your conversion is now. Soon it will be too late.

Thank you, child, for writing. I love you and bless you. Go in peace.

Thank you, Jesus. I love you and bless you, too. Amen.

October 12, 1995

Lord Jesus, do you want to write?

My beloved child, I, the Lord, have given my life as a ransom for many. Now, I come with my heart in my hands. I come as a pauper begging for your love and loyalty. Do you see my wounded heart? If I were not wounded, would I have to beg for your love? Remember, beloved children, I am the Eternal Heart and the Eternal Fountain of Love. My love shall never change. Listen to my words, little daughter. The father that observes my precepts and commandments is a merciful and compassionate father to his children. The spouse that hopes in me is tolerant and loving. The friend who is a friend of mine brings loyalty and compassion to others. How can someone be a welder if he knows not how to weld? How can a doctor perform surgery if he knows not the body?

Oh, children, open your hearts to my teaching. You cannot be a friend to someone else unless you are my friend first. You cannot love another unless you love me first. Who is it that supplies you with the ability to love? I am He, the one who causes the mountains to spew lava, the sun to rise and set each day, and the one who lights the candle of love that I, the Lord, have placed upon each heart. If I had not given the gift of love to each of you, you should be no more than a pile of sand. You should be as a rock that has no feelings when it is kicked. Children, to find love, you must first come to me, the Giver of Love.

Thank you, devoted child, for writing. Go in peace.[75]

I love you, Lord. Amen.

October 13, 1995

Lord Jesus, do you want to write?

Little heartbeat of mine, receive my words of love.

Children of my heart, I am the God of Abraham, Isaac, and Jacob. I am he who determined the continents and spoke to the oceans. I am he who illuminated the sky with brilliant lights. I, the Lord, have placed an unseen staircase between heaven and earth. It is one of the ways the angels travel to and fro. It is one of the ways for you to enter into the gates of heaven. With each step you take towards me, it is as if you have climbed another step on this stairway. Though your journey is long and sometimes discouraging, I, Jesus, have sent my angels to assist you.

So many of you make a mockery of me and, of course, you mock the heavenly court. But little ones, you do not realize the size of the family you have. Your spiritual family is your true family. We are one body and one family. Dear children, those who acknowledge me must also acknowledge the saints and angels. I love you so much that I permit them to assist you on your journey to

---

[75] At the closing of this message the Lord said in a friendly and joking manner, that my room is a mess and I need to dust his altar - a small shrine of statues that I have constructed in my room. He added, "I am very patient with you."

me. It is their constant desire to help you.

You see, my precious ones, the traveler on the road to me, though he be lonely, is never alone. The one who prays has the heavenly family praying with them. Children, I, Jesus, have the utmost respect for family unity, but remember, family unity truly begins in heaven.

Thank you, beloved one, for writing. Do not fear, my little one, I will always help you.

I love you and bless you, Lord. Amen.

October 14, 1995

Lord Jesus, do you want to write?

Children, I am here. I am the Lamb of Reconciliation. I am the Finder of the Lost and the Healer of the Sick.

Beloved children, I grieve as I watch you in despair. You say to the person to the left that you are troubled. You say to the person to the right you are troubled, yet you say nothing to me.

Your lives are empty because your hearts are empty. If you were to visit a large city you would see thousands of people in close proximity to each other, but sadly they are strangers. There is no unity nor camaraderie between them. Many of you seem as passengers on a train; though the train makes occasional stops, you do not get off for you know not where to go.

In my kingdom love flows as freely as a river. In my kingdom there is no difference between one soul and another, for all of us are one heart. This is why I, Jesus, say to you, "do not judge your brother or sister." How can an impure heart judge another? With what clarity shall he make his decision?

Children, imagine a large playground and in the center of this playground is a water fountain. This water fountain delights at the children that will come and drink this water. This water fountain has only one care, to provide drink to those who thirst. In simplicity I, Jesus, give this example. The children will come to the water fountain and their thirst will be quenched. But some of the children will not come, they will seek satisfaction elsewhere. So the water fountain grieves because those children have not accepted the water. I, the Lord, am as that water fountain. I await all eternity to give you water and food.

I, Jesus, am the Gift-Giver. Come, children, come and accept the gifts I desire to give you. I am the only source in heaven and on earth of love. Unless you come to me for nourishment, you cannot nourish others. Unless you make a home in my heart, you cannot share your heart with others.

Truly, I say, "if you are not with me, you are against me." You will be as a stranger in the place you dwell. But if you are with me, you will never feel as a stranger, for my mercy and love shall be your garments.

Thank you for recording my words. Understand that I am the heart of all creation. We shall continue tomorrow. I bless you all.

We love and bless you, too, Lord. Amen.

October 14, 1995 - Evening Message

Have you heard this taught in my Church?

No, Lord.

Children, I shall answer your question.[76] At one point in time the Baptism was

---

[76] This unusual occurrence of having two messages on the same day arose out of need for clarification concerning a theological issue that evolved between two disciples. The subject was "intergenerational healing" and they had phoned to request whether Jesus could resolve their issue. I was totally unfamiliar with the term and said that it is highly unusual that Jesus would respond to "personal" questions. Usually Jesus informs me to have the person seek him directly and he will reveal the answer(s). Nevertheless, I said that I would ask but I needed more information. One disciple related that he was contemplating approaching his parish priest to request an "intergenerational healing mass" be celebrated. The other disciple cautioned against it stating that it might create a wrong perception concerning free will and accountability for sin. To buttress his argument, the latter disciple had produced an article

a baptism of blood. The sins of one were passed through the bloodline from generation to generation, whereby the suffering of this bloodline eventually served as a baptism and thus a reconciliation. But I, Jesus, am the New Covenant, the New Baptism, the New Bloodline. I am the Sacrifice of Reconciliation to the Eternal Father.

There is really one Baptism, children. It is the Baptism into my wounds and the sharing of my passion that purges the soul of sin, thus unshackling other generations. Because of my death on the Cross, each one of you is accountable but reconciled and sanctified by my blood. If one of you chooses not to reconcile with me, I shall not hold this against any other family members. I have not shed my blood for one generation and expected my blood to cover the second, third, and fourth generation. No, my children, I have shed my blood for each of you. Being that I, Jesus, am the Sacrificed Victim of Reconciliation, my blood has

---

written by Bill Reck of the Riehle Foundation on the topic (*Blue Letter* September 9, 1995 p.2). In the article, Reck states:

"Intergenerational Healing is the process of attempting to cleanse our ancestry of past sins to free our present lives from the effects of these sins...There is always great merit in praying for our deceased family members, seeking forgiveness for held grudges, and freeing ourselves from bad memories and unrepented offenses. But there is a much greater danger in trying to blame our current difficulties on what our great-great grandfather did...Make sure you are not tying your present and future to someone else's past."

I took extra precaution to ensure that the evil one would not distort the message by spreading holy water around my room and invoking several times the "testing the spirits formula" which Jesus had taught me. After responding affirmatively to "bowing down to God, the Father Almighty" Jesus inquired of me: "Have you heard this taught in the Church?" This implies that Jesus places great importance on the official teaching of the Church and whether such a concept - "intergenerational healing," was a vital doctrine taught by the Magisterium. In addition, Jesus himself never initiated this topic in the many messages given to the world through me. Nevertheless, Jesus graciously responded to the need of his disciples, delivering a succinct but theologically profound message. Thirty minutes later, I returned the call to the disciples with Jesus' response.

covered mankind for eternity. Baptism frees you from original sin and my blood frees you from everything else.

Do you see, my children, how great my love is?

I have answered your question. I love you and I bless you.

We love and bless you, too, Lord, Amen.

October 15, 1995

Lord, do you want to write?

Dear children, I am the Lord, the Holy Spirit. I am the Spirit of Counsel and Right Judgment.

Children, my mercy is a great net. I shall cast my net into the ocean of sinners and many will be saved. I shall not hoist up my net until it's overflowing with repentant souls. Those who are left behind have chosen their destiny.

If you were to be without rain for a great number of days, by my mercy the trees and most of the other foliage would not die. It is my mercy that sustains all life and rescues the sinner just before he enters the kingdom of hell.

Children, there is a place for sin and there is a place for purity. As separate as the ocean is from the desert, so also are these places separate. Children, search your hearts. Are you drowning in satan's ocean of deception? Call to me and I will lower the net of my mercy and rescue you. I, Jesus, shall rescue you and you shall be satan's prey no longer.

You are a funny and foolish generation. When you make arrangements to fly an airplane most of you prefer a direct flight; you do not like to change planes and wait for another. But I, Jesus, have offered you a direct flight to heaven. I am the Way, my beloved, there is no other. Those of you who sit and wait for different planes to carry you to and from your destination, have chosen the wrong destination. Open your ears to my teaching. View my words with a humble and contrite heart so that you may see and that you may hear.

We shall continue tomorrow, my children. I bless you and love you.

We bless you and love you, too, Lord. Amen.

October 16, 1995

Lord Jesus, do you want to write?

Come, my little child, and record my words of love. Wisdom is speaking. I AM is speaking.

How many of you, children, have taken a journey? If so, then you had to make plans, you had to make many provisions to successfully reach your destination. There is another road and another journey you are traveling. It is the journey to your final destination. If you choose heaven, then there are certain provisions you are responsible for along the way. You must be obedient to my commandments. You must frequent the sacraments, always maintaining a humble and contrite heart. On your earthly journey, many of you will communicate with others either by telephone or radio. But how many of you communicate with me as you travel the road to heaven?

Children, prayer is the way to communicate with me. The moment you utter my name, I hear you. Be persistent in your prayers, my little children. Though the journey to heaven is narrow, I, Jesus, am with you each step of the way. Be aware of my presence, children. Call to me to help you.

Daughter, I know you are weary. Rest, little mercy of my heart, I bless you. *I bless you, too, O Lord. Amen.*

October 17, 1995.

Lord Jesus, do you want to write?

Yes, my beloved disciple. I AM is speaking through you. You are a vessel of grace. I, the Lord, shall explain my views on suffering.

Many of you believe I am cold and callous. You yell out to me in your bitter despair and accuse me of being responsible for all the mishaps and misfortunes you encounter. Children, listen carefully to my words. If a toddler places his hand in a flame, will he not get burned? If you cross the street without paying attention, will you more than likely be struck?

Oh, children, there are so many examples I, Jesus, could give. My point is simple. Follow my commandments and be reconciled to me, thereby receiving grace for each situation. Again, much of your suffering is self-inflicted for you distance yourselves from me. The further you are from me, the less you are surrounded by light. Instead, you are attacked and plagued by darkness. Evil has every opportunity to assault you, for you have shut the door to me and opened the door to satan.

Beloved ones, when heaven sends a trial to you, it is a priceless gift from the Eternal Father. Understand, my little ones, that what is sent by heaven is ordained and sanctified in heaven, and is sent to increase virtue.

Beloved ones, I, Jesus, desire you to unite your suffering with mine. Together, we shall lift up our offering to the Eternal Father and the fragrance of reparation shall delight the heavens. Accept your trials and tribulations with joy. You are a metal in the hands of the Sovereign Welder, who loves you infinitely.

We shall continue tomorrow, my beloved child. I bless you. Go in peace.

I bless you and love you, too, Lord. Amen.

October 18, 1995

Dearest child, I am here. I am Blessed Virgin Mary and Queen of Peace. I am the Mother of Mercy and the Mother of the Sick.

Children, as a messenger from the Eternal City, I have been given the task of bringing more children to full citizenship in heaven. The Eternal City of Glory was created by God for his creation. It is a place of magnificence created by the love of the Sacred Heart.

Children, Jesus is Lord both in heaven and on earth. It is his Holy and Sacred Heart which rules the entire realm of his creation.

Children, think of your own leaders and leaders in other countries. Do they rule by pride and the staff of greed? Which leader amongst you rules by the love in his heart? I assure you, my beloved ones, that Jesus is the only ruler and king who has established his kingdom by love. Yes, it is love which rules. It is love which nurtures and enkindles the passion of souls. It is love which heals.

Oh, children, God grieves because every nation upon the face of the earth is sick. Your leaders cannot heal you nor solve your problems. Only love can solve your problems. Only God can heal and rescue you from the deterioration of your soul. Children, call to me and I will extend my motherly hand to you. I will gather you in my arms and together we will begin the journey back to God and to his Eternal City.

I bless you, my children. I bless you with the immense love of a mother. Go in peace.

Mama, I love you, too, and thank you. Do you want to write, my Lord?

No, my beloved, we shall continue tomorrow. Go in peace.

I love you, O Lord. Amen.

October 19, 1995

Lord Jesus, do you want to write?

My beloved disciple, listen to the words of the One Who Is. Dearest child, Wisdom is speaking.

The crown of a king or queen is usually made of various jewels embedded in gold. Sometimes the number of points on a crown will be indicative of the number of provinces within the king's jurisdiction.[77]

Now, beloved ones, think of me. Think of the crown of thorns placed upon my brow. What could a crown of thorns represent? Ah, children, sadly, the crown of thorns is indicative of my kingdom on earth. Each thorn represents cruelty, abandonment, humiliation, and violent disrespect for human life. Each thorn is

---

[77] When the Lord said the word, "points" he immediately followed it with the word, "spires." He sensed that I did not know the meaning of the word so he requested that I research the word. "Spires" refers to the tapered pointed parts of the crown. In addition, because of the scholarly reference in this message, I began to question whether this is really the Lord speaking. He answered, "do you think it is you?"

as the cruel instrument used to kill the unborn. Each thorn represents the unwelcomed poor and elderly. Each thorn represents the youth and how they carve and mutilate their bodies and minds with drugs and alcohol. Oh, it is true. The crown bestowed on a king's brow surely signifies his kingdom.

Ah, my beloved, in heaven my crown is a crown of roses. The flower representing beauty and life is my crown. The soft velvety texture of the rose signifies the tenderness and compassion of your God. The rose is a flower that has many varieties. This represents the vast garden of my love in which there is no discrimination. There is only love. Oh, beloved ones, each time you praise me another rose is added to my crown. Each time you deny me, another thorn is added to my crown of thorns. Think of me, my beloved ones, which one would you rather see upon my head? Which crown are you willing to share with me? I am Jesus, I am the Eternal Mind and Heart. Accept my love, children.

Thank you for writing, daughter. I love you and bless you.

I love you and bless you, too, O Lord. Amen.

October 20, 1995

Lord Jesus, do you want to write?

My beloved children, thank you for responding to my invitation of love. I, Jesus, am your Holy Teacher and reference to all that is good and righteous. I have extended an invitation to each of you to come aboard the ark of my mercy.

Children, when Noah guided the animals aboard the ark, did he just leave them to care for themselves? No, children, instead Noah carefully provided for each animal. There was none to enter the ark who did not flourish and live. Only those who refused the invitation of Noah perished.

Children, when you receive an invitation to a party, you attend with anticipation and joy. When you are invited to a home of a friend, you go with a glad heart. Truly, you consider these invitations important. I, Jesus, do not wish to remove the entertainment from your lives. Certainly, there are times to celebrate. But I ask you, why do you consider and validate these invitations, but you ignore my invitation? I, Jesus, have invited you to my home. I have invited you to have supper with me, which is the banquet of the Holy Sacrifice of the Mass. Yes, I, the Lord, constantly extend my invitation of love to you.

And now, just as in the days of Noah, I am inviting you to enter aboard the ark of my mercy. If Noah would take care of the animals and they would survive, then how much more would I, Jesus, do for you? Are you not greater than the animals? Those who continue to refuse my invitation of love shall lose all that they have. The door to the ark of my mercy shall be shut to those who reject me. Many will perish just from grief. For those who accept my invitation of love, everything shall be given them.

Children, I, Jesus, compare those who reject me to a piece of coal. This coal is only good for the furnace. But those who accept me, are as magnificent diamonds. They cannot lose their brilliant shine or their strength. Do not take the invitations of the world seriously, my beloved, for the world shall pass away and unless you are a passenger aboard the ark of my mercy, you shall perish as well.

Thank you, my devoted children, for recording my words. I, Jesus, shall grant the confirmations you asked.[78] Be patient, little children of my heart, I bless and love you.

We love and bless you, too, Lord, and may we be faithful passengers aboard your ark of mercy. Amen.

October 21, 1995

Lord Jesus, do you want to write?

Beloved children, I am the Lord, the Holy Spirit.

Dear ones, I have given you a mission. I, Jesus, have asked that you bring my words to the four corners. I have told you that amongst the wolves you would go. I have told you that the arrogant and hardhearted would be the target to

---

[78] Another disciple and I were seeking confirmations concerning specific actions we were contemplating. Both confirmations were granted within a few days.

receive these messages.

Disciples of Mercy, rejoice with me. I, Jesus, have set the table and now the meal is about to be served. Can you not see the glory of the Lord, thy God? Though I have been a beggar for your love, I have offered you mine without any reservations. Oh, what a feast I have prepared.

Disciples of Mercy, go to the hungry that they may receive nourishment by my words. Go to the thirsty that my messages might be as a delicious cold drink on a hot sweltering day. Dearest children, there will be verbal persecutions. You must not fear them. Receive courage and strength from my Sacred Heart. All that you need, children, shall be given you.

Thank you for writing, my devoted children. We shall continue tomorrow. Child, I bless you. Go in peace.

I love and bless you, too, O Lord. Amen.

October 22, 1995

Lord Jesus, do you want to write?

Little children, I am here. I am the Lord, the God of your Fathers from Everlasting to Everlasting.

Oh, beloved children, how easily you are distracted. How easily you lose sight of me. When you lose sight of me your peace escapes you. When you take your eyes from me, it is the same as opening the door for satan. Surely, I tell you, he will not knock and wait to be invited in. As swiftly as lightening strikes a tree, so shall he strike.

My beloved ones, you are not without protection. If you had a friend and you found your friend a place to live, would you leave him in this place without food and water? If you who are wretched can provide for others, think of how much I, Jesus, shall do for you.

A powerful heavenly court lights your way and protects you on your journey to me. Michael, the warrior, immediately comes to defend those who call upon him. The Rosary is a sword of holiness and truth. Though you live upon the earth, I, the Lord, have placed you within my wounds. It is important for you to understand, children, that the evil one waits for you to turn away from me. He is as a spider who has spun his web to catch his food. Yes, children, he spins many webs of confusion and discontent, and of division and jealousy. He creates an atmosphere of friction in the midst of the calm. Beware of him, my children. Do not let your eyes wander from me.

Thank you, my children, for recording my words. I bless you both. Go in peace.

We bless you and love you, too, Lord. Amen.

October 23 and 24, 1995[79]

October 25, 1995

Lord Jesus, do you want to write?

My beloved children, thank you for your sacrifice of love. I, the Lord, have heard the cries of my people, Israel. I have bent my ears to their cries.

Dear children, in the desert of sin you shall hear two voices calling you. You shall hear the voice of the snake, the evil one. You shall hear my voice which is a love song that I send to you on the wings of angels. And yet, my beloved Israel, when on one hand you are presented with sweetness and on the other hand you are presented with bitterness and sour, you reject the sweetness of my love. When you reject the sweetness of my love, all of Israel suffers and drinks from the bitter chalice that satan has prepared.

Children, again, I, Jesus, am referring to my Mystical Body. Every prayer that is uttered strengthens my Body. The sin of one affects the entire Body. Think of a river, my beloved. As the river flows, all the sand and all the life are carried within the arms of her currents. But what if part of the river flowed to the north while part of the river flowed to the east, while part of the river flowed to the west? If you were a fish, which direction would you choose? How would you know the correct direction? Oh, my people Israel, I am the Lord, thy God. I am

---

[79] I was in the hospital receiving chemotherapy and thus the Lord dispensed me from writing the messages these two days.

Holy and I am One. If you do not follow my commandments and return to my heart of love, you shall be as a fish in a river that endlessly takes you in the wrong direction.

I, the Lord, am the fisher of men's souls and I have loosed the nets of heaven that they may catch every soul who desires my mercy. The Spirit of God is circling the earth, capturing the hearts of those who have cried out to their God. Remember, children, I have told you, in the desert of sin you will hear two voices. Pray always for discernment, my little ones, that you will follow the voice of your God and not the voice of the serpent. But do not be afraid, my little ones, for truly I tell you if you are mine, I shall not let you go. Pay attention, my sleeping children. Persevere. Persevere. Persevere.

Thank you for recording my words. I love you and I bless you all.

We bless you and love you, too, Lord. Amen.

October 26, 1995

Lord Jesus, do you want to write?

My beloved child, come to my dinner table and break bread with me. I, Jesus, have given you all of me. I have given you my heart, my soul, my body, my blood. I have given you everything, that there would be nothing left for you to take. Even the crumbs of my broken and rejected heart, I have given you.

Now, I am inviting you to my dinner table. I have set the table and have made a place for you. I am even willing to give you a soft and gentle garment that has been designed to fit only you. My question to you, children, is, will you come? Will you come to my table when you hear me call? I wait for you, my beloved children, in every tabernacle throughout the world. I wait as a parent eagerly waits for his children to come home after being gone all day.

Jesus, are you crying?

Child of my heart, I am grieving. My heart is a sponge of loneliness and isolation. My children do not recognize me and they continue to ignore me. Dear one, if you were to plan a meal for your family, how would you feel if one of the members took the food and threw it in the trash? Would it not break your heart? Oh, my beloved one, at my dinner table there are many empty seats. There are many wine glasses that lips will never touch. There is much food that will not be eaten. I am referring to the infinite amount of graces I have to bestow on each of you. Come with open arms and uncluttered hearts and take, take, take. It is my desire to give.

I love you, child. Thank you for writing. I bless you.

I bless you and love you, too, Lord God. Amen.

October 27, 1995

Lord Jesus, do you want to write?

My beloved children, I am here. I am the God of your Fathers, the God of Abraham, Isaac, and Jacob. Wisdom is speaking.

My beloved children, I shall teach you a prayer to obtain holiness:

> O Spirit of Truth and Righteousness, Protector of the Tabernacle of Each Heart, look with pity upon your children. See the chalices which they themselves have filled and empty them, O Spirit of God, into the ocean of your forgiveness. Set a new chalice in front of each heart and bestow the gift of holiness upon each one of us. Fill every chalice with good works, desires for your love, and graces from the Eternal Gift-Giver. And then, Most Holy God, Spirit of Light and Love, permit us to drink from the cup that you have anointed with your Blood. Let every mouth proclaim the glory of the God Israel. Amen.

Jesus, that was a beautiful prayer.

Beloved children of my heart, if you could only understand the effect of prayer. Prayer is simple, my little ones. It is as the harmony to every melody; it is the melody to every harmony. There is nothing that cannot be accomplished by prayer.

Oh, you poor, foolish doctors and scientists, how much better your patients would be, if you prescribed prayer as well as medication. But my beloved, when you limit your resources, why do you wonder that your solutions are limited? Prayer has no boundaries in heaven. The soul that prays unites his heart eternally to my heart. The soul that prays is heard and answered.

I, the Lord, have so many gifts for you. My children, I am teaching you how to ask for them. The effect of prayer from a humble and contrite heart is more powerful than a hurricane.

My beloved ones, make time for me each day. Ask for the gift of prayer and it shall be granted to you. There is no incorrect or correct way to pray. I do not care for fancy words and false compliments. When you pray, pray in private and speak to me from your heart. Shed the outer garments concealing your heart and be as one who is naked before me. Come to me in humility and I will lift you into my heart of love.

We shall continue tomorrow, my beloved children. Thank you for recording my words. I bless you all. Go in peace.

We thank you, Lord, for your encouraging words. Give us the grace to be united to your heart as we constantly seek the gift of holiness. Amen.

October 28, 1995

Lord Jesus, do you want to write?

Devoted child of mercy, it pleases me that you would write in your circumstances.[80]

Child, it is the man who with heavy eyes says a goodnight prayer to me, that is honored by the Eternal Father. There are many ways to honor me, my precious one. Obedience to my will brings me glory and honor. Perseverance during trials crowns me with roses from my faithful.

---

[80] The last few days have really knocked me for a loop due to the effects of the chemotherapy and the medication I am taking for pain. The Lord is so grateful for our efforts to please him.

Oh, beloved child, I, the Lord, have been preparing you since the day you have been born. You have been born to be my messenger in the wilderness of sin. Go forth, my little daughter, and be not afraid.[81] You shall be granted all you need at the appointed time. Do not worry what you will say, for I will speak through you. The Spirit of Love and Righteousness shall speak through you.

Remember, child, to invoke the Holy Spirit. Call upon St. Michael and cast out demons that will assault you and others. As my disciple, I am giving you this authority. Speak, my child, speak boldly and do not be ashamed of the gifts I have given you. Speak with authority and confidence, my little sparrow, for I, Jesus, have taught you to fly.

I will be with you, little daughter. I love you and I bless you.

I love you and bless you, too, O Lord God. Amen.

October 29, 1995 [82]

October 30, 1995

My beloved children, I am here. I am the Blessed Virgin Mary and the Mother of the Holy One of Israel.

When my children gather together in the name of my Beloved Son, Jesus, know that I am present as well. I come with roses, for I am delighted by your call to my Son.

---

[81] The next day I was to talk for the first time to a large audience (235 people) concerning the messages and how the Lord completely turned my life around.

[82] The Lord is always true to his word regarding his promise to assist me while I spoke to a large audience today. I was initially very nervous but after ten minutes everything flowed so smoothly, as if he was carrying me along. This was particularly true during the question and answer period. The Lord had dispensed me from taking a message on this day because I was physically exhausted after the lecture.

Children of my heart, be concerned for one another. You must not only concern yourselves with the physical well-being of someone. It is your responsibility to be concerned with their spiritual well-being. Those of you who follow my Beloved Son, Jesus, know that it is only the heart that matters and not one's outer appearance.

Children, if God judged you the way you judge others, there would be no heaven. Truly, none of you feel that another is worthy to go to heaven. It is funny how in your prayers you recommend family and friends to God, rarely recognizing your own need.

Let God be the welder in your life. Be as a metal in his hands. Be pliable, my beloved children. Be docile. We have given you the Rosary, my children. The Rosary is a sign of simplicity of the love of God. God's love is not complicated. God's love is peaceful. God's love produces love in others. Those who are simple recognize God's love.

Look at a rose, my beloved ones. It is a flower of magnificence God has chosen for his heavenly garden. God has chosen and ordained a place for each of you, my beloved ones. He who so loves the roses, loves you even more.

As your heavenly Mother, again, I make the appeal for your conversion and reconciliation with God. Extend your hands to me, my beloved ones. Does not an infant reach for their mother from the crib? Reach for me, my beloved, and I will take you to the manger. I will place you in the manger next to my beloved son, Jesus, and I will care for you as I do for him. Come, children, come.

Thank you, my beloved children for your sacrifice of love for my Son. Thank you for the time you have spent with me. I bless you, children.

Thank you, heavenly Mother, for being our advocate. May we always be honorable children.

Jesus, do you want to say anything?

My beloved children, I know you are weary. Persevere my little lambs. Soon you shall see your Savior in the clouds surrounded by the heavenly host. Remain awake, my little lambs, I am coming soon. We shall continue tomorrow, my little children. Go in peace. I bless you.

We bless you, too, Lord and dearest Mother. Give us the grace to follow the words you have spoken in our hearts and through our actions. Amen.

October 31, 1995

Lord Jesus, do you want to write?

Welcome, my little children. I am pleased with your efforts.

Little ones, be not afraid of the invisible world.[83] Who can harm you if I, Jesus, am with you? I am allowing you to share in my trials in the desert. For one to obtain a college degree, they must take many courses, even some they do not deem necessary.[84] You, children, are in my school. Trust the itinerary I have

---

[83] It is uncanny but just prior to receiving this message, another disciple and I were discussing the danger of the evil one intruding in our efforts to follow the Lord's will in everything he requests us to do. Unfortunately, the evil one can often mimic the voice of our Lord and Blessed Mother, thereby leading to confusion. The disciple present said we cannot allow the evil one to intimidate us or attribute to him too much power. The Lord now seems to confirm what had just been said and encourages us to persevere in properly dealing with the deceiver through the use of the weapons he has given to thwart him.

[84] Several hours later, the disciple and I present for this message were conversing about how our Lord seems to utilize metaphors in his message for that day which are attuned to the particular professional background of the disciples who are witnessing the message. In this case the disciple is a college professor who was commenting that the genius of God is demonstrated by the ability to deliver both a personal message to those present and a lesson understandable and directed to all humankind. Suddenly, I heard the Lord speak the following words, which I repeated to the disciple: "My children, you are like the individual branches connected to a large tree, but this large tree, like all other trees, falls within the light of the sun." I responded to the disciple, "See _____, how the Lord wants to be involved in all aspects of life. He wants to be included in our conversations as well." Truly, the Lord is a God of intimacy.

devised to teach you. I, Jesus, am teaching you to be ever on guard against the evil one's persuasions. Did he not try to lure me in many different ways?

Children, do not put your weapons down. Though at times they appear cumbersome, cast them not aside from you. There is a war, beloved. The war is waging. Those who sleep are weakened by the poison from satan's tentacles. No, do not put your weapons aside. When I, the Lord, say, "weapons," what am I referring to? The Rosary, as I have told you, is a sword of holiness and dignity. Scripture is your garment. Prayer is your strength. The Eucharist is your nourishment. If you cast any of these aside, even momentarily, you shall be as a tire that has been punctured. Though the air will leak out slowly, eventually the tire will be completely flat. Aside from these tools I have given you, I, Jesus, have provided you a hiding place. You are to hide within the depths of my wounds.

Children, when a storm approaches, do you try to find a secure building or do you go out in a rowboat? [85]

We love you, Lord.

I love you, too, children.

I have taught you every way to protect yourselves. You must trust me to do the rest. I, Jesus, am the secure building in the midst of the storm. The evil one is the rowboat.

Children, when you go to school, you are tested as a means for you to show how well you have absorbed the lesson. In my school there are tests as well. The main purpose of my test, however, is to strengthen you and sanctify you. All that I, Jesus, wish for you to remember, you shall. But I shall not force you to put all that I have taught you into practice. I leave that to you.

_____

[85] This statement struck a funny chord in me and the disciple present, for if anyone is familiar with storms, it is certainly individuals living in South Florida. It would be totally unthinkable for someone to even consider being in any size boat, let alone a rowboat, during the storms that occur in this area. This incongruity caused us to laugh. I responded to this with the following statement cited at the top of this page, to which the Lord replied, "I love ..."

Thank you, devoted children of my heart. Continue in your efforts to please me. I bless you and I love you.

Thank you, Lord, and may we always seek the security we so desperately need to thwart the evil one in your heart and wounds. Amen.

November 1, 1995

Lord Jesus, do you want to write?

My beloved one, record the words of the Life-Giver. I am He, the Author and Sustainer of Life. I am He who is Love. I am He who is the Sovereign and Holy. I am One God.

Children of my Sacred Heart, I, Jesus, am your Holy Teacher. Each day I present various tasks for you to accomplish. Does the servant not have responsibilities in the master's household? Children, the earth and all its inhabitants dwell within my household.

My little ones, many of you cry out to me saying, "Lord, I desire to do this for you; Lord, tell me what I can do to serve you." Ah, beloved children, first, you must learn to serve me in silence. Do not boast of your accomplishment, rather the Eternal Father who sees all shall reward you for your accomplishment. Be as a tiny flower in a vast and exotic garden. The flower will not be noticed by those who come to view the garden because the flower is unobtrusive.

After each task you accomplish for me, I, Jesus, will assign you another task. Many of you wish only to be associated with the limelight and the large scale evangelizations. But truly, I tell you, it is the small hidden flower that will be granted the most responsibility by the Father. For it is the small hidden flower that seeks no self-glorification or importance, rather to only seek his task accomplished and pleasing to God. Therefore, he shall be granted the most important missions by God.

Children, if you are silent in your work, you will hear the voice of the Comforter, the Holy Spirit. You shall be as one who plants one tiny seed and reaps a tremendous harvest. The loud and boisterous servant shall also plant a seed, but God will not water the garden, for the servant is only self-enterprising. Therefore, let each man cast aside his pride and need for applause, and begin to serve the kingdom of heaven. Begin to serve the one who has died in your place.

Thank you for writing. Be secure in my love. I bless you and love you.

I bless and love you, too, O Lord. Amen.

November 2, 1995

Lord Jesus, do you want to write?

Beloved children of my heart, I am here. I am the God of the Resurrection. I know you are weary, my little lamb. Persevere in your efforts, my child, I will not forsake you. You are only ill temporarily and it is to benefit the Kingdom of God.[86]

I did not come upon this earth to bring illness and suffering. On the contrary, I despise sickness and it is my desire to heal the sick. Many of you wonder why there is so much illness when I, Jesus, am the Divine Healer.

Children, with my bare hands I scooped out part of the earth, filled it with water, and called it an ocean. However, I tell you, because you have placed toxic chemicals and wastes of all kinds into the oceans, you have sickened that part of my creation. But none of you worry if the animals or if the fish are sick because of your efforts, you only wonder why there are diseases and human beings become ill. You cannot cut yourself with a sharp piece of glass and not be scarred. You cannot poison part of my creation without it affecting you. All of creation rests in the palm of my hand. If part of my creation bestows injury and illness upon the other part, how shall the entire creation be not affected?

And now, my children, you have turned the sword of cannibalism and immorality in your direction. You have placed the sword of abomination and it

---

[86] The Lord is assuring me, despite the negative prognosis of my physicians, that the cancer will eventually be eradicated and I need to trust him entirely and that this cross has benefit.

now points to the womb. Do you think it is an unselfish and compassionate person that terminates the life of the unborn child? This is murder. This is murder. This is murder. Do you not send murderers to prison?

Yes, I, Jesus, have come upon the earth to heal the sick and make low the proud. But I have healed you and you have rejected it. I have provided cures for every disease upon the earth but you have aborted them. What more do you wish me to do? In your selfish arrogance you call yourself "god." You shall wear your ignorance as a cloak about your shoulders for all eternity. I carry you in the palm of my hand, but it is you, children, who, by your nature, bring about diseases and pestilences. Your arrogance is a more deadly and virulent disease than Ebola.[87] When you are ready to accept my teachings and to accept my commandments, healings will be plentiful.

Thank you, devoted scribe, for recording my words. Have faith, my little children, persevere in your efforts. I bless you.

We thank you, Lord, for your words of wisdom, admonishment, and consolation. May your people change their ways so that the great day of all healings may come soon. Amen.

November 3, 1995

Lord Jesus, do you want to write?

Yes, beloved daughter of my Sacred Heart. Record my words of love.

Come with me, my little children, and journey into the depths of my wounds. Enter into the embrace and passion of your Savior. Enter into the heart that

---

[87] Ebola is a mysterious and deadly virus that initially surfaced in the rain forests of Zaire. The virus, named after a small river located in a valley north of the Congo, takes only a few days to incubate and sets off a series of chain reactions in the body, which eventually causes the blood to clog and swell in the organs soon spilling out in the major orifices of the body. It is my understanding that very few survive and there is presently no known cure. Quarantine is the only means of defense against contagion.

loves infinitely and patiently.

Children, when a precious soul is baptized I, the Lord, set a place for that soul at the heavenly banquet. The angels, in their delight, begin to make the new garments that soul shall have for eternity. I, Jesus, call the soul to enter a union with me, to die with me, and then ultimately to rise with me. Unless the soul journeys through each of my wounds, this cannot be accomplished.

Child, be not afraid to record my words. I, Jesus, will confirm.[88]

When death comes and the soul is separated from the mortal flesh, the soul begins his journey either to me or to the adversary. The soul that comes to me will encounter a time of "passing through the valley" from death to immortality. The soul is being led through my wounds. The soul is being prepared for heaven and is being sanctified and bathed by the eternal light that emanates from within my wounds. Truly, I tell you, beloved, it is not enough for a soul to look at the wounds of his Savior. No, the soul who is being prepared for heaven must journey through my wounds because the nails pierced my flesh from one side to the other. The soul coming to me must encounter being pierced from the side of death through to the side of eternal salvation. The journey through my wounds is a journey through me, with me, and in me. Thus, we become truly one body.

Little one, I know you are weary. Daughter, you cannot comprehend the magnitude of graces the Eternal Father has granted you. Persevere, my little lamb, and I, the Lord, will help you.

Thank you for writing. Go in peace.

I love you forever, O Lord. Amen.

---

[88] Because of the theological implications of the journey a soul takes both at the beginning of life and at the end of life, I had asked the Lord for a confirmation to assure that what is being recorded is truly from him. I was granted this, a white flower, within the next day.

November 4, 1995

Lord Jesus, do you want to write?

My beloved children, welcome. I have been waiting for you. Children, there shall be many obstacles upon the path you are traveling. As I, Jesus, was taken to Calvary, I had to endure many obstacles. Stones were thrown at me. I was mocked and ridiculed. I was spat upon. Even the hair upon my head was pulled. As the lamb, I was taken to the slaughter.

In some ways, my beloved children, you shall be taken to the slaughter as well. No, you shall not have to face the nails or the end of a spear, but rather the fierceness of verbal ridicule. Many of you wish to be called my disciples, yet you do not want to follow in my footsteps. Many of you wonder what is the correct path to me.[89] It is simple, beloved. See where I, Jesus, have set my feet and then do the same. If you truly recognized my footsteps, then you would also see how I have designed my Church.

Be not afraid, my little lamb, speak the words I, the Lord, am speaking to you. I, Jesus, desire all of you to listen to my high bishop [the Pope] for truly he walks where I walk. I have set my high bishop to be the leader of my Church. I have given the ten commandments to be the walls of my Church. I have given the Scripture to be the life of my Church. I have given myself in the Holy Sacrifice of the Mass that my Church will neither hunger nor thirst. I have given my Spirit that my Spirit may breathe life into my Church, and I have given you my beloved Mother to be the Mother of my Church.

Dear children, to honor me you must honor my Mother. To honor me you must cherish all that I have given you. The Church, my beloved, is my home upon the earth. It is the sanctuary of the most Holy and Blessed Trinity of the Lord God. Every answer that you seek shall be found in the tabernacle. The tabernacle, children, is my footstep upon the earth.

---

[89] Prior to this message, one of the disciples went to a non-denominational prayer service and inquired of me what would be Jesus' reaction to her behavior. I told her I was not sure but the Lord in his infinite wisdom answered her query because the disciple was present for this message, which was the occasion the Lord took to instruct us on his true Church.

Thank you, my beloved children, for your sacrifice of love. I bless you all. We shall continue tomorrow.

I love and bless you, too, Lord. Amen.

November 5, 1995

Lord Jesus, do you want to write?

My devoted child, let us begin. Record my words of love.

Child, how many times do I, Jesus, forgive you? Have I ever turned my face away from you and offered you criticism rather than forgiveness? No, beloved, I, the Lord, forgive and forget each of your offenses. I hold you in my arms and place you near my heart. I cast your offenses into the ocean of forgiveness and I, Jesus, remember them no longer.

Dearest one, be forgiving to others. Do not put a limit on your patience and forgiveness to others.

Let us continue, my dear child.

Child, the gifts that I, the Lord, desire to bestow upon a soul are infinite. If I grant the gift of faith, then this gift has no limits because I am unlimited. Children, my gifts cannot be measured by human standards. Truly, my gifts cannot fit into a gift box, for they are without limit. They are infinite and eternal as I am.

Which of you knows the star that is the last one in the sky? I tell you, there is no last star. There is no limit to anything in my kingdom. The Spirit of the Lord of Hosts moves as he wills. The Spirit of God wills infinity into existence, and so it is with all creation. Oh, yes, my beloved, there are some changes and alterations in my creation, but even these are constant and faithful. Everything that comes from me is constant and faithful.

Lord, forgive me. I am so tired.

Ah, my little one, I know you are weary. We shall continue tomorrow, my child. Rest. I bless you.

I bless you, too, O Lord. Amen.

November 6, 1995

Lord Jesus, do you want to write?

Yes, my child, record my message of hope.

Children, the moment the nails penetrated my hands and feet, hope was born. Until that time, hope did not exist. It did not exist because the door to heaven was shut and locked. But I, Jesus, came upon the earth to bring hope to those who despair and to bring life to those who are dead. Many of you are already dead. I am not referring to a physical death, my beloved ones. Rather, I am referring to a spiritual death which is the most significant. When one dies, there is no reason to grieve if he is reconciled to me and one of my faithful ones. The only time to grieve is if one dies and he is not with me. Oh, then, truly you should grieve. You should fast and tear your garments in two. Put on sackcloth and ashes and grieve. Yes, for truly it is a sad moment. All of heaven grieves when one dies and goes to the eternal pit.

Children, there is no return from the eternal pit. It is a place to cast all hope aside. There is no hope because the Lord, thy God, is absent from the eternal pit. There is no consolation from the unending flame. There is no drink for the thirsty, nor is there food for the hungry. There is no relief from the unending torment of the heart.

Remember, my children, I created the soul, that the soul would return to me and dwell with me for eternity. A great abyss separates heaven from hell. This abyss either guides you to heaven where hope and love pave the streets, or to hell where hope and love do not exist.

Children, I am Jesus. I am the one who desires you infinitely with an incomprehensible love. Open your hearts, my children. I am calling you. I am begging for your love. Repent, children. Change your ways. Hear my voice and accept my teachings. I am the Author of Love and Hope. Satan is the thief of love and hope. Choose wisely, my children.

Thank you for writing, little mercy of my heart. I bless you.

I bless you, too, O Lord. Amen.

November 7 and 8, 1995[90]

November 9, 1995

Lord Jesus, do you want to write?

Come, my beloved one, and record the words of the Divine Heart of Truth and Justice.

Dear children, think of the qualities you would desire to see within a judge. Would you desire him to be humble or arrogant? Would you desire him to be merciful and compassionate or selfish and uncaring? Truly, I tell you that when you come into my courtroom and stand before me, you will be standing before the Love God of Eternity. You will be standing before Mercy. You will be standing before Compassion. You will be standing before Wisdom. You will be standing before Divine Justice. Ah, beloved, as my mercy consumes the humble, so does my wrath consume the arrogant.

For those who approach me in honesty and humility, all shall be granted them. For those who stand before me clutching their arrogance, it shall be their arrogance that will hurl them to their knees. Every knee shall bow before me.

Children, you shall bow in love or you shall bow in fear. Either way, children, I, Jesus, am Lord and every knee will bow. Even the ground that supports your bent knee shall rejoice on that day.

Children, the day of my return is approaching. The chariots in heaven are being prepared for the victory when darkness shall be plummeted into the abyss forever. Do you dwell in darkness, my children? Come to me, my little lost souls. I, Jesus, love you to depths you cannot comprehend. Come to me and become a candle of light upon the earth.

----

[90] I was in the hospital receiving chemotherapy on these two days. While we were waiting to be admitted, my husband and another disciple saw a man wearing a tee shirt with the words, *Jesus is our only hope!* They related this to me and I took it to be a confirmation of the message of November 6.

Thank you, dearest child, for writing. Be not afraid, my little one.[91] I bless you and I love you.

I bless you and love you, too, Lord. Amen.

November 10, 1995

My beloved child, I am here. I am Blessed Virgin Mary and the Mother of Jesus. I am the Mother of the Shepherd. I am the Mother of his Flock.

Dear one, the words I speak come from my Immaculate Heart and from the Sacred Heart of Jesus. Our hearts are joined by his bitter passion. His passion is the umbilical cord that connects our hearts. Though we are independent of one another, we are completely united in our hearts and minds. We are as one because we are united by love.

My beloved daughter, this is what my Son desires of each of his children. He desires perfect union in love. Children, join your hearts to the heart of my Son. Let God's embrace consume you and become one with God. Though you are all part of the body of Jesus, you must be united in love. Allow the Holy Spirit to unite you by opening your hearts to his heart. Listen to the voice of God, children. Has he not called for your conversion and reconciliation with him? Have you not heard my voice begging for your return to God?

Children, you are part of my Son's flock and I am your Mother. When you come to me you will find my arms outstretched and waiting to embrace you. You will find my hands extended, waiting to bring you to my beloved Son, Jesus. I should like to give each one of you a rose from my crown, that you may present it to Jesus in union with your heart and your loyalty. Please, my beloved children, do not cast aside the love of God. This is a grave mistake.

Thank you, my devoted child, for recording my words. Do not be afraid, my

---

[91] The Lord is encouraging me not to lose faith in his word despite the ominous reports I've been getting from the doctors.

child.[92]   I will always help you. I bless you and I love you.

I bless you and love you, too, Mama.

Lord, do you want to write?

My beloved one, meditate on the words of my Mother. Go in peace. Little disciple of mercy, I bless you.

I bless you, too, Lord, and love you. Amen.

November 11, 1995

Lord Jesus, do you want to write?

My beloved children, how great is my joy when you are gathered together in my name.

Little ones, my love is an expression of humility. From the moment of my birth I was bathed in poverty. Poverty was my garment the years that I was with you, that you may know I depended upon my Eternal Father for everything. Does an infant not depend on his mother for everything?

Humility, my children, is when the soul acknowledges its nothingness before God. Humility is when the soul completely accepts its limitations and weaknesses. Just as you would apply an anesthetic ointment to a wound, humility is an ointment to heal the scars of sin. For truly it is a humble soul that is heard and answered. It is the humble soul who is empty and void of material consolation and seeks spiritual consolation from God. This is a soul that is great in the eyes of God. This is a soul who shall be granted all that he asks.

Children, in humility I, Jesus, come to you with my heart in my hands begging for your love. It is humility which breeds courage and patience. It is humility that is the seed in the garden of unlimited virtue. In every garden, children,

---

[92] The Blessed Mother is well aware of my fears regarding the cancer in my body and is echoing the Lord's assurance that there is nothing to fear regardless of what shall occur.

seeds must be planted which produce fruit. I, Jesus, am the Farmer of Virtues. I am the keeper of the rose garden of love and hope. And I am the water to bring all life and virtue into existence. All life grows through me and with me for every beat of my heart is a breath upon the earth. Do you think the earth does not breathe, my children? All creation breathes, my children. The Holy Spirit moves where he wills and breathes existence into all creation.

Remember, beloved, you cannot comprehend all that I have done. Even the sand is humble. Even the sand recognizes its place is to be crushed by billions of tons of water. Yet the sand is appreciative of its existence and gives glory to me, the Lord God.

Many of you wonder why you do not receive an answer from me right away. I tell you, truly, the humble and contrite soul is answered first. It is because the humble and contrite soul recognizes the eternal and sovereign authority of God and the lowliness of his own humanity. Because of his respect for me, I place his needs above all others for he is great in my sight. Ask for the virtue of humility, my children, for the Lord, thy God, considers humility a priceless gem.

Beloved ones, I am pleased with you. Truly, you have heard my voice and are my beloved disciples. Go with my words, children. Teach others as I have taught you. Tell them of my love.

Thank you, my devoted child, for recording my words. I bless you all. Go in peace.

We bless and love you, too, Lord. Teach us to be contrite and humble souls. Amen.

November 12, 1995

Lord Jesus, do you want to write?

My beloved child, listen to the One Who Is. Wisdom is speaking and using your hand as an instrument of grace.

Children, children, the ark of my mercy is sailing from soul to soul. Why do you not come aboard? How many times shall I, Jesus, return to each soul imploring your love and loyalty?

Beloved ones, soon the doors will shut on the ark of my mercy and for those who have not listened, it shall be too late for the hand of judgment is soon to be upon each of you. The chastisement of justice is soon to be upon you. Your souls will be flooded with grief when you shall look into the mirror of your wretchedness. You shall see yourselves as I, Jesus, see you. You shall see yourselves through the eyes of honesty and self-criticism. Children, on this day many of you will be crushed by the weight of your sins. The baggage you carry each day shall be put on the scale of Divine Justice and you shall feel crushed by the weight of your sins.

My beloved, I, Jesus, have provided a way for you to loose yourselves from the weight of your sins. Go to Confession, my children. Go frequently. Each time you go, I, Jesus, place a drop of my holy, Precious Blood upon your hearts, thereby healing you and discarding your burdens. Children, on the day of justice, those of you who have not reconciled with me will perish from fear alone. That is not my desire, my little ones. I desire you to be free from sin and to soar as a bird above your earthly mortality. Frequent this sacrament, my children, and offer reparation on behalf of your lost brothers and sisters.

Beloved one, do not despair.[93] I, the Lord, shall help you. Go in peace. I bless you.

I adore you, O Lord. Amen.

November 13, 1995

Lord Jesus, do you want to write?

Come, little mercy of my heart, record my words of love. I AM is speaking. Wisdom is speaking.

Dearest children, I, Jesus, shall give you a lesson on discipleship. Yes, if you truly desire to be a student in my school, then you must learn what it truly means to follow me.

---

[93] The Lord is very conscious of my feelings of fear and doubt that are surfacing due to the negative reports of the doctors.

Let us continue. The fisherman takes out his boat before sunrise. As he casts his nets, he knows he must wait patiently for the fish to come. Yes, eventually they will come, for the successful fisherman has learned patient endurance. To be my disciple you must be patient. You must be willing to wait upon my instructions.

Children, my way is perfect. My path is perfect. Follow my commandments and you will be following my path. To be my disciple you must be willing to place the needs of other souls first. The soul that is lost from me, should be your first priority. Never lose sight of one who is distant from me, rather as my disciple, you must continuously extend your hands. You must be ready at a moment's notice to help one in need, remembering that their needs are more important than yours. You must not be critical, but rather you must see each one as my child. Remember, there is no discrimination in heaven, for the sun shines over all the earth, not just the few.

Ah, beloved, I know you are weary. Rest, child, in my Sacred Heart. Do not despair, my little heartbeat. I, Jesus, will help you. Trust me.

I love you, Lord, Holy Spirit, and Mama Mary, forever. Give me the grace to always trust in your love for me. Amen.

November 14, 1995

Lord Jesus, do you want to write?

Little ones, I am here. I am Jesus, the Lamb of Reconciliation. I am the Fulfillment of All Hope.

Oh, my little one, your lack of faith grieves me.[94]

---

[94] Jesus is very disappointed in me for my lack of trust and even doubt in his very presence. This day was not a good one regarding the news of my medical prognosis and I was having tremendous turmoil despite the Lord's assurances in the past that my illness is only temporary (see Message of November 2).

I'm sorry, Lord.

Child of my heart, remember I told you that there will come a time when you will doubt my presence. The time is at hand.[95]

Please forgive me, Lord. I'm scared.

Child, as I have told you, I will part every Red Sea. I will carry you in my arms to the other side. You have nothing to fear, my little lamb. You must understand (that I, Jesus, am speaking to all my children) that there are a certain amount of steps to Calvary. There is a certain distance for each of you to walk the path to Calvary. This distance cannot be reduced. It is your willingness to accept my hand that will make your journey easier. Sometimes, children, it may appear that your suffering is far greater than another's. Sometimes, my children, one has only fifty steps to take to Calvary, while another has five hundred steps to take. But do not judge another's situation, for only the Lord, thy God, knows the sufferings of the heart.

Dearest ones, if you won the lottery, you would rejoice on the journey to pick up your prize. But I, Jesus, solemnly assure you that you should rejoice on your journey to Calvary for I am the prize that awaits you.

Beloved ones, never does a soul walk to Calvary alone. My beloved Mother accompanies every soul on their journey to Calvary. I, Jesus, provide Simons to help you carry your cross. The day will come, children, when those of you who did not have a heavy cross, will beg for one. The day will come when those who have had a heavy cross will desire an even heavier one. The cross is priceless. The cross is my gift to each of you.

Thank you, beloved children, for recording my words. We shall continue tomorrow. I bless you, children. Be willing to serve me, children. I have graced you abundantly.

We thank you, Lord, and ask for the graces to carry the cross to Calvary in a

---

[95] Jesus is reminding me of a prophecy he made last year regarding my present doubt and lack of trust in the message of June 6, 1994: "You will thirst for me and doubt that I am with you.."

trusting manner. Amen.

November 15, 1995

Lord Jesus, do you want to write?

Yes, my devoted one. Come and record my words. My words are life. My words are as medicine for the sick and food for the hungry. I AM is speaking. Listen carefully to my words, my little daughter.

I, the Lord, have placed each star in the heavens according to a specific plan. I have placed each planet in accordance to my plan for creation. Oh, you silly, arrogant scientists, you are more foolish than a snail, for at least the snail recognizes he has a roof above his head. The snail with his limited abilities knows that I am the Lord.

Consider the flower, my children. Is the flower not an umbrella for the tiny insects below it? Is the tree not a hiding place for various creatures? Why is the pearl hidden within a shell and not scattered freely as bird seed? Oh, beloved ones, can your scientists answer these questions? No, on the contrary, for I, the Lord, have confounded them. I, the Lord, have given wisdom to the simple and pure of heart.

Dear ones, it is my desire to bestow many gifts upon you. I wish to see each of you become as birds. Yes, children, soar away from your earthly mortality and become unshackled in my love. My love shall become your wings and you shall soar as a bird. I, Jesus, will lead you to rest in my heart where you shall receive nourishment and strength. Oh, my little lambs, the cross is heavy for each of you. As you approach the calvaries in your life, know that I, Jesus, go before you always.

We shall continue tomorrow, my little lamb. Thank you for writing. I bless you.

I bless and love you forever, Holy Spirit. Amen.

November 16, 1995

Lord Jesus, do you want to write?

Yes, my beloved child. Allow me to use your hand as an instrument of grace. I am the Shepherd of My People, Israel.

The cross upholds the earth.[96] The cross upholds the sea and all its inhabitants. The cross upholds the earth and all its inhabitants. The cross upholds all creation. When one accepts the cross as a part of his life, he is given a share in my redemptive work. He is given a chance to help humanity.

Beloved children, the cross brings countless graces to the one who carries it and countless graces to others as well. Although there is not one to be spared a cross, I, the Lord, have given heavier crosses to specific souls. I have done this that these souls may offer reparation for their brothers and sisters. Children, there is not one among you that has not been lost from me at one time or another. There is not one among you who has not fallen under the weight of the cross.

Oh, beloved one, what do you think the arrogant do with their crosses? They accept the cross with the attitude that they do not need my help to carry the cross. With their arrogance comes their lack of humility and they would rather suffer silently then to seek help. Oh, beloved children, do you think I, the Lord, do not weep because of such behavior? Did I not receive help to carry my Cross to Calvary? As I, Jesus, received help, so shall I provide you help. The Cross sustains humanity, for the Cross is covered with my blood and my blood sustains humanity. When you acknowledge the value of the Cross, then truly you are acknowledging the importance and value of my shed blood, hence, my death. Those who acknowledge my death on the Cross as the key to salvation are acknowledging me and the Eternal Father who sent me.

Thank you, beloved one. Rest, little mercy of my heart. We shall continue

---

[96] I was becoming very disheartened concerning the minimal effects the chemotherapy was having on the cancer cells and wondering why we humans suffer in life. The Lord took the opportunity to console me by explaining the value of the cross, particularly his Cross of expiation, atonement, and reparation which he invites us to share in some capacity. He promises that he will never abandon us in our crosses - a promise that I must constantly rely upon in my present trial.

tomorrow.

I bless and love you forever, O Lord. Amen.

November 17, 1995

Children of my heart, I am here. I am the Blessed Virgin Mary and the Mother of God.

Children, my heart rejoices to see you together. I desire to see unity between all of those who follow my Son. My dearest ones, the clock is ticking. The time of mercy is almost over. I am only a messenger, children, and today I have come with the message that the clock is ticking. The hours of mercy are moving away from you. God's justice is soon to be upon you.

My beloved ones, I am calling you to tell others of my words. I have already asked that you be more deeply committed to my beloved Son, Jesus. Now, children, the currents are changing direction. Many of the birds and insects have left their homes in search of hiding places. There is only one hope, my beloved, and that hope is Jesus, my beloved Son. Some of you, my children, say that you believe in God, yet you do not pray nor attend Mass. If you believe in God, why do you distance yourselves from him? You cannot have a relationship with God if you do not pray.

Children, I have listened and heard all of you. Each one of you has a heavy cross. I tell you, children, you cannot carry the cross without the help of my beloved Son.

Children, it is the responsibility of my Son's disciples to tell others of his love and mercy.

Rest, my child, I bless you. Go in peace.

We thank you and bless you, Mama Mary, and may we be always faithful to the discipleship of your Son. Amen.

November 18, 1995

Lord Jesus, do you want to write?

My beloved children, you have brought joy to my heart. Thank you, beloved son, for recording my words.[97] I am the Lord of the Heavens and the Earth. I am the Lord over the Visible and Invisible. I, Jesus, shall instruct you on the virtue of patience.

I, Jesus, walk the ocean floors and I plant different seeds. These seeds will eventually begin a long and perilous journey to the top. These small little seeds which I have planted are a perfect example of patient endurance. They know that their mission shall not be fulfilled until they reach the top of the sea, where other fish will feed upon them. Yet they make their way from the floor of the ocean to the very top with patience, for if they did not, they would be unaware of the incoming attacks of predators.

Children, I am Jesus. I am the one who nurtures and sustains you with an infinite love. I have given you a metaphor, my children. I, Jesus, will explain.

Each of you is a little seed upon the ocean floor. Your journey to the top is the steps that you take throughout your life. Those of you who make it to the top are the ones heaven shall open her gates for. As I have explained, if the little seed swam quickly and impatiently he would not see an oncoming predator. He would be devoured before ever reaching his destination. So it is with you, my children; do not rush from one situation to another. Be prayerful. Be patient, always permitting the Spirit of God to lead. If you rush through your life, you will not see satan when he comes. He is the predator to devour you. Pray for patience, my children. Pray for awareness and discernment. I, Jesus, will help you.

Thank you, beloved children, for your sacrifice of love. I bless you all. Extend my love to others.

We bless you, too, Lord. Thank you for your mercy, love, and such great patience with us. Amen.

---

[97] One of the disciples who lives in a distant state was present to witness and record the message that Jesus was to give. Jesus prefaced his message with an expression of gratitude to this disciple. Jesus rarely does this, which I interpret to be a sign of his endearment to this disciple.

November 19, 1995

Lord Jesus, do you want to write?

My beloved ones, I am here. I am the God of your Fathers, the God of Abraham, Isaac, and Jacob.

Children, where does the wind come from, and where does it go when it is finished blowing?[98] The wise man knows that the wind comes from the great storehouses of heaven. The wind, my children, is a vehicle for graces to be delivered. The wind, my children, is the breath of the Spirit of God. Who can say where the wind begins and the wind ends? Only the wise man knows that I, the Lord, am the master of the winds. Did I, Jesus, not say to the wind, "be still," and it listened to me?

Children who worship false idols are an abomination in my sight.[99] Do your false idols control the winds? Do your false idols watch the unborn in the mother's womb? Tell me, children, what do your idols do for you that I do not? Do they make the sun rise and set each day? When the ground cries out to be watered, do they provide rain? Was it your idols who provided a home for the snail and a place to hide a pearl? Do your idols know how many blades of grass and grains of sand are upon the earth? Your idols are empty, passing fantasies

---

[98] I had asked the Lord if he would not mind giving the message outdoors rather than the usual place in the home. He agreed, so a disciple and I sought a cozy, restful place exposed to the wonderful environment of the open air. It was a beautiful, windy day. The Lord used the experience of the wind gently buffeting our faces to deliver this message.

[99] Yesterday, I was watching a segment of those video magazines that often border on the sensational. To my amazement the segment was addressing the fact that people were now deifying Elvis Presley. They were actually blessing themselves in the name of Elvis and mounting pictures of Elvis on crosses. The Lord interrupted my viewing with a very harsh tone of disgust and anger. This message more fully addresses what will occur to those who violate the First Commandment.

which I, the Lord, shall crush with my bare hands. I shall crush your idols and all those who worship them.

Have mercy, Lord!

Daughter, I am weary. I am sickened by the atrocities and abominations upon this earth. The stench of idolatry has filtered into the Throne Room of heaven. I say to you, "repent, repent, repent."

To those who worship false idols, the next time the wind brushes the back of your neck, you should fall prostrate and beg for mercy for I am the wind. Call to your false idols in that moment, they will not hear you.

Beloved, I am consumed with grief. My heart is sorrowful. I will do anything for a soul that repents but there is nothing that enkindles my wrath more than idolatry. I have crushed evil worshipers since the beginning of time and I will continue to do so! How dare you come in my sanctuaries with your false gods. How dare you use my house to pray to your false gods. Since you have brought evil and ugliness into my home, I shall permit the same to be brought into your home.

Lord, have mercy!

Daughter, my mercy sustains the earth. Go and tell the people. My words are finished. We shall continue tomorrow.

We bless you, Lord, and ask that you carry us along the wind of righteousness. Amen.

November 20, 1995

Lord Jesus, do you want to write?

My beloved children, thank you for responding to my invitation of love. When you call to me I, Jesus, will help you to obtain virtues. In the garden of virtues I, Jesus, shall plant the seeds that will send the fragrance of righteousness to the Eternal Father.

My beloved ones, if you had a vegetable garden, there would be certain steps you would take to secure the life of the garden. I, Jesus, do the same in my garden of virtue. The garden begins when a precious soul is baptized. I water the garden with the water of grace. Grace, my children, is my gift to you. With grace the various seeds of virtue that I have planted will blossom into magnificent flowers. Remember, children, grace flows freely in the garden of virtue if the soul is obedient to my commands. The soul must confess and repent frequently. The soul must frequent the sacraments.

Dear ones, just as there can be attacks on a vegetable and flower garden from insects and other events, attacks can also come upon the garden of virtue. When this occurs, the soul which was progressing in holiness in the eyes of God begins to decay as grace is removed.

Children, why would grace be removed from a soul? Grace is removed when the soul is not reconciled to me and is in disobedience to any of my commandments. Two sins which block the soul from grace are arrogance and pride. There are others, my children, but I, the Lord, say these are the most dangerous ones. These sins are not easily recognized and they become the weeds to suffocate the flower in the garden of virtue. Grace flows freely as a river but sin is as a dam which stops the flow of the water.

Oh, beloved ones, I do not ask you for money or cars or gems. I, the Lord, ask for your loyalty and obedience to my commandments. The soul that follows my precepts is granted all that he asks of me. The soul that follows my commandments is heard and answered by me when he prays.

Children, I am Jesus, the Gift-Giver. Come and accept the gifts I desire to give you. My gifts are priceless.

Thank you, children, for your sacrifice of love. We shall continue tomorrow. I bless you all.

We bless you and love you, too, Lord. Amen.

November 21, 1995

Lord Jesus, do you want to write?

My devoted children, your words have brought me great joy this day.[100] So few spend time with me. Most of my children only pray during times of crises. They believe that I am the reason for their crises but I assure you, it is their sins which bring their catastrophes. I am pleased with you, children. I shall answer your request and teach a prayer to console your Creator.

> Father and Majesty of All Heaven and Earth, what could a wretch like me say to console you? I shall say that I am grieved by my offenses to you. I shall say that I will worship and adore the Union of the Three, the Most Holy and Blessed Trinity. On my knees do I come to whisper love songs to you. Grant me your passion to love you. Grant me your heart to love the world. Grant me your eyes that I may see your crucified body impaled upon the heart of everyone I meet. And when I love the stranger, it is because I love you. When I do my work silently, it shall be to console your grieving heart. When I am forgiving of those who mock and wound me, I will be anointing all your wounds. When I console others, then I am consoling you, my God. Amen.

Children, you have asked how you may console me. Each time you are kind to your brother, you are kind to me. Each time you recognize my sovereign authority, you bring consolation to my heart. The greatest consolation, however, is for me to look into one's eyes and to see them teary with love for me. Oh, how my heart leaps for joy.

Beloved ones, think of this example. When the sea meets the shore, it wets every grain of sand it touches. It ignores none. This is how you can console me,

---

[100] The evening before this message, the Blessed Mother requested that we, the Disciples of Mercy, console Jesus, her Son, tonight. I made the necessary phone calls to the disciples relating the request. Each disciple agreed to do some form of prayer to Jesus hoping to console him for the sins that are committed by mankind. Today, one of the disciples who was present for this message had inquired just a few minutes prior to the commencement of the message that the Lord teach us a prayer of consolation to his heart. The Lord responded immediately to this request as evidenced by teaching this beautiful prayer.

touch every person you meet.

My children, you are the light of my love to shine upon the earth. You are my disciples and my students. Within your hearts, I, Jesus, have lit the candle I have placed there at the moment of your conception. Continue in your efforts, children, and great will be your rewards.

Thank you for writing. I bless you.

We eternally thank you, Lord, in affording us the opportunity to receive your prayer and instruction on how we may console your heart. Give us the perseverance to do so always. Amen.

November 22, 1995

Lord Jesus, do you want to write?

Little mercy of my heart, how I long for you to come to me. How I long for all my children to come to me. I am a father who is cast aside by his children. I am a God who is cast aside by his people.

Hear my words, O Israel. Pay attention to the heavens, children. The time is at hand. Children, there are signs to mark the beginning of each of the seasons. There are signs that are being given to you, now, my children, that you will know the season of mercy is about to end and the season of judgment is about to begin.

Hear my words, O Israel. Pay attention to which direction the wind is blowing. Pay attention to the trees and all plants. On the day of my return, every blade of grass will be standing at perfect attention. Every tree will be bent to face me.

Hear my words, O Israel. Pay attention to the signs all about you. Listen to my messengers and those to whom I have given extraordinary gifts. Pay attention, my children. When I, the Lord, return, I shall not accept excuses. Many of you will deny that I have called to you. I solemnly assure you that every creature on the face of the earth and under the earth will know the moment of my visitation. Every knee will bow. Every heart will skip a beat. Every soul will see itself through my eyes.

Repent now, my children, that on the day of my visitation, you shall be able to face me with happiness. Oh, but many of you shall flee to the mountains, but even the mountains, shall cast you aside on that day.

We will continue tomorrow, my beloved student. Be at peace, little child of my mercy.

I love you, my merciful Lord. Amen.

November 23, 1995 - Thanksgiving

Children, I am here. I am Blessed Virgin Mary and the Mother of God. I am the Mother of Mercy and the Mother of the Sick.

Dear ones, I am weeping. I have come to beg you to repent and turn back to God. Few of you have heeded my requests. Why do you not come to thank my Son? Today, is a day that each one of you should have brought bouquets of praises to the foot of the Cross.[101] Today, children, you were afforded an opportunity to be thankful and gracious in the eyes of God. What have you done with your opportunity, children?

I stand beside Jesus at every Mass.[102] God looks into each heart, children and there he separates the stones from the pearls. When you come to the Mass, children, come with a grateful heart, for it is a grateful heart that sings praises to God. When you come to Mass, children, come with an honest desire to discard your ways and accept God's ways. When you come to Mass, children,

---

[101] Earlier today, I attended Mass and was astonished to see so few expressing their thanks to God through the Holy Sacrifice of the Mass. At Mass I was also told by the Blessed Mother that she was going to give the message today.

[102] Just a few minutes prior to the message, a disciple present for this message suggested that we ask the Lord how we might more properly participate in the Mass, that is, what should be our dispositions so we might experience the fullness of graces available? I related that I would ask Jesus but today the Blessed Mother will be giving the message. To our complete surprise, the Blessed Mother responded to this request.

come as the metal and allow my beloved Son, Jesus, to be the welder. Be pliable. Be docile. Be willing to become an empty vessel so that the Lord may make manifest his glory through you. When you come to Mass, children, be willing to accept the love and mercy which Jesus desires to bestow on each of you. When you come to Mass, make certain that you have reconciled with God, thereby permitting grace to flow freely as a river. Remember what my Son has taught you, children. Sin is a dam that will block the flow of a river.[103] Sin is as a weed to suffocate the beauty of a flower.

When you come to Mass, children, come hungry, thereby permitting my Son to feed you. *Pray to the Holy Spirit, children, that you may hunger and thirst for the things of God. If you pray this before each Mass, you will be nourished both physically and spiritually by the Holy Eucharist.*[104] If you are hungry when you come to Mass, you shall accept the food that Jesus gives you.

My beloved children, why do you close your hearts to my Son? Many of you prepare great feasts on this day; you invite family and friends. Why do you not attend the banquet of the Holy Sacrifice of the Mass first? Is the food that you prepare and serve holy? Is the food that you prepare and serve able to grant eternal life? No, children. You are facing in the wrong direction. Beloved ones, you are facing the king of doom.

I have come as your Mother, children, to guide you to my Son's dinner table. Partake of the Holy Eucharist, children, first in your lives. Allow God to be first in your lives. If you do not, you shall have cast aside your gift of salvation.

I shall not say any more today, my children. Thank you for recording my words. I bless you.

We thank you, Mama Mary, may we be always properly disposed for the Mass and hungry for the Eucharist, the Bread of Life itself. Amen.

---

[103] The Blessed Mother is referring to the message given on November 20, 1995.

[104] The Blessed Mother requested that this exhortation be emphasized. This is the reason for the bold italics.

November 24, 1995

Lord Jesus, do you want to write?

Devoted children, I am here. I am the God of your Fathers, the God of Abraham, Isaac, and Jacob. Wisdom is speaking.

It brings me great joy, children, when you invoke my name and the name of my beloved Mother.[105] So few believe in my Real Presence at these moments. When you are gathered together in my name I, the Lord, am present. When I am present so shall you find my beloved Mother.

Children, praise is when the soul accepts with humility his nothingness before me. Praise is when the soul acknowledges that I am the One, True, Eternal God.

At the moment of your conception I, the Lord, placed a candle upon the altar of each heart. If it is your desire to praise me, then, in essence, you are saying, "Lord, come and light the candle upon my heart." Ah, my beloved ones, this is a candle of faith. This is a candle of love. Once I, Jesus, light this candle, no man can extinguish it. Each day you are given an opportunity to walk with me or to walk away from me. I leave this decision to you. Those who walk with me become as candles upon the face of the earth. There is no limit to praise and love. There is no limit because I am not limited.

Children, you cannot praise me and love me enough with your heart. You must ask to love me and praise me with my heart. When you ask this, I will place your heart within mine. I will seal your heart by my blood and the candle upon your heart will begin to glow with a brighter intensity. Praise is when the soul realizes it can do nothing apart from me. It is, therefore, my desire that the soul acts in complete union with me. Again, children, you cannot accomplish anything on your own. For the soul who is in union with me is completely

---

[105] A few minutes before this message, a small group of disciples prayed over me for a healing, invoking the presence of the Lord and the Blessed Mother. This group was present for the message where the Lord confirmed their faithfulness.

sealed by my blood.

Children of my heart, each time you accept my teachings, you are accepting me and the Eternal Father who sent me. I, the Lord, am the one to look into men's hearts. What joy it brings me when I see a soul trying to please me. I do not desire fancy gifts. A little soul who desires me, makes me weep with joy.

I am again inviting you, children, to come to my dinner table. When you break bread with me, you have accepted my invitation of love. When you accept my body and blood, it is the greatest form of praise.

Thank you, children, for your love and faithfulness. I bless you all. Go in peace.

We, love, bless and praise you, Almighty Lord. May you continue to fan the flame of the candle of love in our souls. Amen.

November 25, 1995

Lord Jesus, do you want to write?

Children, I am here. I am the Lord, the Holy Spirit. I am One and the same as the Holy Trinity. I am the One God.

Today, I shall teach you how to "rest." I have made my creation to rest and renew its strength. I desire that you rest physically as well as spiritually.

Children, many of you believe if you are physically weak, you will be spiritually weak. I, Jesus, solemnly assure you strength begins in the soul and strength ends with the soul. If you were to take the word "rest," let the "r" represent reassurance, let "e" represent eternal, let the "s" represent salvation, let the "t" represent trust.

Do you see, my beloved ones? Come to me when you are weary. I am the only strength and consolation of the soul. Children, though it is important that your physical bodies be maintained, it is the heart that I make my dwelling place. Just as I desire for you to rest in me, I desire to rest in you.

Many will mock this revelation of my love. I am willing to accept this mockery in exchange for those who will invite me into their hearts to rest. My heart is consumed with love and mercy for each of you. My heart is as an inn for a weary traveler; when you come into my heart I, Jesus, will help you to unload the baggage you are carrying.

The "t" in the word, "rest" also means "together." Together we will unload the baggage you are carrying. I will help you. After you have rested and you continue on your journey, you will be refreshed. Your burdens will be lighter.

Children, many of you travel in a circle. You go to the source of your burden to find release from that burden. Search your hearts, children. You know what I am referring to. But I, Jesus, am not the source of your burdens. I am the one who hides you within my heart. I am the one who provides the shade on a hot sunny day. I am the one who awaits an eternity for you to love me. I am humble, children. I do not expect you to give your entire heart to me. I only wish that it would be so. But if you give me even a little of your heart, soon you will desire to give me more. It is because every soul was created by me to serve me and rest in me.

Where shall you find me, you shall ask? Come to me in the Blessed Sacrament. I wait there day and night. Imagine this to be a resting place when you come to me in the Blessed Sacrament. I will grant you all that you need so that you may continue on your journey.

Remember what I have taught you, children. The letter "t" in the word "rest" means "trust" and "together."

Thank you, beloved son, for recording my words. I bless you all, my children. Go in peace.

Thank you, Lord, and may we always practice the word, "rest" in its fullest expression - always abiding in trust and your Presence. Amen.

November 26, 1995 - The Feast of Christ the King

Lord Jesus, do you want to write?

My little one, come into my arms. Oh, how I, Jesus, cherish you. I cherish each one of my little souls.

Today, my children, my kingship and authority over all creation is honored by my Church. Oh, yes, but I, Jesus, look into the hearts of each of you. Many of you are as the good thief who was crucified with me. He humbly asked for my forgiveness and was awarded eternal life. Ah, but many of you are as the man who refused to recognize my kingship. If you do not recognize my authority, then I shall not recognize you before my Eternal Father.

Children of my heart, consider a village where the ruler is a king. The people of the village pay taxes and homage to their king, thereby remaining loyal subjects. I, Jesus, am also a king who desires loyal subjects. What can you do, my children, to show me your loyalty each day?[106] Begin each day dedicating yourselves to be a servant to the Kingdom of God. Ask me to utilize all your works and intentions to benefit the kingdom. If you do this, then you may consider your entire day a prayer of service.

There are many different types of prayers, my children, as I, Jesus, have taught you. If you wish to offer your daily tasks as a prayer, then bring them to the foot of the Cross. I, Jesus, will accept this whereby another king shall ask you to pay taxes to enhance his kingdom. Offer your life to me and permit me to use you as I desire. This is where many of you falter. You place conditions on what you are willing to give me. Pray for the willingness to give me everything. Have I not given you everything? Hold nothing back from me.

Also, realize that a good king will use the tax money wisely to increase the wealth of the kingdom. The villager who has contributed his share need not be concerned where the money goes. I, Jesus, ask the same of you. Offer me everything and I shall plant fruitful trees everywhere. Do not be concerned where I use what you have given into the kingdom of God. Am I not wiser than the wisest of all earthly kings?

Thank you, child, for writing my words. Go in peace, daughter of mercy.
I bless you, God of mercy, forever. Amen.

---

[106] Two days prior to this message a disciple inquired how we might make our entire day a prayer. The Lord graciously responded in this message. The Lord always heeds our requests when it is for the benefit of our souls.

November 27, 1995

Lord Jesus, do you want to write?

Come, my little lamb, and record my words of love and hope.

Beloved one, my flock is growing. Today all of heaven is rejoicing. Today a lost child has returned to me. Ah, the pleasure that is upon my heart. Heaven is rejoicing, my children. The angels are singing in glorious melodies and harmonies. There is one less empty seat at my dinner table.

Child, what does the father do when a child who has been lost returns home? Does he not weep with joy and contact all his relatives and friends. Did he not go to sleep that evening with a peaceful and content heart?

My beloved one, I, the Lord, have no greater joy then when one of mine returns to the flock. When one of mine who has been astray decides to return, I recall my death on the Cross in delight. I see that the price I paid to purchase that one lost soul was surely worth it, for love has no limits. I am a God of infinite love and I would return to Calvary for just one sinner. I would die again for just one little soul.

Come home, my little lost lambs. Come and join me at my dinner table. Come home to me, my precious children.

Daughter, you are weary. Rest, little mercy of my heart. We shall continue tomorrow.

Thank you, Lord. I love and bless you. Amen.

November 28, 1995

Lord Jesus, do you want to write?

Children, I am here. I am the Lamb and the Eternal Guardian of the Soul. Be not afraid, my little children. Let your faith in me be your cloak of armor. The evil one shall not harm you.[107]

Children, I am the Alpha and the Omega, from Everlasting to Everlasting. Why did I choose to die on the Cross? Why did I not choose to be stoned or beaten to death? Why would I, the Lord, permit two pieces of wood to be the trademark of your salvation? I shall tell you, my beloved ones. Every work of my hands is productive and has special significance. What is a primary purpose of wood? It is used in the fire to keep the fire burning and alive for a long period of time.

Remember, that I, the Lord, have placed a candle upon the altar of each heart. I also desire for this fire to burn eternally. I use the wood of the Cross to keep the spiritual fire within each heart alive as well. Everything in my creation has a three-fold purpose. This is something you cannot understand but it stems from the Holy Trinity. The wood of the cross was used to light fires in those days. And as the means of my death, I use it to burn the fire in each heart. What does it mean to come to the foot of the Cross? [108]

The Holy Sacrifice of the Mass is a re-enactment of my Crucifixion. Those who consume my body and blood will reap the full benefits of my Resurrection as

---

[107] I was becoming more and more agitated and anxious for no conscious reason as I was approaching the time for the Lord to give this message. From previous experiences when this happens, I generally sense it is the evil one's doing and that the message contains information he *definitely* does not want disseminated. The disciple who recorded this message and I sprinkled holy water and said prayers for banishment of the evil one's presence through the Wounds and Precious Blood of Jesus and the intercession of St. Michael.

[108] I had asked the Lord earlier in the day to clarify the use of the phrase "at the foot of the Cross." Our Lord and the Blessed Mother has used it several times in previous messages in different contexts. The Lord said he would answer the question in this message, which is probably why the evil one was lurking around to disrupt it in any way he could. The Cross is our salvation.

well. If you could visualize the events of the Mass, you would see me nailed to the Cross. You would see a priest holding a chalice under each one of my wounds to collect the blood. You would see my death and Resurrection. This is why you cannot comprehend the magnitude of the graces at the Holy Mass.

However, my beloved ones, because I have made an altar on your heart, you can come to the foot of the Cross in prayer. Because it is the wood from the Cross on Calvary that keeps the fire alive in your heart, when you kneel in prayer, you are kneeling at the foot of the Cross.

There is yet another way. The soul that fully acknowledges my death and resurrection on the Cross at Calvary is given the grace by the Eternal Father to come to the foot of the Cross each time he prays. Children, love and mercy flows from the Cross. The soul that acknowledges my kingship and authority is taken spiritually by the Eternal Father to Calvary when he prays. He is given the blessings as if he was actually present on that day.

Everything upon the heavens and the earth is done in a three-fold manner. The Holy Trinity of God is as the roots to a tremendous tree, the tree being all creation, and being sustained by the Holy and Blessed Trinity.

You must pray for your brothers and sisters, children, for my other flock. They are not brought to the foot of the Cross by my Eternal Father. Children, how can they be brought to a place they do not believe exists? I have many graces for them but they will not accept them. It is the gift of faith from the Holy Spirit that permits the soul to embrace the Cross. This is why I, Jesus, have told you that faith is a priceless gem. Always pray for faith, my beloved ones.

Thank you, my beloved scribe, for recording my words. I bless you all.

Thank you, Lord, for such profound words and incomprehensible blessings. May we always be at the foot of the Cross. Amen.

November 29, 1995

Lord Jesus, do you want to write?

My beloved children, I am here. I am the Lord, the God of my people, Israel.

My beloved ones, each day you prepare for events in your life. You decide what you will wear according to the weather. You decide what you shall eat according to the time of day. Children, open your hearts to my teaching. There is not one among you that does not follow an itinerary each day. As you move from place to place and plan to plan, why do you not include me? Who do you think wakes you up each day? Who do you think it is telling your eyes to open in the morning?

Children, I am Jesus, the one who loves you with an infinite and passionate love. Continue to speak my words. You must learn to find me in the midst of distractions.[109]

Children, my children, many days the seas are calm and the waves gently come to meet the shores. But many days, my beloved ones, the seas are angry and the waves come crashing to the shoreline. I, Jesus, give you this example in simplicity, my beloved ones. Though the shoreline acknowledges the seas will be very rough at times, the shoreline welcomes every breath of the ocean. The shoreline does not say, "I shall leave you, ocean, for you are angry today." No, on the contrary, children, the shoreline realizes that I, the Lord, shall be its strength when the stronger waves approach.

In each situation you encounter, children, I, the Lord, am your strength. Do you think your strength comes from a bottle of vitamins or a cup of coffee? If that were so, what shall you say has happened to the lion? What shall you say about the bear? If you include me in your daily plans, I, Jesus, shall grant you the strength to endure every situation. Remember, my children, always allow my Holy Spirit to lead you. Never go in front of my Spirit of Counsel and Right Judgment.

Thank you, children, for your sacrifice of love. I bless you all.

We bless you, too, Lord. Thank you, Lord. Amen.

---

[109] I was interrupted during the message by the activity of the children in the next room. At times this exasperates me and my patience is tested. The Lord sensed this and gave me a lesson to see that even distractions can be opportunities to discover his presence. The Lord has infinite patience and I must learn to imitate him in this respect on all occasions.

November 30, 1995

Lord Jesus, do you want to write?

Welcome, my beloved and devoted children.[110] I am pleased that you have gathered together in my name. I am in the midst of you, my precious ones.

There are pinpoints of light standing apart from the darkness which permeates this earth. They are my beloved priests, my daughter. In the heavenly gardens there are many varieties of flowers. These gardens represent my consecrated souls. In the heavenly gardens it is the rose with its unique beauty that represents my priests upon the earth. I have explained that I, the Lord, have placed a candle upon the altar of each heart. For those that I have desired to follow me in the priesthood, I have placed a drop of my blood upon their souls. I have done this at the moment of conception. I have called them to be mine and I have sealed them with my blood. I, Jesus, have given my priests a great responsibility.

Children, how many of you have gone to a State Fair or an equally large event? There are small booths throughout the grounds whereby the employee gives information and directions. This is so the people who are visiting will not become lost and confused, but rather enjoy the event in a peaceful way. I, Jesus, am giving you an example in simplicity. I have my priests responsible to provide information and guidance to those desiring the kingdom of heaven. You must understand, my beloved, satan wishes to destroy each of my priests. Aside from my youth, my priests are his largest target.

Beloved ones, many of you mock and ridicule my beloved priests. You blame them for your own shortcomings. Remember, little ones, they are my lights of love to shine upon the dark earth. Who among you has the right to criticize one of my beloved priests? Silence your tongues, children. Speak not against them. Think no evil about them but rather pray for them. Encourage them, always remembering that I, Jesus, have chosen them above all others to be soldiers in my army.

---

[110] There were several disciples present for this message, one of whom is a priest.

I ask each of you, children, what would you do to serve the kingdom of God? Would you be willing to detach from all material consolations, to accept the consolations I desire to give you? There is something else, my children. I have asked my priests to serve me unselfishly and to place the needs of the community before their own. I have asked them to discard their concept of time to accept unlimited service on my behalf.

Children, I have told you time is my adversary. Your concept of time blocks you from fully giving your heart to me. For all those who desire to be my disciples I, Jesus, am asking you to pray for my priests. Cast aside your criticisms and mockeries, for I, the Lord, stand beside each one of my priests. When you mock and criticize my priests, you are doing so to me and to the Eternal Father who sent me.

Continue in your efforts, my beloved children. Though the road to salvation is narrow and often difficult, remember I, Jesus, go before you always. I bless you all, my children. Go in peace.

We thank you, Lord, for the wonderful blessings that you provide through your priests. May you instill in us the spirit of prayer for your beloved sons as you continue to send us holy priests. Amen.

December 1, 1995

Lord Jesus, do you want to write?

My little one of mercy, come and record my words of mercy. My words are food for the hungry and medicine for the sick. My words comfort and refresh the soul.

Beloved children, think of a staircase. It serves a two-fold purpose for you can either reach a destination at the top or a destination at the bottom. However, one cannot be at the top destination if one is climbing down the staircase. Silly children, the examples that I, Jesus, give you are simple. My love is simple and heaven is a place where only the simple and humble of heart are brought.

I, Jesus, am also the Shepherd of a flock of sheep that do not know me.[111] They are the ones who are not going in the upward direction on the staircase to heaven. They are the ones who do not follow my ways. They follow other religious practices and instead of walking on the path with me, they feel they are walking alone. These poor children do not believe in my existence. They are my flock of sheep that do not recognize their Shepherd. Some of them are searching for me and others do not believe in my existence. Others do not believe in the need for my existence.

Children, if you wish to go to the second floor of a house and there is a staircase in the house, then there is only one way available to reach the second floor. Many of my children do not see things in this way, for their hearts have been hardened by arrogance and pride.

I, Jesus, have two flocks of sheep to guide. One flock acknowledges me as the Shepherd and accepts my guidance. They see that my shepherd's staff is the cross. My other flock does not accept the cross nor what the cross represents. Their shepherd is materialism. Their shepherd's staff is money. The food they hunger for is spiced with greed and malignant life styles. Some worship false idols. Others are still waiting for my visitation. Their hardness of heart has blinded them to my kingship. This flock of children does not accept the most Holy and Blessed Trinity and does not place any value on the cross.

But, children, it is my mercy that consumes and protects these foolish and prideful ones. It is my continual desire for their conversion that keeps me as their invisible shepherd. Truly, I tell you that I watch over all creation, though only a few even know my name. Only a few know that my name is above all other names, that my name is Holy. Blessed are those that know.

Thank you, Lord, for clarifying to whom the "other flock" refers. Truly, your mercy exceeds our comprehension. I love you, Lord, and Mama Mary, too. Amen.

---

[111] In the message of November 28, the Lord requested that we pray for the "other flock." One of the disciples had asked just a few days prior to this message, of whom does the "other flock" consist? The Lord, in his infinite mercy responded to this inquiry.

December 2, 1995

Lord Jesus, do you want to write?

My beloved children, I am here. I am the Lord, the Holy Spirit.

I, the Lord, have designated great contrast within my creation. Think of the desert, my children.

Think of how the desert is in contrast to the North Pole. Think of how the ocean is the contrast to the seashore. Think of the contrast between a stone and a pearl. Think of the contrast between light and dark.

My beloved children, I, Jesus, am teaching you the ways of truth. There is only one Truth and I am He. All those who claim that the truth lies elsewhere are not part of my flock. All those who place their faith in material possessions and not in me are not a part of my flock. These children are the same distance from heaven as the rock is from the pearl. Their hearts are as cold as the North Pole and their tongues as deceitful as the desert mirage. Those children who desecrate my Church and the Sacred Host are not a part of my flock.

My flock, children, is surrounded by the gates. The gates are made of wisdom and humility. My flock thirsts only for the things of God. My flock quenches its thirst from the chalice of love and mercy, which I provide them. The children who are not of my flock shall drink from the chalice of despair for who shall be their consolation? How can I console them when they reject me?

Thank you, my beloved ones, for your sacrifices of love. My blessing shall be with all of you tomorrow.[112]   Do not be afraid, but rather go forth and speak my words to others. Go in peace, my dear children.

Thank you, Lord, for your words of wisdom. I love you. Amen.

---

[112] The next day the disciples and I were to travel a 250 mile journey to speak at a prayer group concerning the book, *The Heart of God, Vol I.*

December 3 1995 [113]

December 4, 1995 [114]

Lord Jesus, do you want to write?

My beloved child, I am here. I am the Lord, the God of All Creation. I am the God of the weak and of the strong. I, Jesus, am the architect of my Church. I am the designer and master builder of my Holy Jerusalem.

Daughter, every structure has certain components that contribute to the fullness of the structure. In a building sometimes a small screw can be just as important as a large steel beam. But you may say that such a small screw is insignificant! But I, Jesus, assure you that if enough of these metal screws are missing, the building will eventually collapse . The metal beams cannot support the building alone.

Now, children, think of my Church. I am referring to my religious brothers and sisters. I am referring to all those participants in my Church who are not considered to be as important as the beams of steel in the building. Surely, without these people supporting my priests and encouraging my flock, my Church would crumble. Is my Church not a structure made of various parts as well?

Remember what I, Jesus, have previously taught you. It is the smallest hidden flowers in a vast garden that are given the most important tasks by the Eternal

---

[113] I was speaking before a prayer group in the middle of the state today and I did not return home until it was very late. The Lord dispensed me from recording a message.

[114] Just a few hours prior to this message one of the disciples informed me of how another disciple had initiated the process of becoming a deacon. The disciple with whom I was speaking said, "Wouldn't it be beautiful if the Lord were to give a message, as he did for his priests on November 30, concerning his consecrated souls - the religious brothers, sisters, and deacons who also serve the Church?" The Lord heard this request and responded with the following message.

Father.[115]

Children, though my priests are the beams of steel within my church, consider the brothers, and sisters, and deacons, and even the secretaries to be the walls and windows of my church. Have respect and admiration for all the members of my church beginning with my high bishop and extending to someone who may occasionally run an errand for one of my priests. Remember, the small hidden leaf is loved just as much as the mighty tree by the Eternal Father.

Daughter, thank you for writing my words. Go in peace, my little lamb. I bless you.

I love you, too, Lord. Amen.

December 5, 1995

Lord Jesus, do you want to write?

My children, I am here. I am the Consolation of the Heart. My beloved children, I am closer to you than ever before. The heavier the cross, the closer I am to you, children.[116]

---

[115] I can attest to the reality of this statement and how everyone is important in building the Kingdom of God on earth. The Lord has spoken to me when I get anxious concerning all the jobs that need to be done to promulgate his messages and there doesn't seem to be a person available with the proper skills to perform the requisite function. However, he always seems to send us the "hidden leaf" to do the job. Love and humility appear to be the two virtues that truly find great favor with the Lord and through which he manifests his glory.

[116] Today I was particularly sensitive to the weight of my cross because I wasn't feeling very good due to my physical condition. I also was ventilating a lot of other frustrations to the disciple present for this message. In the course of our conversation, we both became critical of our situations in regard to the other disciples, who appeared from our perspective to have less of a burden than we. Nevertheless, the Lord, pointed out how such conversation can only

Be unified, my little disciples. On the last day, every person upon the face of the earth will receive a crown. If you are with me, you shall receive a crown of roses. If you are against me, you shall receive a crown of thorns. On that day, those of you who are crowned with thorns shall be left as food for the vultures, the scorpions, and the snakes. They will feed upon you and your bones will cover the earth. Those of you who have been crowned with roses, will be escorted by the angels to the heavenly banquet. I, the Lord, shall dictate a period of mourning whereby we will grieve and say good-bye to all the lost. After this period of mourning has ended, we will feast. I shall no longer remember the lost. After the period of mourning which I shall command every soul to participate in, the lost shall not be mentioned again.

Children, you do not realize the seriousness of my words. I, the Lord, am flooding the earth with my mercy. But soon, beloved, the Eternal Father will bang the gavel of judgment. Each of you will receive a crown and it is up to you what type of crown you will receive.

A great abyss separates heaven and hell, my children. It is this abyss that will stand between those crowned with thorns and those crowned with roses. As far as the East is from the West shall these two groups be separated.

Every sin committed places a thorn in my brow as well as a thorn in yours. Every charitable act places a rose on my brow as well as yours. Truly, I tell you that I, Jesus, have placed roses on each side of the path that you travel to me. Accept the roses I desire to give you, children.

My beloved children, I know that you are weary. I, the Lord, am your strength and consolation. I will grant all that you need. We shall continue tomorrow.

Thank you for writing, my beloved child, I bless you.

We thank you, Lord, the God of Consolation. May we always choose roses for your brow as well as our own. Amen.

----

be divisive and that he alone is our only consolation.

December 6, 1995

Beloved child, I am here. I am the Blessed Virgin Mary and the Mother of the Lamb. I am the Queen of Heaven and Earth, and the Refuge of Sinners.

Dearest children, most of you have already begun your holiday preparations. You have decided what you shall cook and who shall be invited. Have any of you given any thought to my beloved Son, Jesus? Have any of you given any thought to the true meaning of Christmas?

Children, because of the birth of Jesus, Israel has been granted an eternal place at the banquet table of the Eternal Father. Hope has been born and each wineglass shall be filled with the wine of mercy and forgiveness. My Son once turned water into wine, but that eventually ran out. In heaven, the wine of love shall never run out. Glasses shall never be empty. No one shall thirst or hunger. There shall be no tears, for my Son shall dry every tear by his own hand.

Children of my Immaculate Heart, heaven is a place created by Love and sustained by Love. Every heart is satisfied because every heart finally rests in its Creator. My beloved children, the most magnificent places upon the earth are as barren wastelands when compared to heaven. Love, in its purest form, radiates incomprehensible beauty. Every soul was created by God to desire God. But each soul is sick with sin. Each soul is separated from God, and only my beloved Son, Jesus, can heal the soul. Go to him, my precious children. Go to him, soon.

Thank you, daughter, for writing. Little child, trust in my Son completely and give all your burdens to him. I bless you and love you.

I love you and bless you, too, Mommy. Amen.

Are we going to write, Lord?

No, child, we shall continue tomorrow. I love you and bless you.

I love you and bless you, too. Amen.

December 7, 1995

Lord Jesus, do you want to write?

Beloved children, I am here. I, the Lord, am the Eternal Fountain of Mercy and Forgiveness.

Children of my heart, each day you must pray for faith. Faith is a priceless gem given freely by the Eternal Father. Without faith, one could not accept my death and Resurrection. Without faith one is doomed to return to the land of the dead. I, the Lord, am a God of the Living.

Each time you come to Mass, children, I am presented as the sacrificial lamb to the Eternal Father.[117] Each time you come to Mass, I permit you to place all your grievances and sufferings upon the altar with me. Your difficulties, children, are nailed to the Cross with me and an offering is made to appease the Eternal Father.

It is by my Body and Blood that I, the Lord, nourish the congregation. Think of the miracle of the fish and loaves and how I, Jesus, fed the entire multitude. At each Mass, again, I feed the multitude a meal of my own Body and Blood. All who are hungry are fed. Once you have been fed, you are given the opportunity to share in my Resurrection, because my Body and Blood empowers you with supernatural life. All those who partake of me in Holy Communion are truly reaping the benefits of my Resurrection as well.

Children, the gift of salvation actually begins on earth. During Holy Communion, you are closer to heaven than any other time. My Body and Blood brings you from the land of the dead into the sanctuary of the living. Faith is the

---

[117] Just a few minutes prior to this message a disciple had acknowledged how the Lord in his messages often speaks of the Mass as "being at the foot of the Cross at Calvary." The disciple inquired whether the Lord would expound on how we also participate in his Resurrection at the Mass. In essence, the disciple was asking how the Mass is a foretaste of the heavenly banquet. To my amazement the Lord responded with this most profound message.

vehicle that transports you to the land of the living where I dwell. Those of you who acknowledge my death at Calvary, and my Resurrection, have been recorded in the Lamb's Book of Life. Only those who share in my Resurrection shall have their names recorded in the Lamb's Book of Life. At each Mass an angel comes carrying this book. In it he records the names of those who partake of me in Holy Communion. The angel only records the names of those whose hearts are humble and contrite. The angel returns the book to the Throne Room of Heaven.

Children, it is because of my incomprehensible love for each of you that while you are on earth I, the Lord, have brought heaven to you. It is at the Mass where heaven and earth actually become one time and one place. It is because of this union that you are given the power to share in my Resurrection. As I told you before, no man can comprehend the magnitude of the graces offered at the Mass. In a way, time is suspended at the Mass. In a way, the East meets the West, and the North meets the South. Only those with faith will believe my words.

Thank you for recording my words, my beloved scribe. Go in peace with my blessing.

Thank you, Lord, for always responding to our needs. Give us the gift of faith so we may always come hungry and approach your table in the spirit of humility and contriteness. Amen.

December 8, 1995 - The Feast of the Immaculate Conception

Lord Jesus, Do you want to write?

I do, my precious child. Record my words of love.

Children of my heart, when you do not honor my Mother, then you do not honor me.[118] Many of my children refuse to accept my Mother. They refuse to accept

---

[118] Earlier in the day I made note of how meager was the number of parishioners who were attending the Mass in honor of our Mother's Immaculate Conception. Later in the day the Blessed Mother related to me how saddened she was because so few of her children honor her.

my Mother's intercessory hand. They refuse to accept the refuge my Mother offers to sinners.

Oh, beloved children, I, Jesus, am asking you to recognize and honor my Mother. I came through my Mother and it is through my Mother's Immaculate Heart that my children shall return to me. The heart of my Mother acts as a filter to purify the sinner on his return to me. This happens whether you believe it or not.

My beloved Mother was given to each of you at Calvary. This is one of the greatest gifts ever given to mankind by the Eternal Father. But most of you cast my Mother aside just as you would cast aside a piece of coal. But does not a diamond come from a piece of coal, my children? My beloved Mother is as a brilliant shining diamond. Her beauty and innocence consumes the sinner and enables the sinner to come closer to me. As I, Jesus, have told you, my beloved Mother is a stepping stone to union with me. She is the Queen of Heaven and of Earth and the Refuge of Sinners.

Children, there is nothing that is denied my Mother by the Eternal Father. Just as my beloved Mother said the humble and selfless "yes" to God, so it is that God always says "yes" to my Mother. Those with wisdom will run to her and hide themselves in the arms of her embrace. She loves each of you infinitely and passionately as I, the Lord, do. Remember, children, our hearts are joined by the bonds of my passion.

Daughter, I thank you for writing and honoring my Mother today. I love and bless you.

I love and bless you, too, O Lord and Mama Mary. Amen.

December 9, 1995

Lord Jesus , do you want to write?

Ah, my little lamb, how patiently I have been waiting for you.

My beloved ones, how many of you have planted a vegetable garden? With great precision you plant certain seeds at different times of the year. You water them every day and with great anticipation you wait. You wait for the joyous day that the small seed you planted will become the vegetable plant you desire and worked for. You wait patiently for each seed you planted to take root and successfully produce and live. I, Jesus, do exactly the same with each seed of faith I plant.

At Baptism, the seeds of faith that I, the Lord, have planted at the moment of conception are watered. Truly, I am the Farmer of the Harvest of Souls. I am the Farmer of the Garden of Faith.

Children, if faith does not produce fruit, then it is useless. If you are waiting for tomatoes to ripen and instead they never reach maturity, then the farmer is disappointed. What he has planted has not grown, it has wasted away. Many of you disregard the precious gifts that I, the Lord, have given you. You do not nurture them and they eventually wither and die. Only those with a simple and contrite heart realize the value of the gifts sent by Heaven. Only the simple and contrite rise early each morning to water the seeds planted by me.[119] They do everything possible to make sure the gifts they have received from me blossom and produce fruit.

Each time I, Jesus, see a soul diligently trying to please me and treasuring the gifts I have given him, my heart is delighted. I help that soul and even bestow more gifts upon him. If you saw a small child trying to reach an object above his head, would you not try to help him? Think of how the child would either get a chair or climb on top of the counter top to reach this object. Do you see the perseverance and effort of the child? Be as children, my dear ones, and the Kingdom of Heaven shall belong to you.

Thank you for writing, my little child. I love you and bless you.

---

[119] Since many of the messages over the last two weeks dealt with what occurs at the Holy Sacrifice of the Mass, I believe we can safely assume that the Lord is referring to attendance and participation at this incomprehensible gift - his paschal mystery. More gifts are bestowed upon us by Almighty God during the Mass than at any other time.

I love you and bless you, too, O Lord and Mama Mary. Amen.

December 10, 1995

Lord Jesus, do you want to write?

Come, my little lamb, and record my words of love.

Dear children, each day I, the Lord, hear the voices of gossip and idle chatter. Gossip is the same as a bitter herb; it adds a foul taste to any food. It dampens any relationship. My little ones, who among you are worthy to gossip about another? Have you completely swept your house before you decide to sweep the floor of another's house? All of you could learn a great deal from observing small children. Their entire world revolves around their mothers and fathers. When they are brought into a situation they will immediately seek the comfort and solace of their parents' arms. They do not criticize or gossip. They do not worry after tomorrow. They trust their lives to their parents.

This is how I desire you to be. When I, Jesus, say, "be as children," it is truly for your benefit and happiness. I, the Lord, am your Eternal Father. Seek me in every situation and I will come and comfort you. You shall never have to be alone. The truly lonely are the ones who do not know me. Thank you for writing, child. I know you are weary.

I love you forever, O Lord. Amen.

December 11, 1995 [120]

December 12, 1995 - The Feast of Our Lady of Guadalupe

My beloved ones, I am here. I am the Blessed Virgin Mary and the Mother of

---

[120] The Lord gave a message today but it was directed solely to the Disciples of Mercy - those whom the Lord had specifically called to formally assist him in disseminating his messages (See August 16, 1994 message). In addition, they have formally acknowledged their willingness to follow his directives in their spiritual lives.

God. I am the Mother of All Creation.

My beloved children, you have brought me joy in your efforts to honor the feast of my Most Immaculate Conception.[121] When my little ones come together to honor me in this fashion, the Eternal Father permits the heavenly court to participate as well. Truly, it becomes a bonding of my children in heaven and on earth as well.

I, your Most Immaculate Mother, have been making my sorrows known throughout the world. Reparation has been asked for, but only a few of you have complied with my requests. Most of the reparation is now coming from my young children and the unborn. But alas, my beloved, you do not see it in this way. If more of my Son's beloved ones would offer themselves as victim souls, the little ones would suffer less.

There is a place for each of you in heaven, my beloved children, but love does not force the hand of another. Love waits patiently accepting anything you desire to give. This is how we wait, my beloved Son and I.

The little ones know my Son and myself. Their hearts have not been cluttered by materialism and pride. They are pure, unspotted lambs in the eyes of God. This is the purpose of the Sacrament of Reconciliation, to make you a pure, unspotted lamb in the eyes of God. Before going to Confession, you should pray to the Holy Spirit the words that I, your Mother, shall teach you:[122]

---

[121] The Disciples of Mercy had honored our Blessed Mother on the feast of her Immaculate Conception by attending a chapel nearby which has exposition of the Eucharist. We said the "Eucharistic Rosary" - a Rosary written by Fr. Martin Lucia SS.CC. and circulated by the Apostolate for Perpetual Adoration (P.O. Box 46502, Mt Clemens, MI 48046-6502).

[122] The previous day, one of the disciples had requested that possibly the Lord would provide a prayer assisting us in the proper reception of the Sacrament of Reconciliation. Our Lady answered this request today with this beautiful prayer of honest admission of sins in the loving atmosphere of her arms and before a most forgiving and merciful Lord.

Eternal Father, I am a sinner; have mercy on me. Beloved Jesus, I am a sinner; have mercy on me. Beloved Holy Spirit, I am a sinner; have mercy on me. My heart and my soul are blackened by my offenses. Grant me a voice of confession and not one of omission. Permit my most holy Mother, the Blessed Virgin Mary, to place her loving arms about me as I confess my sins. Permit her to obtain for me mercy and forgiveness from you, my God. Grant me your eyes to see my iniquities. I place them at the foot of the Cross and I ask you to cover them in your Holy Precious Blood. Heal me of the scars of my sin, O Lord, and make me a pure, unspotted lamb in your sight. Amen.

Children, continue in your efforts to please my Son. Listen to him. My mantle of love covers you. Go with my blessing and love.

Lord Jesus, do you want to write?

No, my little child, meditate on the words of my Mother and go with my blessing.

Thank you, Jesus, and most Holy Mother. May we be worthy of becoming pure, unspotted lambs in your eyes. Amen.

December 13, 1995

Lord Jesus, do you want to write?

Yes, my beloved disciple, child of my Sacred Heart. Unity begins with the Holy Family. The blessed Holy Family is the model of love and shared unified living. Imitate my beloved Mother and St. Joseph, my dearest children, and you will find joy in abundance.

Heaven is as a large rose garden. Each day petals from the heavenly roses fall to the earth, carrying infinite graces and gifts. Every time one of my gifts is accepted and nurtured, it is as if a shrine of love is built upon the earth. Are there not shrines of despair and grief? Are there not wailing walls and cemeteries of holocaust and AIDS victims? Are these not shrines of the sign of the times? I, Jesus, am offering you shrines of holiness, shrines that come directly from heaven. Though these shrines may not be visible to the naked eye, I assure you they are visible to the faithful heart.

Yes, my children, slowly the heavenly roses are blossoming upon the earth as well. Heaven and earth are mingling in various places. As I have already told you, during the Holy Sacrifice of the Mass heaven comes to earth and there is the communion of saints and angels. There is communion of the mortal with the immortal. There is communion of the heavenly rose gardens and the flowers at the foot of each altar. Eventually, there will be communion between the lion and the lamb. But this I assure you, my beloved ones, the abyss between heaven and hell shall stand firm as the eternal wailing wall and cemetery of souls. This abyss can either mark a heavenly shrine or a symbol of terror and grief. Which side of the abyss are you facing?

Thank you, child of my heart. I bless all of my disciples of mercy. Go in peace.

We love you and bless you, too, O Lord. Amen.

December 14, 1995 - The Feast of St. John of the Cross

Lord Jesus, do you want to write?

My beloved children, I am here. I am the Lord, the God of Abraham, Isaac, and Jacob. I AM is speaking. Wisdom is speaking.

Reparation is the means by which every soul can enter into the fire of purification prior to death. As I have told you, for a metal to be pliable, it must first be placed in the fire by the welder.

Children, many of you do not understand the concept of reparation.[123] Let us

---

[123] A disciple and I were discussing the message of the Blessed Mother two days previously where she stated "most of the reparation is now coming from young children and the unborn." We were unsure of this meaning and fearful that it might infer that the Lord "imposes" his reparation upon the weakened ones of our humanity if he does not get a sufficient number of willing victim souls. The Lord clarified the meaning of reparation and how his mercy utilizes the suffering that we perpetrate upon others, particularly, the innocent

look at an ordinary bush as an example. The small leaf hidden in the belly of the bush is offering reparation for the entire bush. This is so because this small leaf is denied the same amount of sunlight and rain as the rest of the bush.

I, Jesus, do not desire to instill reparation upon you. However, your sins are so grievous and your ways so abominable that acts of reparation are accepted to tilt the scales from wrath to mercy. Yes, I am a God of the strong and of the weak. And sometimes, it is by a person's very status in life that he has a much heavier cross than another. Think of a seesaw at a playground. If you were to place your offenses on one end, the seesaw would automatically be tilted in the direction of hell. What could you possibly do to raise the seesaw that your offenses may face the gates of heaven?

I, Jesus, am a God of mercy. I place every act committed against one of my innocents on the other side of the seesaw. I place every offering and sacrifice you are willing to give. I do this so that your offenses, though they be pointed toward heaven, in essence, are cleansed by the very acts of reparation I have accepted. I accept reparation from many who are unaware they are offering it. It is funny how I will place the weakest and simplest of all my children to balance the offenses committed by the strong and mighty.

As I have said, though your sins be ever before me, the light of my love shall always prevail. It is the small hidden leaf which by its very placement is forced to subordinate to the surrounding leaves. Yes, I, Jesus, have taken the weak and lowly and they have become the vessel to give strength to my entire creation. I have asked for willing hearts. I have asked you to be as a small hidden leaf. When the time comes to face the Eternal Father, which side of the seesaw would you prefer to be on?

Thank you for writing, my beloved scribe. We shall continue tomorrow.

Thank you, Lord, for clarifying our understanding of reparation. May we have the grace of willing hearts to balance the offenses committed against you. Amen.

---

and the unborn.

December 15, 1995

Lord Jesus, do you want to write?

Yes, my beloved one. Allow me to use your hand as an instrument of grace. I AM is speaking. Wisdom is speaking.

I, the Lord, had shed tears for every one of my children. Every soul that has ever been born has been infinitely precious to me. I see each one of you as a precious rose, waiting to blossom. The soul can only blossom to the rays of my love. The thirst of the soul can only be quenched from my heart of mercy. Drink, therefore, my beloved children. Drink freely. Come to me often throughout the day and drink from my infinite heart of love.

Many of you journey to a friend's house during the day. You go for enjoyment from the camaraderie you share. Why do you not share some of your time with me? Can any human being give you more than I can? Who is a better friend? Who is a more faithful friend?

Children, many of you are the borrowers in a relationship and many of you are the lenders. This is true in both personal and professional relationships. But I solemnly assure you that I, Jesus, am neither a borrower or a lender. I am a Giver. I am a Nurturer. I am the Eternal Gift-Giver. When I give you a gift it does not have to be repaid.

Children, is not the truest of all friends the one that gives but does not lend? All those who give shall receive great favor from the Eternal Father. Blessed are the charitable for their hearts shall receive abundant graces and the gates of heaven shall open for them.

We shall continue tomorrow, my little sparrow. Be blessed, child of mercy.

Be blessed, my merciful God. Amen.

December 16, 1995

Lord Jesus, do you want to write?

My beloved children, I am the Lord, the Holy Spirit. I, the Lord, shall answer your question.[124]

Heaven is an ongoing revelation of my love. It is the source of all love and it is the infinite apostleship of love. Only I, the Lord, comprehend heaven. Heaven is an ongoing revelation even to my closest angels, for heaven is infinite; it cannot be defined.

Just as human beings are part of my Mystical Body upon the earth, my Heavenly Court is part of my Body as well. This is why heaven and earth become as one during the Holy Sacrifice of the Mass. When I, the Lord, say, "Heavenly Court," I am referring to the Lamb's army of intercessors. I am referring to all those who spend their heaven assisting my children upon the earth. It is a combination of saints and angels, and holy creatures. This was partially revealed in the Book of Revelations.

There are many saints that have not been recognized by my Church. There are many roses in an ordinary garden. Those who become saints are the ones who have always spent their time trying to please me. They are charitable and conscientious about my ways. They are, as I have already explained, the small hidden leaf in the belly of a bush.

It is my greatest desire, children, to see each one of you become a member of my Heavenly Court. It is there that you are given garments of love and mercy, and a heart of infinite love. All those who desire to spend their heaven assisting people upon the earth become a part of my Heavenly Court.

There are many other jobs as well, my beloved. As an example, there are those

---

[124] Approximately ten minutes prior to this message two disciples who witnessed this message had inquired about the meaning of the term, "Heavenly Court" which both the Lord and the Blessed Mother have frequently mentioned in the messages. The disciples were wondering whether the term refers to angels only, or angels and saints, and if saints are included, does it consist of only those who are officially acknowledged as such through the canonization of the Catholic Church? In addition, the Lord teaches us another lesson: the promptness with which the Lord responded to this question pales in comparison to his instantaneous acknowledgment of his presence to those who utter his very name.

who guard the Lamb's Book of Life. There are those who prepare heavenly garments.

Oh, my little beloved ones, do you see how quickly I, Jesus, come to answer your questions? The moment you utter my name, I AM is by your side.

Children, my children, tell others of my love. I am lonely for my children's love. How long would you wait for someone to love you? I, the Lord, wait an eternity.

Thank you, children of my heart, for your devotion to me. I bless you all. Go in peace.

Thank you, Lord. May we become the hidden leaves in your holy bush, worthy members of your Mystical Body on earth, and hopefully, citizens in your Heavenly Court. Amen.

December 17, 1995

Lord Jesus, do you want to write?

My beloved one, I invite you to share my heart of love. Will you share my heart with me, my little one?

Yes, Lord.

Will you always love me? My love does not change, little disciple. Can a rose become a carnation? I shall love you despite your wickedness. I, Jesus, am extending an invitation of love to each of you. Will you accept, my children? My promise is eternal bliss. I do not promise you earthly riches. I do not promise that you shall live problem-free. On the contrary, children, if you choose to accept my heart, then you will also be accepting the very sword that pierced it. You will be accepting the Cross that I was nailed to, that I may give you my heart. If you accept my heart, do not expect earthly riches. Do not expect freedom from prison or freedom from poverty. Do not be as those who cast away their Messiah in lieu of earthly freedom and wealth.

I, Jesus, have come to free you from your sins. I have come to free you from an eternal life of bondage in hell. I have come to give you treasures beyond your imaginations. But these treasures will not be found upon the earth. They are kept in the storehouses of heaven and they are for all those who accept my invitation of love.

Remember, my children, your life on earth is passing. Why do you spend so much time preparing for your retirement and so little time preparing for eternal life where there is no retirement?

Go in peace, daughter of my Sacred Heart. Thank you for writing my words. I bless you.

I bless and love you, too, O Lord of my heart. Amen.

December 18, 1995

Lord Jesus, do you want to write?

Little child of mercy, thank you for your perseverance.

My child, it is by perseverance that bridges and highways are built. Do they not connect one area with another? Surely, your perseverance shall connect your heart to my heart. Your perseverance shall be the highway that carries you across the great abyss. This is the chasm that separates heaven and hell.

Children, listen to my teaching. I, Jesus, am giving you examples. Does not an airplane take one across the ocean from one country to another? Children, it shall be your faith that shall be as the airplane to deliver you into my waiting arms. It is your perseverance that shall make you a passenger.

O Lord, I'm sorry. I'm so distracted.[125]

Be distracted in my love, my child. Consider my Mystical Body to be a continent

---

[125] I was having a hard time focusing because my daughter, who was on leave from the Army, was to return tomorrow for her new assignment - Korea. The Lord was consoling me stating that my daughter, the Lord, and I are never really separated, since we are part of his Mystical Body and a mere act of love or a prayer made to Jesus on our part brings all three of us together.

unto itself. All those who are a part of my Body are as close as an act of love and a prayer.

Rest, my little heartbeat. We shall continue tomorrow. I love you.

I love you, too, Lord. Amen.

December 19, 1995

Lord Jesus, do you want to write?

My beloved children, I am the God of your Fathers, from Everlasting to Everlasting, I AM.

Beloved ones, many of you are placing a great emphasis on signs. This is dangerous as it gives the evil one more opportunities to confront you.

I am a God of the heart, children. I am a God who desires faith and loyalty. Blessed are those who believe in me yet do not see. I, the Lord, wean each of you from my breast of love. I nurse you as a mother nurses her newborn. But then, my beloved ones, you are weaned from my breast. This does not mean I love you any less. On the contrary, my children, I am giving you the grace to feed yourselves from the holy food I provide you.

When you become as toddlers spiritually, it is because I have increased my gifts. I have sent the heavenly manna but it is up to you to eat it. It is often at this stage that many of you feel forsaken by me. I do not change. Will a mighty tree uproot itself and find another dwelling place? When I led the Israelites out of Egypt and their captivity I nursed all of them as tender newborns. I provided many signs that they would accept me as the one, true, eternal God. But then, when I left them to be toddlers, they abandoned me. They waited for more signs and wonders but I, the Lord, held them back. Do not be as they were, my children. Be patient and wait upon my answer in every situation.

Is the sun rising and setting more faithful than I am? Do not give the evil one an opportunity to place a cloak of signs and wonders about you. Understand that as you grow in faith, many times signs from me will decrease. It is because I desire your faith to increase. I desire for you to unite your heart to mine. Must you see my heart to do this? Again, I repeat what I have said, "Blessed are those who believe yet do not see."

Thank you, children, for recording my words. I bless you all. Go in peace.

Thank you, Lord. May we be people of faith and not of signs and wonders. Amen.

December 20, 1995

Lord Jesus, do you want to write?

Beloved children, thank you for responding to my cries from the Cross. You have before you a piece of the wood from my Cross at Calvary. Though this is an actual piece of wood taken from my Cross, each time you come to Mass, you are again brought to Calvary.[126] The Holy Sacrifice of the Mass is a re-enactment of my Crucifixion and Resurrection.

Children, my children, unless you die to things of this earth, the wood of my Cross has no meaning for you. Many of you are so busy collecting relics and ornaments that you fail to see the miracle of the Mass. Each time the host becomes my Body and Blood, Soul and Divinity, it is a miracle granted by the Eternal Father. I cannot emphasize enough the importance of receiving me in the Eucharist. It is then that I place a drop of my Blood upon your heart. The Blood that I place upon your heart is the same Blood I shed at Calvary.

So many of you come to Mass with unholy and wicked thoughts. You obtain me in Holy Communion with irreverence and disrespect. I assure you, children, one day you will stand before the Eternal Father and have to account for your actions. Change your ways, my children, before it is too late.

Thank you for writing, my dear children. Go in peace with my blessing.

---

[126] One of the disciples present for this message was a seminarian home for the Christmas holidays. He had in his possession a relic of the true Cross. This relic had papers from the Vatican attesting to its authenticity. Interestingly, the Lord seems always to bring us back to the Holy Sacrifice of the Mass as the most sublime religious expression the Church and the faithful can celebrate.

Thank you, Lord, for sharing the value of the Mass; forgive us for our hardness of hearts. Amen.

December 21, 1995

Lord Jesus, do you want to write?

Beloved children, I am here. I am the Lord, the Holy Spirit. I am the Counselor and Protector of Souls.

Children of my heart, to be a part of my flock you must always keep your eyes on me, the Shepherd. You must follow the direction that I lead you. To accomplish this, you must frequent the sacraments and be in a state of grace at all times. Grace is as an invisible armor. When you are in a state of grace, the evil one is held in abeyance.[127] Grace surrounds you as a protective wall that the evil one will not penetrate. Once you break away from my flock, you automatically will begin to follow the other shepherd. He is a deceiver who carries a shepherd's staff as well. He mimics me and my beloved Mother in many circumstances. If you are not in a state of grace, he will be able to hear you. If you are not in a state of grace, he will try to convince you that you are, thereby distancing the soul from me even further.

Children, fill a plastic bag with air and seal it. Then place the tiniest pinhole in it. Because the covering of the bag has been weakened, the air will eventually escape. If one is not in a state of grace, then it is as if the cloak of armor has holes in it, thereby giving the evil one access.

The evil one's ploy is to pretend he does not exist and to come under the appearance of good. But I assure you, when you look at the flock, you will see one lamb trying to lead the others away from the shepherd and then you will

---

[127] In the message of December 19, the Lord raised the issue of not looking for "signs and wonders" because this makes us too vulnerable to the machinations of the evil one. About ten minutes prior to this message today, a disciple had raised several questions regarding how we are to discern the evil one's subterfuges in our lives both personally and as members of the group, the Disciples of Mercy. The Lord subsequently delivered this instruction.

know that the lamb is satan.

I am a simple God, children. My love is simple and uncomplicated. Those who continuously ask for "signs" pay no attention to the voice in their soul. There is a difference between "signs" and "answers." Most of you have so little faith that you will only believe that which you see. When you are looking, you will not see. When you are focusing outside your soul, you will not hear the voice of the Holy Spirit speaking to your soul.

Children, the evil one carries a shepherd's staff as well. Many times he will try to distort the visual signs that you ask for. I, the Lord, have taught you what to do daily that you may be protected from these snares. Be reconciled to me. Be in a state of grace. Pray for wisdom. Pray for discernment. Pray to your guardian angel. Pray to St. Michael. Pray to all the saints and angels to help you each day. Hold the hand of my beloved Mother.

There is a great war for souls right now, my beloved ones. It is because of this war that I desire you to live more by faith than by any other way, for in the end it will be your faith to secure my mercy.

On certain occasions, I, the Lord, permit an individual to seek additional "confirmations" from me. In this instance it is because I, Jesus, am working closely with this person and permitting this event.

Many of my children come to places where my beloved Mother appears. They are so busy looking for signs that they have missed the point! Never does a soul come into my presence or the presence of my beloved Mother and that soul does not leave with a gift. Each time you come to me in the Blessed Sacrament, you are given priceless gifts by the Eternal Father.

Children, I, Jesus, desire each of you to pray for more faith. Pray for my children who are not in a state of grace, for they are easily influenced by the evil one. I have taught you, my children, but it is up to you to prepare.

Thank you for recording my words. I bless you all, my dear little children. Go in peace.

We thank you, Lord, for the gift of responding to our inquiry. Truly, you are the Eternal Gift-Giver. Armor us with your grace and feed us in the way of faith.

Amen.

December 22, 1995

My beloved child, I am here. I am the Blessed Virgin Mary and the Mother of God. Come with me, my beloved children, to Bethlehem. Come with me and behold my Son, the Lamb of God. Children, come and witness the birth of salvation and the death of death. How can such a wonder begin in a stable and end with the Resurrection of the Messiah?

There is a process, my children, whereby an ordinary piece of coal can become a diamond. But I tell you, that only my beloved Son, Jesus, is the flawless diamond. Only Jesus shines more brilliantly than the noonday sun. I, Mary, am the Mother of the Flawless Lamb who shed his blood to defeat death. I, Mary, am the Mother of the Flawless Lamb who defeated sin and reconciled all of mankind to the Eternal Father. I, Mary, am the Mother of the Precious Child born in a stable who offered his life as a ransom for many.

Come with me, my precious children, to Bethlehem and witness the birth of a star. This star is different from all the other stars in the heavens, for this star was the first star and shall be the last. This star always was and always will be. This star is Jesus, the King of Heaven and Earth.

My beloved children, never judge another by one's outer appearance. Though you may be looking at a piece of coal, always does my Son see a precious diamond. Always does a weed become a rose when it responds to the love of God. Come to Bethlehem, my children, and pick a rose from my Son's garden of virtues.

Thank you for writing, my child. I love you and bless you.

I love and bless you, Mama Mary. I love you, Jesus, forever. Amen.

I love you, too, child of my heart. Go in peace.

December 23, 1995

Lord Jesus, do you want to write?

My beloved children, thank you for responding to my invitation of love.

Children, I, Jesus, am looking for souls to go with me from the manger to Calvary. It is by one's willingness to offer themselves to me completely that I, Jesus, will make manifest my glory. I, the Lord, am looking for hearts that I may possess. Would the shepherd hurt one of his flock? I, Jesus, have shed my blood that you may spend eternity with me.

See me in the manger, children? Who would have thought that such a small seed would grow into a mighty tree? It is at Calvary, my children, that the instrument of my death became the instrument of your life.

My little ones, I am calling for my faithful ones to come to Calvary with me. All those who drink from the chalice of suffering shall also drink from the chalice of consolation and glory. I am a mighty tree whose branches envelop the sinner for eternity. Remember, children, a tree is mighty because of its roots. Let your roots be the manger in Bethlehem and the Cross at Calvary, and you will be mighty as well. Do not be afraid to give your life to me. All that you give to me will be used for the glory of the Kingdom of God. When the storms come, you will have my mighty branches of love to protect you.

Many of you are afraid to make a commitment to me. You are afraid of the unknown, but I, Jesus, solemnly assure you that nothing is kept hidden from the heart that loves me.

Thank you for recording my words. Be not afraid to follow in my footsteps for I go before you always. I bless you all. Go in peace.

Thank you, Lord, for your invitation and words of encouragement to pick up our crosses and follow you. Amen.

December 24, 1995

Lord Jesus, do you want to write?

Come, my little student, and record the words of the God of Israel. I am one God. I am Holy. I am One.

Have you made a place for me in your homes this year, my children? First, I, the

Lord, am asking you to make room in your heart for me. Surely, I tell you, the person whose heart is far from me has the wrong gifts under the Christmas tree. Do you think that the Heavenly Father does not place gifts under the tree as well? Ah, beloved, are you more generous to your children than the Eternal Father is to you?

Beloved ones, though the gifts you receive from heaven are not always visible at first, I solemnly assure you that they will eventually become visible. What dwells in the heart is manifested in the eyes and in the mouth. What is given to the heart is eventually seen by all. If you accept my birth and my death, then you are also saying "yes" to God, as my beloved Mother did. Oh, children, I have gifts for you as well. Are my gifts so unimportant to you that you refuse even to acknowledge them?

Remember, my dearest children, that it is by my birth in Bethlehem that you were granted this day of rich blessings. Ask that the heavenly gifts be placed under the tree as well.

Thank you, my beloved one, for recording my words. Go with my blessings.

Forever, I bless you and love you, Jesus and Mama Mary. Amen.

December 25, 1995 - Christmas Day

Lord Jesus, do you want to write?

Yes, my beloved one, record the words of the Holy One of Israel.

My beloved ones, there is a manger in the Throne Room of Heaven, a shrine to represent the Birth of Hope. The manger of the Lamb contains spiritual gifts. Ah, beloved ones, this manger now rests in the Throne Room of the Lord God. In it rests the keys to the gates of heaven and the keys to the padlock of hell. Angels guard the precious vault.

What is a vault, my beloved ones? Is it not a place to store priceless possessions? Is it not a place where people go to be sure a valuable possession is guarded carefully? Even on earth the manger was a vault where your Messiah rested. But now, my beloved children, I, Jesus, am asking you to make your hearts my manger, my most precious resting place. Yes, the heavenly manger is now the storehouse for the keys to eternity.

But, my children, the manger on earth was also the storehouse for the keys to eternity. For, I, Jesus, am the only way to heaven. I possess the key to the heart of the Heavenly Father for we are one.

My children, on this day of victory, lift your eyes to heaven and pursue my mercy and compassion. Today, more gifts are given from earth, and from heaven, than any other time. Peace be with you all, my precious children. I love you all.

Child of my heart, thank you for honoring my birthday.[128]

Lord, I adore you and praise you. Thank you for all the gifts. Thank you for everything. Amen.

December 26, 1995

Lord Jesus, do you want to write?

Beloved dear ones, I, the Lord, am here. I am the Shepherd of My People Israel.

Dearest ones, consider casting a stone into a pond. When you do this, you will see the ripples the stone has made. Sin, my children, is as the stone. Sin not only affects the sinner but it affects my entire Mystical Body. It is as a domino that knocks the other down. You must begin to learn, my children, how each one of you can either contribute to or damage my flock.[129]

---

[128] Today my husband and I made the effort to spend some time before Jesus at a nearby chapel that has daily exposition of the Blessed Sacrament from 9 a.m. to 9 p.m.

[129] When one of the disciples read this message he said that this is very similar to a fundamental principle in chaos theory known as the "butterfly effect," that is, the very fluttering of a butterfly in Idaho affects the weather in Asia. How this occurs I have no idea but it too brings about the realization that nothing is done in a isolated manner; that every "single" act does have its effect on other persons or events.

Children, consider the flock. If one sheep were to leave, would not the ones who were close to it take their eyes from the shepherd to see where it was going? Once those other sheep take their eyes from the shepherd, there now is a chance they will be lost as well; and will not the sheep who are near these others take their eyes from the shepherd to follow what these other sheep are doing? This is the ripple effect of the stone being cast into the pond. The person who sins loses sight of me, the shepherd. Those who are close to that person begin to focus on what this sinner has done and they lose sight of me as well.

Do you see, my children, how one sin can affect many people? If you were to take a drop of poison and place it into a container filled with water, would only the water where you placed the poison be affected, or would the entire container of water be affected?

Be reconciled to me, my children, thereby purifying and bringing grace to my entire Body. The Sacrament of Reconciliation removes the poison that sin has brought upon my Mystical Body.

Thank you, my little children, for recording my words. Go in peace, my dear little disciples, I bless you all.

Thank you, Lord, for bringing to our consciousness the "social" effects our individual sins have upon your Mystical Body. Purify us in your mercy and give us the grace to take advantage of the Sacrament of Reconciliation whenever the opportunity arises. Amen.

December 27, 1995

My beloved children, I am here. I am the Blessed Virgin Mary and Mother of God. I am the Mother of the Church and the Mother of every heart that loves my Son. I have come from heaven to help my children to recognize my beloved Son, Jesus. I have come from heaven to help my beloved priests recognize the voice of my Son. I have come as a messenger and servant of the Most High God.

When the disciples recognized my Son, Jesus, on the road to Emmaus, their eyes were opened to the fullness of faith the Eucharist affords.[130] Each one of you travel the road to Emmaus every day. It is the road between life and death. It is at the intersection of good and evil that you must be able to recognize Jesus. The road to Emmaus is as a large quilt to warm every member of the Body of Christ. Those who do not recognize my Son shall find themselves cold despite the warmth of the quilt.

The road to Emmaus is a long winding road running through every Mass as well. At the Holy Sacrifice of the Mass it is as if the road divides; those with faith will see my Son, Jesus, in the breaking of the bread and will continue their journey with abundant graces. Those who approach the altar without faith and with hardness of heart will not see Jesus in the breaking of the bread. They are as travelers who have lost their way.

The road to Emmaus is the one that a precious soul travels all the days of his life. The traveler with faith and a humble heart will see my beloved Son walking with him. Remember, there are two ways to travel any road: you can go someplace or you can return from someplace. Those who walk with Jesus and who are fed by him, by the Holy Eucharist, will never be lost on this journey. There are intersections, my children, but those who see Jesus in the Holy Eucharist will not take the wrong path.

I thank you, beloved ones, for recording my words. Be at peace, little ones, on the road to Emmaus. My Son and I are with you always.

----

[130] Earlier in the day one of the disciples indicated that he was always fascinated by the story of the disciples on the road to Emmaus. The Emmaus story recounts how, soon after the Lord's resurrection, he appeared and journeyed with them for quite a while, discussing the manner in which Jesus of Nazareth fulfilled the Scriptures, but the disciples did not recognize him. It was only after requesting this knowledgeable stranger to have dinner with them did they discover who their companion really was. It was precisely at the moment of "breaking the bread" when they were illuminated with the realization that it was the resurrected Jesus. Ironically, at that very moment he was gone. The disciple always wondered whether this story was a confirmation in the reality of the Eucharist and the continued presence of the resurrected Lord in the Mass. The Blessed Mother confirmed his belief.

Jesus, do you want to write?

No, my child, we shall continue tomorrow.

Thank you, Lord Jesus and Mama Mary, for responding so rapidly to our inquiry regarding the "road to Emmaus." Truly, you are our Father and Mother, so watchful and solicitous for all our needs. We pray that all mankind may come to this realization. Amen.

December 28, 1995

Lord Jesus, do you want to write?

My beloved children, thank you for responding to my calls from the Cross.[131] Many of you have heard my anguished cries, yet you have ignored my calls from Calvary. You have ignored the prodding of the Holy Spirit to call you to conversion and reconciliation with God.

Little lambs of my heart, many of you are floundering in your faith. It is to you that I direct these words. I shall teach you a prayer to call your attention to my most Sacred Heart:

> Father, Eternal Wisdom and Majesty, transfuse my entire being with the light of your love. Place my heart within yours. Place my mind within yours. Place my spirit within yours. I consecrate my life to the Sovereign and Omnipotent God of All Creation. Help me to be mesmerized by your love. Help me to forsake my earthly attachments. Help me not to be distracted by the things of this earth. Lord, I come before you on my knees, completely willing to empty the blood from my veins

---

[131] The Lord constantly amazes me. One disciple had asked that the Lord teach us a prayer to say before Mass so we can be ever mindful and fully participating in what transpires in the Mass. Another group of disciples just prior to this message had requested a prayer of total consecration to his Sacred Heart. Just as we began the message the Lord told me that he would answer both requests in this one message.

and to accept your blood. Help me to be hungry for your Body and Blood every day, as you desire to nourish me in the Holy Eucharist. I ask now for my seat at the heavenly banquet, that my seat remain empty until you, Lord, call me home to heaven. I consecrate and offer my life as reparation, that I may obtain by this offering a seat at your banquet for someone who is lost from you. With abundant gratitude I accept the blood you have shed for me at Calvary. Let me be distracted in your love and nurtured by your blood. May the name of the Lord be blessed forever. Amen.

Children, the heavenly banquet begins on earth, as you partake of me in the Holy Eucharist. Come to my dinner table. Come, children.

We shall continue tomorrow, my little children.

Is that all you want to say today, Lord?

Yes, meditate on the words I said. It is enough.

Thank you, Lord, Almighty God and Merciful Father, your prayer has answered the longings of our souls. May we worthily say it with our hearts each day of our remaining lives on earth. Amen.

December 29, 1995

Lord Jesus, do you want to write?

My beloved children, I speak to you through a simple and humble servant. I desire, children, that you know the voice of your Savior.

My beloved children, the evil one is strengthening his forces. Each day more of my youth are giving their souls to the evil king. My children, satan has cast a heavy veil upon your eyes. He has created many divisions to hide the seriousness of these days. If this were not so, many of you would see that your lifestyles are evil and abominable. Many of you laugh at my words. When my messages speak to you, you laugh at them and mock them. But I tell you truly, satan is so cunning he could make the water of the ocean appear as the flames of a fire. He is the deceiver, my children, the malignant one. Each day he takes hostages of sin and lures them by deceptive tactics to his side; this is the side of darkness.

What can you do to protect yourselves from his deception? Become a consecrated soul.[132] Make the Immaculate Heart of my Mother your resting place. Make my Sacred Heart your pillow. Let the Holy Scriptures be your garments. The Rosary is a sword of holiness. Stay reconciled to me and frequent the sacraments. If you do these things, I, the Lord, shall place a wall of holiness about you. The evil one shall not enter.

Children, do not be so quick to cast my teachings aside. I am teaching you my ways which are the ways of truth and life.

Thank you, my little one, for recording my words. Go in the peace of my blessing.

Lord Jesus, we love you so much. Amen.

December 30, 1995

Lord Jesus, do you want to write?

My beloved disciple, record the words of One Who Is. I AM is speaking. Wisdom is speaking, child.

You say you love me, my little one, and yet you are reluctant to completely trust your life to my care. My little one, you have nothing to fear. You are a precious soul who is a consecrated lamb. However, if the lamb takes his eyes from the shepherd, even if only for a short while, he will become lost.

Daughter, my daughter, there should be no fear in the heart that belongs to me. There should be no fear in the consecrated heart. Though you may endure many

---

[132] The prayer of consecration to the Sacred Heart which Jesus taught me is found in the December 28 message. The prayer of consecration to the Immaculate Heart of Mary is found in the Appendix. The Blessed Mother has told me she enjoys the prayer composed by St. Louis de Montfort. We are encouraged by both Jesus and the Blessed Mother to say these prayers daily.

trials, I, Jesus, am always by your side. I shall never forsake you. You are a precious rose in my garden of love.

How many of you, children, desire to become roses in my garden of love? Call to me with your heart and I shall answer you with mine. I shall make a place for you at the heavenly banquet and I shall dwell within the temple of your heart. You are weeds, my little children, but I, Jesus, desire to make you into roses. Consecrate your lives to my care and become a rose in the heavenly garden.

Child, thank you for recording my words.[133] Go in peace.

I love you, Lord. Amen.

December 31, 1995

Lord Jesus, do you want to write?

My beloved children, I am the Lamb of Reconciliation. You have been in my school, children, and I, Jesus, have been your Holy Teacher.

Many will mock you and verbally crucify you for being my students. Blessed are those who accept these scourgings on behalf of their love for me. As in any school, children, tests are given. But when the Heavenly Father sends tests, it is not to see your intelligence level. It is to see your faith and to increase it. It is the same as polishing silver, it brings out the shine and enhances the beauty.

Another year is beginning, my children. Are your houses in order? Are you prepared to meet me? I solemnly assure you, I will come as the wind. When the wind blows, you know not its origin or destiny. Yes, I shall come as the wind. To those who have been faithful, it shall feel as a kiss. But to those who have mocked me and who have mocked one of mine, it shall feel as fire.

---

[133] I was feeling very sick during the entire day and being attentive to the message was pushing my endurance to the limits. I asked the Lord if he would mind that we cease the message. He graciously acquiesced to my petition.

Blessed are those who hear my words and obey them. Though you cannot see, the battle for souls is all about you. Those who consecrate themselves to my Sacred Heart and the Immaculate Heart of my Mother, have nothing to fear. Call to me, my beloved children, and I, Jesus, will shower you with abundant gifts. The gates of heaven shall open for you, for our hearts are as one. Those who share in my suffering will also share in my glory.

Children, begin the new year with grace and peace of heart. Cast away sin as you would discard trash. Become a student in my school for my teachings are holy and priceless. In my school receive dignity and faith. When you graduate you shall receive the gift of salvation; no other school can grant you such a gift.

Thank you, beloved ones, for responding to my invitation of love. I bless you and love you all.

Lord, we are most unworthy of your invitation of love, but with your grace may we be assiduous students and worthy graduates. Amen.

This page is deliberately blank.

Index

This page is deliberately blank

APPENDIX

Prayers Jesus and the Blessed Mother Taught Lori

1995

Prayer of Consecration to the Sacred Heart[134]

Father, Eternal Wisdom and Majesty, transfuse my entire being with the light of your love. Place my heart within yours. Place my mind within yours. Place my spirit within yours. I consecrate my life to the Sovereign and Omnipotent God of All Creation. Help me to be mesmerized by your love. Help me to forsake my earthly attachments. Help me not to be distracted by the things of this earth. Lord, I come before you on my knees, completely willing to empty the blood from my veins and to accept your blood. Help me to be hungry for your Body and Blood every day, as you desire to nourish me in the Holy Eucharist. I ask now for my seat at the heavenly banquet, that my seat remain empty until you, Lord, call me home to heaven. I consecrate and offer my life as reparation, that I may obtain by this offering a seat at your banquet for someone who is lost from you. With abundant gratitude I accept the blood you have shed for me at Calvary. Let me be distracted in your love and nurtured by your blood. May the name of the Lord be blessed forever. Amen.

Act of Consecration to the Immaculate Heart of Mary[135]
(St. Louis De Montfort's Consecration)

I, N., a faithless sinner—renew and ratify today in thy hands, O Immaculate Mother, the vows of my Baptism; I renounce forever satan, his pomps and works; and I give myself entirely to Jesus Christ, the Incarnate Wisdom, to carry my cross after him all the days of my life, and to be more faithful to him than I have ever been before. In the presence of all the heavenly court I choose thee this day, for my Mother and Mistress. I deliver and consecrate to thee as thy slave, my body and soul, my goods, both interior and exterior, and even the value of all my good actions, past, present and future; leaving to thee the entire and full right of disposing of me, and all that belongs to me, without exception, according to thy good pleasure, for the greater glory of God, in time and in eternity. Amen.

---

[134] This prayer was taught to Lori on December 28, 1995. Our Lord has requested that this prayer and a prayer of consecration to his Mother be said daily.

[135] There are many prayers of consecration to the Blessed Mother. Lori had requested such a prayer of the Blessed Mother and she responded, saying, "I favor the DeMontfort Consecration."

Prayer for Docility
(January 17, 1995)

Redeemer of Israel, Sanctifier and Purifier of Souls, we long to dwell in the land of the righteous. We desire to build a new house which we may call the Temple of the God of Israel, who is Holy, who is One. Let the fire of your love purify us. Make us pliable and useful to you that we may become upright in thy sight. Close not your eyes. Make not your ears deaf to our pleadings. O Lord, drown us in your mercy and hear our lamentation, for the Lord is our God, and holy is his name. Blessed be the name of the Lord forever. Amen.

Prayer for Humility
(March 1, 1995)

Father, Eternal Master, grant us the garments of humility that we may come before you desiring reconciliation. For in that hour, Father, surely you shall not chastise the truly humble and repentant of heart. Though we be naked before you, take away our layers of pride and greed of heart, and gently cover us in the sweet fragrance of humility. Dear Father, turn not your face nor your ears from our cries, but in your mercy hear and answer us. Amen.

Prayer for Increase of Faith
(May 10, 1995)

Father Eternal, Majesty Most High, I desire to love you with a pure love. Grant me the grace of faith that I may ponder your marvelous works. Father, I cannot approach you without faith. I pray that despite my sinfulness, you will hide me under the umbrella of your love and let your lovely countenance shine upon me, and I shall bless your Holy Name forever and ever. Amen.

Prayer for Healing
(May 15, 1995)

Father Eternal, by the merits of your most obedient Son, our Lord Jesus Christ, we come before you sick and wounded by our sins. Heal us, O Lord, and take our iniquity from us by the passion of our most merciful Savior, Jesus Christ. Heal us of all our suffering both in body and soul, and fill our hearts with the fire of your love. O Holy Master, grant us new hearts. Mend our wounds Transform us into your image, that by our healing we may bring glory and honor to your Holy Name. For all thy benefits we thank thee and bless thee forever. Amen.

Prayer of Praise
(August 6, 1995)

Gracious God, humble and generous in thy affections, compassionate and loving in thy responses, consumed with love and mercy for the wretched, I come to offer you nothing but praise. I come acknowledging you as Lord and God. I come seeking your counsel and wisdom. But most of all, my gracious God, I come to adore you and praise your Holy Name. May the name of the Lord be blessed and adored, forever and ever. Amen.

Prayer to Love with the Heart of Jesus
(September 6, 1995)

Infinite God, source of love and comfort, source of all creation, blessed be your Holy Name. Teach me your ways, O God. Reveal your heart to me that by your love, my heart shall burn as a candle upon the eternal altar. O Father Eternal, set a flame in my heart. Teach me your ways. Teach me to love with the Great Heart of Love. May the name of the Lord be blessed forever and ever. Amen

Prayer for Holiness
(October 27, 1995)

O Spirit of Truth and Righteousness, Protector of the Tabernacle of Each Heart, look with pity upon your children. See the chalices which they themselves have filled and empty them, O Spirit of God, into the ocean of your forgiveness. Set a new chalice in front of each heart and bestow the gift of holiness upon each one of us. Fill every chalice with good works, desires for your love, and graces from the Eternal Gift-Giver. And then, Most Holy God, Spirit of Light and Love, permit us to drink from the cup that you have anointed with your Blood. Let every mouth proclaim the glory of the God Israel. Amen.

Prayer of Consolation
(November 21, 1995)

Father and Majesty of All Heaven and Earth, what could a wretch like me say to console you? I shall say that I am grieved by my offenses to you. I shall say that I will worship and adore the Union of the Three, the Most Holy and Blessed Trinity. On my knees do I come to whisper love songs to you. Grant me your passion to love you. Grant me your heart to love the world. Grant me your eyes that I may see your crucified body impaled upon the heart of everyone I meet. And when I love the stranger, it is because I love you. When I do my work silently, it shall be to console your grieving heart. When I am forgiving of those who mock and wound me, I will be anointing all your wounds. When I console others, then I am consoling you, my God. Amen.

Prayer Prior to the Sacrament of Reconciliation
(December 12, 1995)

Eternal Father, I am a sinner; have mercy on me. Beloved Jesus, I am a sinner; have mercy on me. Beloved Holy Spirit, I am a sinner; have mercy on me. My heart and my soul are blackened by my offenses. Grant me a voice of confession and not one of omission. Permit my most holy Mother, the Blessed Virgin Mary, to place her loving arms about me as I confess my sins. Permit her to obtain for me mercy and forgiveness from you, my God. Grant me your eyes to see my iniquities. I place them at the foot of the Cross and I ask you to cover them in your Holy Precious Blood. Heal me of the scars of my sin, O Lord, and make me a pure, unspotted lamb in your sight. Amen.

[This page is deliberately blank]

Please clip or photocopy to order more books

Disciples of Mercy Foundation
P.O. Box 4074
Deerfield Beach, FL 33442

Please send me the following:

_____ copy (ies) of *The Heart of God Vol III* at the cost of $12.95 per book plus shipping and handling. (S & H)

_____ copy (ies) of *The Heart of God Vol II* at the cost of $11.95 per book plus shipping and handling. (S & H)

_____ copy (ies) of *The Heart of God Vol I* at the cost of $8.95 per book plus shipping and handling. (S & H)

I enclose my check payable to: *Disciples of Mercy Foundation* or I prefer to call in my order *toll free*: 1-888-722-7332 (Sacred 2); or order through the web page: http://disciples-of-mercy.org

Please allow 2 - 3 weeks standard service for delivery.

Please Print

Name: _____

Address:_____

City: _____ State _____ Zip _____

Phone: _____ Email: _____

Quantity	Volume	Price/Book	Subtotal
_____	Vol III	$12.95	_____
_____	Vol II	$11.95	_____
_____	Vol I	$8.95	_____
_____	Vol I (Spanish)	$8.95	_____

+ Shipping and Handling $3.95 for any orders less than $50.00. For orders $50 or more - No Charge   _____

Grand Total: _____

[This page is deliberately blank]